# Data Acquisition and Analysis in Animal Breeding

**R.Venkataramanan**
Professor
Department of Animal Genetics and Breeding
Tamil Nadu Veterinary and Animal Sciences University
Chennai, Tamil Nadu - 600 051

NIPA® GENX ELECTRONIC RESOURCES & SOLUTIONS P. LTD.
New Delhi-110 034

**NIPA® GENX ELECTRONIC RESOURCES & SOLUTIONS P. LTD.**

101,103, Vikas Surya Plaza, CU Block
L.S.C.Market, Pitam Pura, New Delhi-110 034
Ph : +91 11 27341616, 27341717, 27341718
E-mail:newindiapublishingagency@gmail.com
www: www.nipabooks.com

For customer assistance, please contact
Phone: + 91-11-27 34 17 17
Fax: + 91-11-27 34 16 16



ISBN: 978-81-19103-29-4



Composed and Designed by NIPA.

# Data Acquisition and Analysis in Animal Breeding

NIPA® GENX ELECTRONIC RESOURCES & SOLUTIONS P. LTD.
New Delhi-110 034

# Preface

Animal Breeding is the selective mating of individuals to obtain desirable traits in future generations. Animal breeding has played a crucial role in shaping the relationship between humans and animals for thousands of years. From the period of domestication, the practice of selective breeding has been both an art and a science. However, with the dawn of the information age, the landscape of animal breeding is evolving rapidly. Today, data-driven approaches are paving the way for ground-breaking advancements in genetic improvement and conservation efforts.

Statistics is an integral part of the science of animal breeding and the process of genetic evaluation and conservation involves analysis of data, diverse in nature. The voluminous and unique nature of animal breeding data warrants need for maintenance, storage, retrieval, processing, classification, analysis, validation and interpretation for effective application in selection of animals. In this context the book on "Data Acquisition and Analysis in Animal Breeding" was conceived and within these pages, we can delve into the essential aspects of collecting and analysing data, unlocking the potential for use in practical animal breeding.

The inspiration for this book emerged from my personal experiences as an animal breeder and researcher. Throughout my career, I witnessed the transformative power of data in decision-making processes. I could also realise the intricacies, assumptions and other challenges in analysing animal breeding data and without proper guidance there is a possibility for wrong interpretation due to lack of precision and bias in estimates. Thus, it was sought to create a comprehensive resource that equips readers with the tools to harness the potential of data-driven breeding programs.

I must acknowledge that this work would not have been possible without the support of numerous mentors, colleagues, students and my Institution, the Tamil Nadu Veterinary and Animal Sciences University (TANUVAS) for the contribution to my growth as a breeder and researcher. Dr. M. Murugan, Professor and well-wisher was instrumental in creating this opportunity and as always my family members (Suseela, Dr. Vijayarajeswari, Sanjay & Diya) have been a big support. I must thank Dr. N. Kandasamy, Professor and my postgraduate teacher, who instilled the basics of animal breeding and

Dr. M. Iyue, Professor who introduced me to the FoxPro database management system. I must also mention my postgraduate students; Dr. B. Gowrimanokari, Dr. S. Vinothraj, Dr. V. Arthy and Dr. Vrinda, B. Ambike for various research work completed on animal breeding data analysis. Their passion and dedication have served as a guiding light in shaping the contents of this book.

May this book empower you to approach data acquisition and analysis for all your animal breeding needs with confidence and ease.

Happy reading!

**Author**

# Contents

# 1

# Introduction

Domestic livestock plays a major role in meeting the food requirement of human beings. Especially with dwindling resources, improvement in production efficiency is primary to meet the ever-increasing demand for animal protein. The role of an animal breeder is to bring about a sustained improvement in the quality and quantity of such products. Over the years, there has been an enormous improvement in the production ability of livestock and statistical analysis has played a predominant role in the application of principles of animal breeding to improve the productivity of animals. The combination of genetics and statistics developed into a separate branch of science called biometry.

Selection of superior animals to breed is an age-old practice that goes back to as early as Jacobs (1800 BC), who selected the fitter rams for his flock. In the early nineties, selecting superior animals was a skill rather than an art, and was based on external appearance or phenotype. Gregor Johanne Mendel proposed the laws of Mendel, which described the mode of inheritance of qualitative characters such as color. However, most of the economically important traits were quantitative in nature and improvement was essential. These traits are under the influence of thousands of genes with infinitesimal effects (Fischer's infinitesimal model) and are subject to greater variation by the environment. Hence the challenge was to find the breeding value of individual animals concerning different polygenic quantitative traits after adjustments for environmental effects. Animals with good breeding values could produce better offspring and maintain superiority in future generations. The estimation of the breeding value of an animal from its phenotype, without knowing the genetic architecture of different traits involved complex statistical analysis.

Statisticians like Galton, Pearson, Yule, and Fisher added to the early knowledge in the field. Fischer (1918) used the analysis of variance (ANOVA) to partition the genetic variance into additive and dominance variance. Wright (1921) used the path coefficient to arrive at the same results. He also contributed significantly to the analysis of inbreeding, which has been used in the development of several important breeds of livestock existing even today. Fischer also demonstrated that the mendelian factors could explain the resemblance between relatives. The resemblance between relatives was used to partition the variance component like genetic comprising of additive, dominance, and interaction variance and environmental comprising of permanent and temporary environmental variances. Other methods of estimation of variance to suit the typical nature of animal breeding data helped in obtaining precise and unbiased estimates of variance components. Initially, the least-squares method was used to correct for different fixed effects and variance estimated. The maximum likelihood method is a powerful technique used extensively in the estimation of variance components (Fischer, 1921). The residual or restricted maximum likelihood (REML, (Patterson and Thomson, 1971) estimate is more robust and takes into consideration the degrees of freedom lost in the estimation of fixed effects. The Bayesian method based on Baye's theorem is robust and advantageous in certain situations (Gianola and Fernando, 1986).

After 1940, Lush and Hazel developed the principles of the selection index to optimize artificial selection based on the relationship between individuals and phenotypic trait information. The selection index also called the best linear prediction proved to be a remarkable methodology for practical breeding and it also had the scope to predict selection gains. The different variance components estimated by partitioning are used in the formation of the selection index. Charles Henderson (1912-1989) established the famous mixed model equation (MME) for estimating breeding values (BLUP). The BLUP enables fixed effects and the breeding value to be estimated simultaneously. He also revolutionized the principle of multisource information by the use of an inverse numerator relationship matrix in arriving at the value breeding value. BLUP has been used worldwide for the improvement of different species of livestock. The response to selection depends on the accurate estimation of components of variance and statistical analysis play a major role in their estimation.

These developments along with advancements in computing power has benefited national and international breeding programs in almost all animal species (Gilmour, 2010). The statistical analysis in animal breeding is inevitable as the data sets for different selection objectives are large and varied. Most of the data are multivariate, seemingly normal or non-normal in a few cases, and under influence of selection bias. The data structure could be cross-classified or longitudinal and with missing observations. A variety of statistical tools are required to deal with such a varied set of data. Most of animal breeding applications involve complex equations which are solved through matrix inversion or iterative techniques. This involves huge computational powers and the emergence of several breeding software like Harvey, DFREML, ASREML, VCE, BLUP, PEST, GEN STAT, SAS, R, etc., and machines with superior computing ability have made the task easy.

The application of various principles of animal breeding has improved livestock production several folds and to achieve the different objectives, a breeder has to depend on a variety of analyses in the form of correction of data for environmental effects, estimation of variance components, calculation of genetic parameters, prediction of breeding value, evaluation of response, etc., for which is required a variety of statistical tools, database management and computer software. This book covers the various aspects of animal breeding analyses and will guide the reader on various aspects including the objectives of an animal breeder, the economic traits, types of data, database management and linear models.

# 2

# Maintenance of Records and Economic Traits

Maintaining the required type of information in the form of records is primary for any type of animal breeding analysis and this chapter explains the importance of records and ways to maintain them in the form of registers or computer databases. The formats for different types of registers to be maintained are also given as a template in appendix. Any breeding plan is formulated to improve the economic traits depending on the utility of species reared and the chapter lists important economic traits of livestock and poultry with definitions and formulae, where ever required.

Basic record maintenance is a must for any animal breeding program. Every farm or breeding program is expected to maintain records in the form of registers or computerized databases. The goal of animal breeding is to select mates with the objective to improve economically important traits. In this chapter, the most common economic traits in different species of livestock are described. Even though the list is not exhaustive the basic economic traits that have been worked for improvement are explained. Breeders also explore new composite traits which are a combination of these base traits.

## Record Maintenance

Animal performance records are fundamental for a livestock farm. They guide us to scientific breeding, feeding, health care and culling of farm animals. The purpose of Animal Performance records are :

- Farm records are essential for ascertaining the pedigree that assists genetic selection.
- Identify best performers.
- Keeping track of various farm efficiency indicators.
- Identify surplus animals for marketing.
- Computation of ration and economic feeding
- Calculation of economics of profit and loss

- Helps the manager in decision-making regarding carrying capacity, type of animal etc.
- Culling of under-productive animals.
- Designing and generation of reports.

## Recording of Data

The important points to be borne in mind while recording livestock data are accuracy, regularity, timely recording of data, integrity, raw data, avoiding duplication, legibility,

## Animal Identification

Record keeping begins with individual animal identification. Animals are usually identified by a unique identification number at the time of birth of the animal. Apart from the identification number, certain basic particulars/records should be kept to monitor herd/flock performance. These normally include breed, lambing/kidding/calving/farrowing, date, sire and dam, sex of newborn, etc. We may also want to record particulars such as the coat colour of the animal, natural marks, difficulties during parturition, retention of the placenta after birth, etc.

Animals should be weighed periodically to assess the growth rate. Weaning, six months, nine months and yearling weights are recorded and the growth rate is arrived at. Other records may be maintained according to the goals of the individual breeding unit. Standard formats are available for different species of livestock for performance recording and for different production systems. The formats are annexed in appendix.

**Table 2.1:** List of registers commonly used in different species of livestock (Formats of important registers are given in Appendix)

| S.No. | Sheep | Goat |
|---|---|---|
| 1 | Lambing Register | Kidding Register |
| 2 | Growth Register | Growth Register |
| 3 | Adult stock Register | Adult stock Register |
| 4 | Insemination Register | Insemination Register |
| 5 | Weighment Register | Weighment Register |
| 6 | Death & Disposal Register | Death & Disposal Register |
| 7 | Sales Register | Sales Register |
| 8 | Medicine Register | Medicine Register |
| 9 | Breeding Register | Breeding Register |
| 10 | Deworming & Vaccination Register | Deworming & Vaccination Register |
| 11 | Daily Stock Register | Daily Stock Register |

| | | |
|---|---|---|
| 12 | Rams Performance Register | Buck Performance Register |
| 13 | Ewes Performance Register | Doe Performance Register |
| 14 | Veterinary Register | Veterinary Register |
| 15 | Feed Register | Feed Register |
| 16 | Wool Register | |
| | **Rabbit** | **Fodder** |
| 1 | Birth Register | Seed Stock Register |
| 2 | Grower stock Register | Fertilizer Stock Register |
| 3 | Adult stock Register | Pesticides Stock Register |
| 4 | Feed Register | Fodder Production Register |
| 5 | Daily stock Register | Fodder Distribution Register |
| 6 | Weighment Register | Tree Register |
| 7 | Death & Disposal Register | Tree Fodder Register |
| 8 | Sales Register | Manure Register |
| 9 | Medicine Register | |
| 10 | Breeding Register | |
| | **Chicken** | **Turkey / Japanese Quail** |
| 1 | Stock Register | Stock Register |
| 2 | Technical Data Register | Feed Register |
| 3 | Feed Register | Mortality Register |
| 4 | Mortality Register | Sale and Disposable Register |
| 5 | Death & Disposal Register | Egg Account Register |
| 6 | Sale Register | Hatchability Register |
| 7 | Egg Register | Vaccination and Deworming Register |
| 8 | Candling Register | Brooder Register |
| 9 | Chick Receipt Register | Grower Register |
| 10 | Hatchability Register | Production Performance Register |
| 11 | Hatch weight Register | Pen-wise Egg Production Register |
| 12 | Fumigation Register | |

## Utilization of Farm Records

Farms records are not just a repertoire of animal numbers. It contains and conceals information on potential performers and they need to be used in the selection process. To be used properly in the selection, all records need to be adjusted to a common basis. Growth measures such as weaning weight and subsequent periodical weights need to be adjusted for various factors like breed type, year and season of birth, type of birth/rearing and age of dam.

## Computerized Record-keeping and Analysis of Farm Data

There are several commercial software packages that can be used to keep production records. Specific packages to suit livestock enterprises are on offer with free demo versions of their software. Various other types of commercial spreadsheets (e.g. Excel) and databases (e.g. Access) are also available, which can be used to record, sort, and analyze performance data.

Selections based on phenotype are not generally sound. Some animals appear more desirable, more productive on phenotype but are genetically poor. Computer-generated statistical analysis of performance data eases the decision-making process. Programs are also available to calculate Estimated Breeding Values for any number of genetic traits. Predictions that define high-performing animals on the basis of the performance of their dams, their sires, and ancestors are far more realistic than calculations that simply list animals on the basis of body weights or phenotype

## Economic Traits

Livestock are mainly reared for some utility. Cattle, buffalo and goats for milk, meat & hide; sheep for meat and wool; poultry for egg and meat; horses for racing, etc., Apart from the main utility there are some secondary utilities such as manure, fancy, companionship, draughtability etc., The main objective of the breeder is to improve these desirable traits so as to improve the economics of the rearing of livestock. In this regard, it is important to understand various economic traits of livestock and poultry. The nature of these traits will also determine the type of animal breeding analyses, which is to be explained in a separate chapter on types of data.

## Economic Traits for Dairy Cattle and Buffaloes

Information on animal identification, sire, dam, date of first service, date of first successful service, number of services per conception, date of first calving, milk yield registers, date of drying off and disposal available from the farm records are used to calculate the following economic traits.

### Production Traits

- **180-day milk yield**

  The cumulative milk yield (kg) for the first 180 days of lactation. For lactation less than 180 days, the yield for that period has to be taken as the 180-day yield.

- **305-day milk yield**

  The cumulative milk yield (kg) for the first 305 days of lactation or less.

- **Lactation length**

  The period in days from the date of calving till cows are dried up / dried off

- **Total lactation milk yield**

  The total milk production (kg) from the date of calving to the date of drying up/ drying off.

- **Peak yield**

  Maximum yield of milk (kg) on a particular day in a lactation.

- **Days to attain peak yield**

  The period (days) from calving to the date of peak yield.

- **Persistency of lactation**

  It can be described as the ability of the cow to maintain production following peak yield.

- **Milk yield per day of lactation length**

  It can be obtained by dividing the lactation yield by the lactation length and expressed in kg.

- **Milk yield per day of calving interval**

  It can be obtained by dividing the lactation yield by the calving interval and expressed in kg.

## Reproduction Traits

- **Age at first service**

  Age of the heifer at first service expressed in days

- **Age at first calving**

  Age of the cow at first calving expressed in days.

- **Weight at first calving**

  Weight of the cow at first calving expressed in kg.

- **Service period**

  Period in days between calving and subsequent service resulting in fruitful conception.

- **Calving interval**

  Interval between two successive calvings expressed in days.

- **Dry period**

  The duration in days from the date of drying to the next initiation of lactation

- **Number of services per conception**

  The number of services to make a cow fertile for the particular calving

## Fertility Traits

Conception rate (CR) is measured as a binary trait with 1 (conceived) and 0 (not conceived) both for the cow and bull.

## Lifetime Production Traits

- **Productive life**

  Number of days in milk during the lifetime of an individual cow
- **Herd life**

  Period from first calving to disposal from the herd
- **Total life or longevity**

  Period from birth to death/disposal
- **Lifetime milk yield**

  Milk yield during the total life
- **Milk yield per day of productive life**

  Calculated by dividing the lifetime milk yield by the productive life and expressed in kg
- **Milk yield per day of herd life**

  Calculated by dividing the lifetime milk yield by the herd life and expressed in kg.
- **Milk yield per day of total life**

  Calculated by dividing the lifetime milk yield by the total life and expressed in kg.

## Semen Traits

Semen production traits are important especially in a bull station were bulls are evaluated based on these parameters.

## Semen production traits

- Ejaculate volume (EV), the volume of semen in each ejaculate measured in ml
- Sperm concentration (EV), the concentratioon of spermatozoa expressed as million sperms per ml

- Initial sperm motility (ISM), the motility of sperm in the collected semen expressed in percentage. It is a subjective measure based on the observer.
- Post-thaw motility (PTM), the motility of sperm in frozen semen after thawing expressed as a percent. It gives an indication of the freezability of semen.
- Total number of spermatozoa per ejaculate (TNS) and the theoretical number of semen doses (TNSD) are composite traits.

  TNS = EV x SC

  $$TNSD = \frac{EV \times SC \times PTM}{10 \text{ million}}$$

## Sperm abnormality traits

Sperm abnormality traits give the percentage of defective spermatozoa present in fresh semen. These traits included head abnormality (HA), mid-piece abnormality (MA), tail abnormality (TA) and total abnormalities (A) which are expressed as percentages.

## Draughtability Traits

In India, several breeds such as the Kangayam, Pullikulam, Hallikar etc. have been developed for draught work such as carting and ploughing. Some animals are even known for the bull baiting game such as the Jallikattu. Traits to measure the draughtability include Ploughing speed, Stride length and Horse power.

- **Ploughing speed**

  The speed of ploughing is calculated by measuring the time taken to cover a particular distance
- **Stride length**

  Stride length is measured as the distance covered per stride.
- **Horsepower**

  Horsepower of a bull is estimated with a spring balance by using a modified technique ( Maurya and Devadattum, 1982b) as Draught X Speed (m/s)/75, where 75 is the constant. Draught is the product of pull (in kg) of the spring balance and Cosθ, θ being the angle the beam of plough makes with the horizontal ground.

## Economic Traits for Sheep and Goat

### Production Traits

- **Body weight:** Body weight in kilograms recorded at birth (BW), weaning (WW), six months (6W), nine months (9W) and 12 months (YW).
- **Average daily gain:** Average daily gain (ADG) is the change in body weight over time and calculated as $(y_{t2} - y_{t1}) / (t_2 - t_1)$ where y refers to body weight and $t_1$ and $t_2$ refers to age in days. ADG is also called as absolute growth rate which is expressed as grams per day. ADG shall be calculated for pre-weaning (birth to 3 months) and post-weaning (3-6, 6-9, 9-12, and 3-12 months) periods.

### Reproduction/ Functional Traits

- **Age at first lambing/kidding:** Age of the ewe in days when it lambs/kids first in its lifetime.
- **Lambing/kidding interval:** Period in days between two successive parturitions.
- **Lifetime productivity:** Number of lambs/kids born per ewe over a given period of time per ewe exposed. The lifetime productivity estimated as lifetime productivity (ewe available) and lifetime productivity (ewe lambed).
- **Survivability:** Pre-weaning survivability (0-3 months) and post-weaning survivabilities (3-6, 6-9, 9-12 and 3-12 months) are studied as a binomial trait, with '1' for survival and '0' for died.
- **Age-specific death rates**: were calculated from one mating to next using the equation,

$$d_i = (N_i - N_{i+1})/N_i$$

Where, $d_i$ is the death rate for $i^{th}$ age interval, $N_i$ and $N_{i+1}$ denote the number present at the beginning and end of the $i^{th}$ interval respectively. Death rates for six age intervals starting from 1½ - 2½ to 6½ - 7½ years are recorded.

### Reproductive traits specific to sheep

- **Tupping percent:** The percentage of number of ewes covered to the number of ewes put to ram.
- **Lambing percent:** The percentage of lambs born including still–births and abortions to the number of ewes. The lambing percent is estimated as lambing percent (ewe available) and lambing percent (ewe covered).
- **Twinning percent:** The number of twin lambings expressed as percent.

- **Fertility** studied as a binary trait (with a measure of 1 or 0), indicates whether a ewe exposed to a ram lambed or did not lamb, expressed in percentage.
- Number of lambs born per ewe mated
- Number of female lambs born per ewe mated
- Number of lambs weaned per ewe mated
- Number of female lambs weaned per ewe mated
- Number of lambs born per ewe lambing
- Number of female lambs born per ewe lambing
- Number of lambs weaned per ewe lambing
- Number of female lambs weaned per ewe lambing
- Total number of lambs born per ewe over lifetime
- Total number of female lambs born per ewe over lifetime
- Total number of lambs weaned per ewe over a lifetime
- Total number of female lambs weaned per ewe over a lifetime
- **Replacement rate:** Replacement rate indicates the female lambs reaching reproductive age per ewe mated or number of ewe lambs reaching joining age per ewe mated. It is calculated as the product of number of ewe lambs weaned per ewe mated and number of ewe lambs reaching joining age (1½ years) per ewe lamb weaned.
- **Net reproduction rate or selective value:** The female lambs reaching reproductive age per ewe over a lifetime is measured as the number of ewe offspring, produced by each ewe during her lifetime in the flock, reaching joining age. Contribution by the ewe in terms of the offspring to the next generation is called the selective value of the individual.

  Net reproduction rate = $\sum ( L_{\tau} L_{EJ.J} )$

  Where, $L_{\tau}$ = probability of survival to lambing age

  $L_{EJ.J}$ = number ewe lambs reaching joining age per ewe mated

## Reproduction Traits Specific to Goat

- **Litter size:** No. of kids born in a kidding inclusive of still-births.
- **Twinning percent:** Number of multiple births expressed as a percent,
- **Post-partum estrus:** The interval in days from the date of kidding to the occurrence of first heat symptoms.

- **Survivability:** Pre-weaning survivability (0-3 months) and post-weaning survivability (3-6, 6-9 and 9-12 months) are studied as a binomial trait, with '1' for survived and '0' for died.

## Economic Traits of Pig

The raw data available in farm records are information on individual animal identity, sire, dam, date of birth, birth weight, sex, date of weaning, weaning weight, date of service, date of farrowing, litter size at birth, litter size at weaning, date of disposal, type of disposal and reason for disposal. Economic traits in the pig could be broadly classified as individual and Sow performance traits.

## Individual Traits

- Birth weight: Body weight of individual piglet at birth in kg
- Weaning weight: Body weight of individual piglet at weaning in kg
- Pre-weaning average daily gain: Daily weight gain of piglet in grams from birth to weaning
- Market weight: Weight of the individual pigs at marketing age in kg (7-9 months)

## Feed efficiency

- **Weaning to 154 days**: Weight of feed consumed in kg for producing one kg of live weight from weaning to 154 days.
- **Weaning to 210 days**: Weight of feed consumed in kg for producing one kg of live weight from weaning to 210 days.

## Sow Performance Traits

- Pre-weaning mortality: Calculated as number of piglets that died up to 42 days of age and expressed as percent.
- Age at first fertile service: Age in days at first service/mating resulting in conception.
- Litter size at birth: The total number of piglets born per sow/ farrowing including stillbirths.
- Number born alive: The number of piglets born alive at birth excluding stillbirths.
- Litter weight at birth: The sum of individual birth weight of piglets born in a litter.

- Litter size at weaning: The number of piglets weaned in a litter.
- Litter weight at weaning: The sum of individual weaning weight of piglets born in a litter.
- Farrowing interval: The period in days between two subsequent farrowings.

## Economic Traits of Rabbit

### Production Traits

- **Growth:** Weight of the rabbit at weaning (six weeks), ten weeks and twenty weeks in kg.
- **Pre-weaning and post-weaning average daily gain** in g.

### Reproduction Traits

- **Age at first mating: Age in days from birth to date of first mating.**
- **Total births per litter**: the no. of young ones born in a litter inclusive of stillbirths.
- **Total live births per litter**: The no. of young ones born live in a litter
- **Litter weight at birth**: Weight of young ones from a litter at birth in kg
- **Litter size at weaning**: The no. of young ones from a litter that survived until weaning.
- **Litter weight at weaning**: Weight of young ones from a litter that survived until weaning in kg
- **Fecundity:** Fecundity is defined as the product of fertility (number of kindlings per doe per unit of time) and prolificacy (number of young per kindling).

### Mortality Traits

- **Pre-weaning mortality**: The number of deaths from birth to weaning expressed as a percent of the total no. of births.
- **Post-weaning mortality**: The number of deaths from weaning to one year of age.

## Economic Traits of Poultry

### Production Traits

- **Body weight gain**

  The body weight gain in birds for various ages can be determined as a difference between the final body weight and the initial body weight or day-old weight

- **Feed Efficiency**

  Feed efficiency is the quantity of feed required to produce one kg body weight in meat-type birds. In layers, it is defined as the quantity of feed required to produce one kilogram or one dozen of eggs.

$$\text{Feed Efficiency in broilers} = \frac{\text{Total feed consumed in kg}}{\text{Total final body weight in kg}}$$

$$\text{Feed Efficiency in layers per kg egg produced} = \frac{\text{Feed consumed in kg}}{\text{Egg mass (in kg) produced}}$$

$$\text{Feed Efficiency per dozen eggs produced} = \frac{\text{Feed consumed in kg}}{\text{Number of eggs (in dozens) produced}}$$

- **Hen day egg production (HDEP)** is the percentage of egg produced by the survivor population. It can be expressed both in number and percentage. A farm or flock average of 92% or more than 335 eggs per year or above are desirable

$$\text{HDEP / day} = \frac{\text{Number of eggs laid}}{\text{Number of live birds on that day}} \times 100$$

$$\text{HDEP / period} = \frac{\text{Total number of eggs produced during a period}}{\text{Total number of hen days during that period}} \times 100$$

Hen days = sum of opening balance of live hens on each day

- **Hen-housed egg production (HHEP)** is egg production based on the initial number of hens housed in the flock. It can be expressed both in number and percentage. HHEP values 88% or higher are desirable.

$$\text{HHEP / day} = \frac{\text{Number of eggs laid on given day}}{\text{Number of hens housed at the beginning}} \times 100$$

$$\text{HHEP / period} = \frac{\text{Average daily number of eggs laid / day}}{\text{Number of hens housed initially}} \times 100$$

## Mortality Traits

$$\text{Mortality}(\%) = \frac{\text{No. of birds died}}{\text{Number of birds at the start}}$$

Livability (%) = 100 - mortality %

# 3

# Nature of Animal Breeding Data and Database Management System

Animal breeding data is unique in terms of volume, statistical analysis, type of information required etc. The large volume of data extended spatially and temporally warrants additional tools in the form of databases to handle data and enable accuracy, retrieval, efficient utilization and adaptability to software. This chapter explains the nature of animal breeding data and the importance of databases with examples and explanations.

Animals are raised for some utility including meat, milk, hide, wool etc., and efforts are on to continuously improve the quality and quantity of these products. Some of the important economic traits in this regard were already discussed in earlier chapters. Record maintenance is primary for decision-making with respect to the selection of animals. The details of record maintenance including the format of registers are already explained in chapter 2. Apart from the actual information required for economic traits, pedigree information forms an important part of animal breeding data.

Traditionally only phenotypic traits and pedigree information were recorded. In recent years genomic selection is applied the world over and as this information is available at birth, genetic gain becomes rapid through the reduction in the generation interval. Similarly, the number of breeds/strain/varieties within a species are more and information on the classification is very important to draw meaningful inferences. The phenotype observed is a combination of genotype and environment and thus correction for various measurable non-genetic factors is an important pre-requisite in animal breeding analyses, for which information on various factors are to be recorded.

Animal breeding data analysis is not restricted to the animals currently available on the farm. It includes all the animals from the founding population as Henderson's BLUP made it possible to utilize the information from all the relatives through the Numerator Relationship Matrix. Thus the voluminous data to be handled warrants additional resources in the form of Data Base Management System.

## Animal Breeding Data

### Unique Features of Animal Breeding Data

- Pedigree information including Individual, Sire, and Dam from the initial founder population
- Economic traits of importance which are the selection objectives
- Other traits which are selection criteria
- Factors which are required for the correction of data
- The date of birth of individual animals which are needed for knowing the generation interval
- The genotype of individual animals if known could be useful in genomic selection.

### Characteristics of Animal Breeding Data

This multidimensional structure of the data which is spread spatially and geographically makes the data voluminous and diverse in nature. Some of the important characteristics of animal breeding data could be explained.

- **Large voluminous data:** The multifaceted information required for an animal breeding analyses makes it voluminous with a large number of fields and numerous observations.
- **Spread over time (From founders to current stock):** Animal breeding data is not limited to the current period as information right from the foundation stock is required for the estimation of breeding values and other parameters including inbreeding. Thus data on animal breeding is temporal in nature
- **Spread over the region (Several farms, Field performance recording):** The type of breeding programme could include several locations and this makes animal breeding data geographically spread with information from several locations.
- **Diverse in type (quantitative, qualitative, date, logical, binary etc.,):** The trait of interest and factors affecting them could be classified into several types of data, which would require special assumptions and types of analyses. Details of the type of data are provided in other chapters.
- **Diverse in units (kg, g, per cent, time to event):** The units of measurement for various traits are different, while the same trait also could be expressed in different ways, each having its own advantage depending upon the objective. For eg., Mortality as a descriptive measure could be expressed as a percentage, while for the estimation of genetic parameters, the same trait is to be expressed as a binary outcome.

- **Diverse in the method of recording (eg. Test day yield, Complete lactation):** The nature of recording also is different depending on the breeding programme and availability of resources. A field performance recording utilises the test day recording system, for which estimation and other analysis varies. In a large farm complete data for all the days are available for analysis.

## Data Base Management System (DBMS)

A set of computer programmes that control the creation, maintenance and retrieval of the information related to an organisation. Difficulty to handle voluminous and diverse animal breeding data in the form of registers and records necessitates additional tools especially the DBMS for efficient handling, retrieval, analysis and interpretation. Computers and database management form an integral part of the data management system.

## Advantages of Data Base Management System (DBMS)

- Easy to manage large volumes of data
- Instant retrieval of the required data for analysis
- Storage of large volumes of data with less effort, space and money
- Transfer of data is instantaneous
- Entry of data is simpler with a DBMS. An interface such as Visual Basic makes data entry customized and easier
- DBMS enables a single entry and multiple retrieval systems which helps in saving data entry time and labour.
- It is possible to specifically denote the type of data such as numeric, string, or logical at the time of entry.
- DBMS enables multiple file formats such as .txt. .xls, .sdf, .csv for use in various analytical software. For eg. the R platform uses .txt or .csv formats
- Coding of factors such as period, season, parity etc., is easily done from the date of birth in a DBMS.
- Sorting and indexing features help in data editing, identification of outliers and data retrieval for specific breeding purposes including age-wise, sex-wise, and production-wise classifications.
- Maintenance of data as DBMS enables the use of computer programmes which in turn will help in the calculation of economic traits; eg. Lambing interval from the date of lambing; litter size of the sow from birth data; average daily gain from weighment data, calculation of composite traits from individual traits.

- Software management systems such as HERDMATE – Any animal management system requires data in the form of a DBMS for efficient outputs which help in decision making, such as estrus detection, vaccination and deworming due, culling pattern etc.
- Estimation of genetic parameters and breeding value which is the main objective of the breeder is possible only if input data is provided in a prescribed format and this could be done easily from a DBMS.

There are a plethora of applications that have been used for DBMS. Microsoft Access in MS office, Visual Foxpro, Oracle etc. Each has its own advantages with respect to the cost, type of data to be handled and expertise available. The R platform itself provides several features of DBMS for handling animal breeding data. The data which is too large for the computer's memory can be stored outside R and it can be organised using a database and only the part of data that is required for the current analysis could be brought into the data frame. Packages such as the 'dplyr' work behind the scene and

- Translates R code into SQL
- Submits it to the database
- Translates databases response into R data frame

## Important operations with R for handling animal breeding data include

- Reading data from a spreadsheet like Excel
- Writing data after analysis into other forms such as text or excel
- Recoding of data to suit different animal breeding analysis
- Merging of datasets
- Forming subsets of data with a specific condition
- Changing the format of data such as string, numeric, factor, date, integer etc.,
- Use of 'if else' conditions to work in a programme
- To incorporate various functions of existing data such as polynomial, square, square root, log etc.,
- To visualize data in the form of graphs or other diagrams.

## Structure of Data Bases for Animal Breeding Data

Depending on the requirement, the structure of a database could be designed in a customised way by the breeder. The structure usually followed is individual animal based with all details from birth to death of the animal forming a single case. However, an example of databases for cattle could form a template for use by animal breeders.

**Table 3.1:** Structure of a Database File

| S.No. | Name of Field | Type of Data |
|---|---|---|
| 1 | Animal No | Character |
| 2 | Date of birth | Date |
| 3 | Sire | Character |
| 4 | Dam | Character |
| 5 | Breed | Character |
| 6 | Sex | Character |
| 7 | Birth weight | Numeric |
| 8 | Weaning weight | Numeric |
| 9 | Date of weighment | Date |
| 10 | Weight | Numeric |
| 11 | Date of first heat | Date |
| 12 | Date of first service | Date |
| 13 | Weight at first heat | Numeric |
| 14 | Weight at first service | Numeric |
| 15 | Date of subsequent service | Date |
| 16 | Date of pregnancy verification | Date |
| 17 | Pregnancy | Logical |
| 18 | Date of first calving | Date |
| 19 | Weight at first calving | Numeric |
| 20 | Peak yield | Numeric |
| 21 | Days to attain peak yield | Numeric |
| 22 | Date of second service | Date |
| 23 | Date of pregancy verification 2 | Date |
| 24 | 180-day yield | Numeric |
| 25 | 305-day lactation yield | Numeric |
| 26 | Date of drying | Date |
| 27 | Date of second calving | Date |
| 28 | Calving interval | Numeric |
| 29 | Date of disposal/death | Date |
| 30 | Mode of disposal | Character |
| 31 | Remarks | Character |

These structures could be decided according to the breeding programme and once data entry is done the database file forms the base for all analysis needed for selection and breeding. Simple programme files could be coded to obtain data in the prescribed form or retrieval of data required for further analysis. Some of the example programme files used are illustrated here

## Foxpro Programme File Models

### Interface Programme to Add Basic Data of a New Born Animal

```
CLEAR
USE TEMP
ANS="Y"

ACCEPT " TAG : " TO MTAG
LOCATE FOR AN = MTAG

RECNO=RECNO()
DO WHILE ANS="Y"

INSE BLANK
CLEAR
@ 10 ,15 SAY " ANIMAL NO: " GET AN
@ 14, 15 SAY " DOB     : " GET DOB
@ 16, 15 SAY " BR      : " GET BR
@ 18, 15 SAY " SEX     : " GET SEX
@ 10, 40 SAY " SIRE    : " GET SIRE
@ 14, 40 SAY " DAM     : " GET DAM
READ
CLEAR
RECNO=RECNO+1
CLEAR
@ 10,10 SAY "CONTINUE  Y/N" GET ANS
READ
IF ANS="Y"
LOOP
ELSE
RETURN
ENDIF
ENDDO
```

----------------------------------------------------------------------------------------------------

## Prog for Arriving Age-wise Daily Stock for Sheep

```
CLEAR
SET TALK OFF
USE Sf
COPY TO AGEPRG.DBF FOR STATUS=" "
*@ 14,10 SAY "IF YOU REQUIRE A PRINT OUT, SET PRINTER READY"
use
USE AGEPRG.dbf

REPLACE ALL DAYS WITH CTOD(DTOC(DATE()))-CTOD(DTOC(DOB))

COUNT FOR BR="N".AND.SEX="F".AND.DAYS>=366.AND.DAYS<730  TO MN1
COUNT FOR BR="N".AND.SEX="F".AND.DAYS>=731.AND.DAYS<1095 TO MN2
COUNT FOR BR="N".AND.SEX="F".AND.DAYS>=1095.AND.DAYS<1460 TO MN3
COUNT FOR BR="N".AND.SEX="F".AND.DAYS>=1460.AND.DAYS<1825 TO MN4
COUNT FOR BR="N".AND.SEX="F".AND.DAYS>=1825.AND.DAYS<2190 TO MN5
COUNT FOR BR="N".AND.SEX="F".AND.DAYS>=2190 TO MN6

COUNT FOR BR="S ".AND.SEX="F".AND.DAYS>=366.AND.DAYS<730 TO MS1
COUNT FOR BR="S ".AND.SEX="F".AND.DAYS>=730.AND.DAYS<1095 TO MS2
COUNT FOR BR="S ".AND.SEX="F".AND.DAYS>=1095.AND.DAYS<1460 TO MS3
COUNT FOR BR="S ".AND.SEX="F".AND.DAYS>=1460.AND.DAYS<1825 TO MS4
COUNT FOR BR="S ".AND.SEX="F".AND.DAYS>=1825.AND.DAYS<2190 TO MS5
COUNT FOR BR="S ".AND.SEX="F".AND.DAYS>=2190 TO MS6

COUNT FOR BR="DN".AND.SEX="F".AND.DAYS>=366.AND.DAYS<730 TO  MD1
COUNT FOR BR="DN".AND.SEX="F".AND.DAYS>=730.AND.DAYS<1095 TO MD2
COUNT FOR BR="DN".AND.SEX="F".AND.DAYS>=1095.AND.DAYS<1460 TO MD3
COUNT FOR BR="DN".AND.SEX="F".AND.DAYS>=1460.AND.DAYS<1825 TO MD4
COUNT FOR BR="DN".AND.SEX="F".AND.DAYS>=1825.AND.DAYS<2190 TO MD5
COUNT FOR BR="DN".AND.SEX="F".AND.DAYS>=2190 TO MD6

STORE MN1+MN2+MN3+MN4+MN5+MN6 TO TMN
STORE MS1+MS2+MS3+MS4+MS5+MS6 TO TMS
STORE MD1+MD2+MD3+MD4+MD5+MD6 TO TMD

STORE MN1+MS1+MD1 TO TA1
STORE MN2+MS2+MD2 TO TA2
STORE MN3+MS3+MD3 TO TA3
```

```
STORE MN4+MS4+MD4 TO TA4
STORE MN5+MS5+MD5 TO TA5
STORE MN6+MS6+MD6 TO TA6
STORE TMN+TMS+TMD TO TAA

CLEAR
SET PRINTER ON

?'TANUVAS,SBRS,SANDYNALLAH'
?
?'SHEEP STOCK AGE WISE PARTICULARS AS ON ',DATE()
?REPLICATE ("*",110)
?'                    AGE GROUP  WISE'
?REPLICATE ("*",110)
?'                    1-2        2-3        3-4          4-5         5-6         >6         TOTAL'
?REPLICATE("*",110)
?'NILAG-F',MN1,MN2,MN3,MN4,MN5,MN6,TMN
?REPLICATE("*",110)
?'SANDY-F',MS1,MS2,MS3,MS4,MS5,MS6,TMS
?REPLICATE ("*",110)
?'DNCRO-F',MD1,MD2,MD3,MD4,MD5,MD6,TMD
?REPLICATE ("*",110)
*?'ADULTS ',MA1,MA2,MA3,MA4,FA1,FA2,FA3,FA4,MA5,FA5
*?REPLICATE ("-",125)
?'TOTAL  ',TA1,TA2,TA3,TA4,TA5,TA6,TAA
?REPLICATE ("*",110)
*?" TOTAL:    MALES :",  GTM ," FEMALES : ", GTF, "GRAND *TOTAL",GTM+GTF
*?REPLICATE ("=",125)
SET PRINTER OFF
WAIT
CLOSE ALL
ERASE ageprg.DBF
CLEAR
CLEAR ALL
SET TALK ON
RETURN
```

---

## Programme to Count the Number of Sires or Dams Repeating in A Data Base

This programme will count for no. of progeny per sire or dam in a genetic parameter estimation using half sib design. It is also useful in deleting the records for a particular parity. For eg. the programme will count the parity for dam based on repeating progeny and if required only the first parity records could be included in the analysis.

```
use temp3
set talk off
do while.not.eof()
cnt=0
store SI_NO to ms
do while SI_NO=ms
skip
if SI_NO=ms
cnt=cnt+1
REPLACE COUNT WITH cnt
endif
enddo
enddo
```

---

## Programme to Delete Sire With Less Than 3 Progeny

(Useful in sire model to have data with more than specific no. of progeny per sire)

Clear

```
use temp3
set talk off
do while.not.eof()
cnt=0
store si_no to ms

do while si_no=ms
skip
if si_no=ms
cnt=cnt+1
```

```
endif
enddo
if cnt<2
dele for si_no=ms
pack
go top
else
endif
enddo
```

-----------------------------------------------------------------------------------------------

## Programme for Entering Consecutive Numbers in Database

```
CLEAR
SET TALK OFF
mfile=space (8)
accept " File ::"to mfile
USE &mfile
*OCATE FOR RECNO()=721
SNO=1
DO WHILE.NOT.EOF()
REPLACE SLNO WITH SNO
SKIP
SNO=SNO+1
ENDDO
SET TALK OFF
RETURN
```

-----------------------------------------------------------------------------------------------

## Programme for Calculating Lambing Interval or Calving Interval Based on Date of Birth of Lamb/Calf

```
clear
use SANDYNO1
set talk off
do while.not.eof()
```

```
LI1T=0
LI2T=0
LI3T=0
LI4T=0
LI5T=0
LI6T=0
LI7T=0
LI8T=0
LI9T=0

store AN to ms

do while AN=ms

if AN=MS.AND.LAMBPARITY=1
LI1T= LI1T+AFL
ELSE
ENDIF
*SKIP

IF AN=MS.AND.LAMBPARITY=2
LI2T=LI2T+AFL
REPLACE LI1 WITH LI2T-LI1T
ELSE
ENDIF
*SKIP

if AN=MS.AND.LAMBPARITY=3
LI3T=LI3T+AFL
REPLACE LI2 WITH LI3T-LI2T
ELSE
ENDIF
*SKIP

IF AN=MS.AND.LAMBPARITY=4
LI4T=LI4T+AFL
REPLACE LI3 WITH LI4T-LI3T
ELSE
ENDIF
```

```
*SKIP

if AN=MS.AND.LAMBPARITY=5
LI5T=LI5T+AFL
REPLACE LI4 WITH LI5T-LI4T
ELSE
ENDIF
*SKIP

IF AN=MS.AND.LAMBPARITY=6
LI6T=LI6T+AFL
REPLACE LI5 WITH LI6T-LI5T
ELSE
ENDIF

IF AN=MS.AND.LAMBPARITY=7
LI7T=LI7T+AFL
REPLACE LI6 WITH LI7T-LI6T
ELSE
ENDIF

IF AN=MS.AND.LAMBPARITY=8
LI8T=LI8T+AFL
REPLACE LI7 WITH LI8T-LI7T
ELSE
ENDIF

IF AN=MS.AND.LAMBPARITY=9
LI9T=LI9T+AFL
REPLACE LI8 WITH LI9T-LI8T
ELSE
ENDIF
SKIP
enddo
LI1T=0
LI2T=0
LI3T=0
LI4T=0
```

```
LI5T=0
LI6T=0
LI7T=0
LI8T=0
LI9T=0
STORE AN TO MS
enddo
```

---

## Programme to Get Adjusted Body Weight Corrected for the Actual Day of Weighing

(For eg. If a lamb was born on the 85th day, then to calculate 3-month body weight (90 days) 5 days of weight gain is to be added based on the average daily gain of that particular animal)

```
SET TALK OFF
mfile=space (8)
accept " File ::"to mfile
USE &mfile
Replace ALL bIRTHwt WITH 0
Replace ALL weight3 WITH 0

REPLACE ALL DAYS1 WITH dom1-dob FOR DOM1#CTOD(' ')
REPLACE ALL DAYS2 WITH dom2-dob FOR DOM2#CTOD(' ')
REPLACE ALL DAYS3 WITH dom3-dob FOR DOM3#CTOD(' ')

GO top

DO WHILE.NOT.EOF()
STORE dom1-dob TO D1
STORE   dom2-dom1 TO D2
STORE dom3-dom2 TO D3

IF  DAYS1>=70 .AND. DAYS1<130
        REPLACE WEIGHT3 WITH ((ACTWT1)-(((D1-90)*((Actwt1-2.5)/D1))))
ENDIF

SKIP
ENDDO
```

---

## Programme to Add a Record for the Same Animal

(eg. Date of birth based on a common field animal number. This will help in data entry, we can enter the common details such as sire, dam, dob etc., for an animal once and this could be filled using the programme where ever the animal repeats in the programme)

```
set talk off
use TEMP1
DO while.not.eof()
STORE bull_no TO MAN
STORE dob TO mdate
skip
if bull_no=man AND dob=CTOD(' ')
*SKIP -1
REPLACE dob WITH mdate
*DELE
ENDIF
*skip -1
*IF DAM=' '
*DELE NEXT 2
*DELE
*ENDIF
Enddo
```

---

## Programme to give numerical numbers for animal ids such as name or other character strings

(sort the file on bull names so as to avoid repeat numbers)

```
clear
use temp2
set talk off
cnt=1000
do while.not.eof()
store bull_no to ms
replace count WITH cnt
skip
if bull_no#ms
cnt=cnt+1
endif
enddo
```

---

## Programme to Calculate the Age of Dam

```
USE PHD
SET TALK OFF
DO WHILE .NOT. EOF()
STORE DAM TO MDAM
STORE RECNO() TO MREC
STORE DOB TO MDATE
LOCATE FOR AN=MDAM
STORE DOB TO MS
GO MREC
REPLACE DAMAGE WITH MDATE-MS
SKIP
ENDDO
```

---

# 4

# Basic Statistics, Experimental Design, Types of Data and Probability Distribution

Basic knowledge of statistics is important to understand animal breeding analysis. In this chapter, the hypothesis testing, principles of experimental design, types of data and probability distribution are described with examples using appropriate software.

## Basic Statistics

Any researcher will have a scientific question in mind and the main objective would be to generalize the results obtained from a sample for the actual population under question. Statistics is the study of methods and procedures for collecting, classifying, summarizing, and analyzing data and for making scientific inferences from such data. Statistics increases the confidence of a researcher in expressing his results. The concept map (Figure 4.1) indicating the steps involved in animal research is nicely depicted by Seltman (2008).

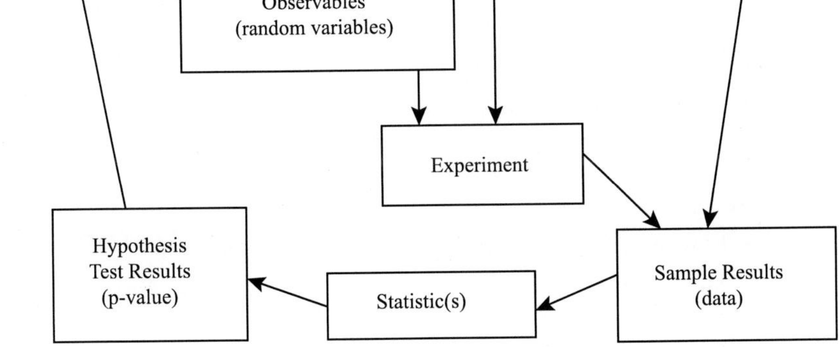


**Figure 4.1:** Concept map of a research experiment (Seltman, 2008)

Once a researcher decides on the concept or hypothesis, the first step is to identify the observables (parameters, random variables). The experiment is conducted on a sample (to do the experiment on an entire population is impossible) on which the various parameters are recorded. The sample point estimate is the value of a character in the sample, and this is not the true population value. Statistics provides an interval estimate, the range within which the true estimate lies and this range would vary according to the confidence level.

## Hypothesis Testing

1. Null hypothesis: set up null hypothesis $H_0$.
2. Alternative Hypothesis: Set up alternative hypothesis $H_1$, which is complementary to $H_0$ and will indicate whether a one-tailed (right or left-tailed) or two-tailed test is to be applied.
3. Level of significance: Choose an appropriate level of significance ($\alpha$), $\alpha$ is fixed in advance.
4. Test statistic (or test of criterion)
5. Inference: We compare the computed value (in absolute value) with the significant value (critical value) to take decisions. A P value of less than 0.05 indicates significance at 5 per cent level and less than 0.01 significance at 1 per cent level. This indicates that the null hypothesis is rejected
6. If significant, pair-wise comparison of means can be done using Post-hoc tests

## Hypothesis: Null and Alternate hypothesis

| | | |
|---|---|---|
| $H_o$: | Distribution of pop. A and pop. B are the same, i.e. A = B | |
| $H_A$: | Distribution of pop. A and pop. B are not the same, i.e A = B | Two tailed test |
| $H_A$: | Distribution of pop. A is shifted to the right of pop. B, i.e. A > B. | One tailed test |
| $H_A$: | Distribution of pop. A is shifted to the left of pop. B, i.e. A < B | |

## Type I and II error

Inference from the probability of extremity (P-value) is either acceptance or rejection of the Null-hypothesis. Based on the truth of this result in the whole population arises two errors; Type I and Type II errors. Type I error (α) is also called the level of significance and could be explained as the probability of a true null hypothesis (in the population) getting rejected (in the sample experiment). This could be fixed by the experimenter and is also called a false positive. The alternative to this is the Type II error (Beta) or false negative which is the probability of a false null hypothesis getting accepted or false negative. These errors are important in designing an experiment as the power of the experiment depends on β, which in turn is dependent on the α

| | The truth | |
|---|---|---|
| Conclusion | No effect | Has an effect |
| Reject H0 | Type I error | ✓ |
| Fail to reject H0 | ✓ | Type II error |

## Types of Data and Probability Distribution

The nature of the variable to be studied and the probability distribution it is expected to follow will decide the type of analysis.

Data can be qualitative or quantitative. Usually, qualitative data such as colour, sex, breed etc., are measured as counts and they are discrete with less number of classes. Quantitative data usually measure a quantity and the number of classes is too high, thus forming a continuous distribution. Such data can be represented as a frequency distribution, which illustrates the frequency of various class limits. In large samples, such data can also follow theoretical probability distributions. Qualitative data are data of a kind and are further classified as nominal or ordinal data. Different types of data used in animal breeding can be classified as shown in Table 4.1 which would form the basis for any animal breeding data analysis.

**Table 4.1:** Type of data for various traits and factors affecting them in animal breeding

| Traits | Type of Variable | Factors Affecting | Type of Variable |
|---|---|---|---|
| **Milk Production traits** | | | |
| • 305-day milk yield<br>• Fat yield<br>• SNF Yield<br>• Protein yield<br>• Test-day milk yield | Quantitative continuous | Species, breed, season, period, herd, milkman, milking frequency | Qualitative nominal |
| | | Parity | Quantitative discrete/ qualitative ordinal depending on the number of classes |
| | | Feed and water intake, temperature | Quantitative continuous |
| **Reproductive traits** | | | |
| Age at first calving<br>Calving interval | Quantitative Continuous | Species, breed, season, period | Qualitative nominal |
| Conception rate/ fertility | Qualitative binomial | | |
| Semen production traits | | | |
| Ejaculate volume<br>Total sperms<br>Toral motile sperms | Quantitative continuous | Species, breed, season, period, semen collector, ejaculate number, | Qualitative nominal |
| Mass activity | Qualitative ordinal | Age of the bull<br>Collection interval | Qualitative continuous<br>Qualitative ordinal |
| **Growth traits** | | | |
| Birth weight<br>Yearling weight<br>Weanining weight<br>Average daily gain | Quantitative continuous | Species, breed, sex, herd, season, period<br><br>Age of dam | Qualitative nominal<br><br>Quantitative continuous |
| **Carcass traits** | | | |
| Weight at Slaughter<br>Dressing percent<br>Carcass conformation scores | Quantitative continuous<br>Qualitative ordinal | Species, breed, sex<br><br>Age | Qualitative nominal<br><br>Quantitative continuous |

## Types of data

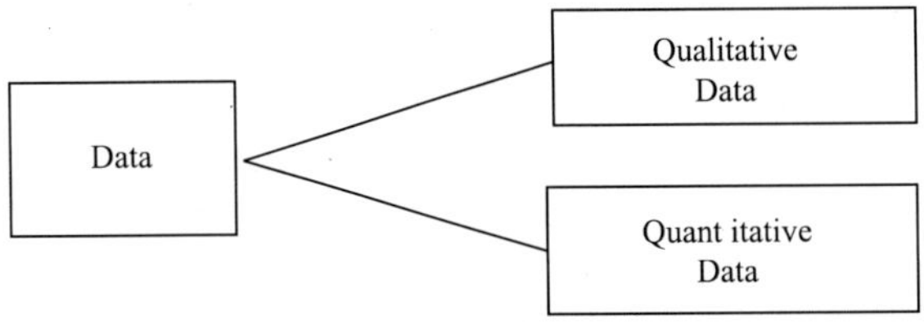


## Qualitative

- Nominal – having 2 or more categories and lack order (Eg. breed, sex)
- Ordinal – 2 or more categories and have order (Eg. Mass activity of spermatozoa; Small; Medium & Large animals) but differences are not meaningful.

## Quantitative

- Interval or scale – Quantitative Variables having own scale; lacks '0' and divisions are not meaningful (temperature in Celsius)
- Ratio – Quantitative variables, valid '0' and divisions are meaningful (Yield, Germination etc.)

Probability is the extent to which an event is likely to occur, measured by the ratio of favourable cases to the whole number of cases possible. A numerical measure of uncertainty is probability and it measures the relative frequency of a particular event happening by chance. In other terms, it is the likelihood of the occurrence of an event.

**Examples:**

1. Getting a head when we toss a coin
2. Getting a normal birth or dystocia
3. Sex of the calf to be born

- To draw inferences about the population understanding the theoretical distributions is essential.
- In a population, the value of the variable may be distributed according to some definite probability law which can be expressed mathematically and the corresponding probability distribution is known as a theoretical probability distribution.

A probability distribution is a distribution of probabilities for various values, which the random variable can take. These distributions have been formed by statisticians based on the function of the variable in terms of parameters (mean and variance for a Normal distribution). Some of the distributions are Binomial, Poisson, Normal, Chi-square, F, Student's t, etc., Most of the statistical tests are dependent on these distributions for comparison and hence termed parametric tests. Some of the tests include large sample Z test, t-test and F-test. For use of any of such tests, it is important that the data follow the respective distribution. Most of the statistical tests are dependent on the assumption of Normal distribution as the majority of data are found to follow this distribution. Exploratory analysis of data can be done to ascertain that the data follow a normal distribution. The type of data will determine the statistical test used.

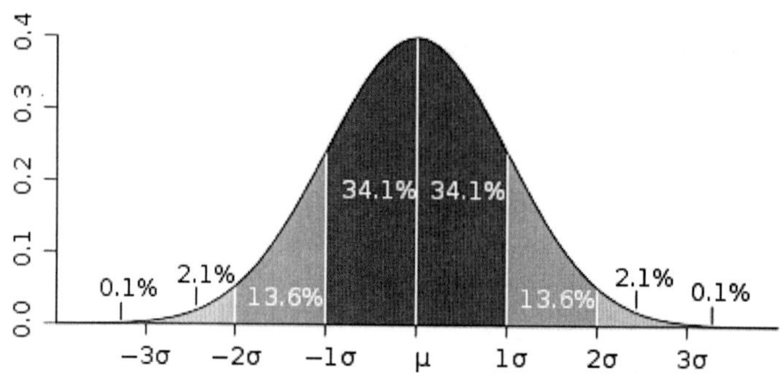


**Figure 4.2:** The normal bell-shaped curve.

When data fail to follow any of the theoretical distributions, the regular statistic tests described above are no more valid. Options are available to transform such data and analysis can be performed on the transformed data, provided the transformed value follows the theoretical distribution. When transformations also don't work, non-parametric tests are available to analyse such data. Some of the non-parametric tests are Wilcoxon rank test, Mann-Whitney test, Kruskal Wallis test and others. In general, the parametric tests have greater power (to be explained later in the chapter) and thus the required sample size would be small.

All kinds of estimations and analyses in animal breeding would vary depending on the type of data.

## Experimental Design

The study design is the blueprint for the experiment and is to be clearly formed before the start of the experiment. A proper design of the experiment helps in increasing the efficiency of trial by providing maximum power with a minimum sample size. The basic principles of an experimental design are **replication, randomization and local control**. Replication takes care of the individual-to-individual variation, while randomization provides unbiasedness by providing an equal chance for every experimental unit. Local control helps in removing heterogeneity by blocking for known external sources of variation. Blinding is the technique in which the treatment and control identities are kept secret in order to avoid bias that creeps in.

Once the hypothesis is fixed, the number of treatments and control are to be decided and based on this the sample size, which is the number per group could be derived. Similarly, for each experiment, the type of controls is to be specified. In the study design depending on the type of parameter, it is important to differentiate between the experimental unit and the animal unit. In certain cases, there can be more than one animal for each experimental unit (for eg. Feed efficiency). In order to explicitly represent our study design, NC3R has a web tool called as Experimental Design Assistant (Figure 4.3).

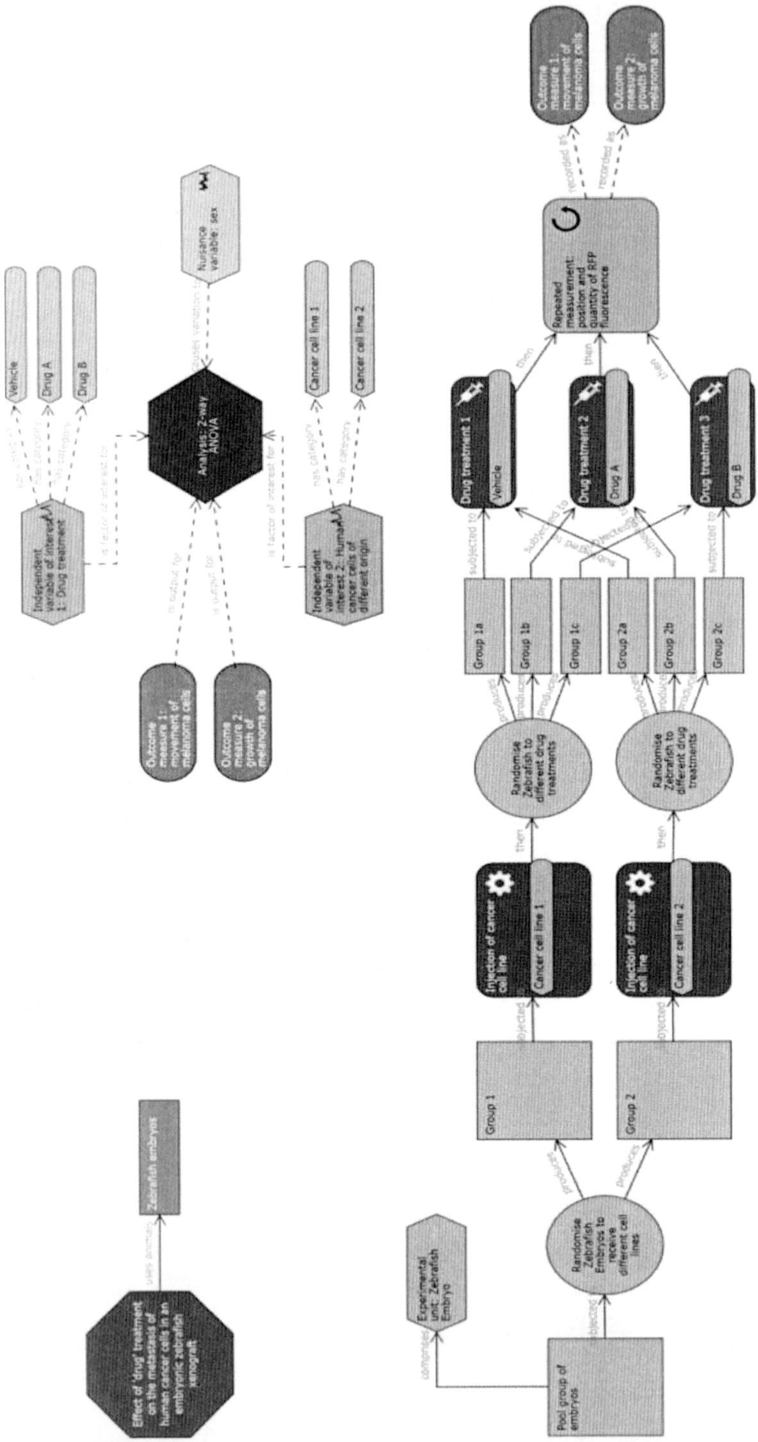


**Figure 4.3:** A template from Experimental Design Assistant (EDA -https://www.nc3rs.org.uk/experimental-design-assistant-eda)

## 1. Sample size (replication)

The sample size is one of the important aspects of experimental Design and represents the replication. As a laboratory animal scientist, the use of the right number of lab animals is essential as too few animals will lead to misleading results, while more animals will lead to ethical issues. Sample size, the second important ARRIVE guideline is the first challenge in front of the researcher and to decide up on the sample size, there is no universal solution. It is highly arbitrary as the sample size would depend upon several factors unique to the experiment.

A. The response variable will determine the sample size depending on the type of data and probability distribution. The details of this have already been explained.

B. **Variability of data:** The greater the variability of data, that is the response measure, the more samples would be required to test the hypothesis. Variability is represented by the standard deviation of the trait.

C. **Level of significance (Type I error or alpha):** As explained earlier α is the type I error and is fixed by the scientist usually at 5% or 1% and lesser the type I error, more stringent is the experiment and sample size required will also increase.

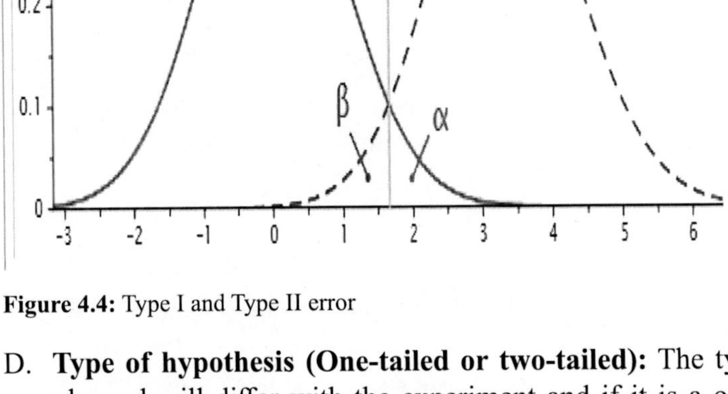


**Figure 4.4:** Type I and Type II error

D. **Type of hypothesis (One-tailed or two-tailed):** The type of difference planned will differ with the experiment and if it is a one-tailed test the difference is expected for only one side of the probability distribution (either lesser than or greater than) and hence α becomes larger, bringing down β. This power is more for a one-tailed test and the sample size will be less. On the other hand, for a two-tailed distribution, α is halved leading to a greater β and thus reduction in power will necessitate more sample size.

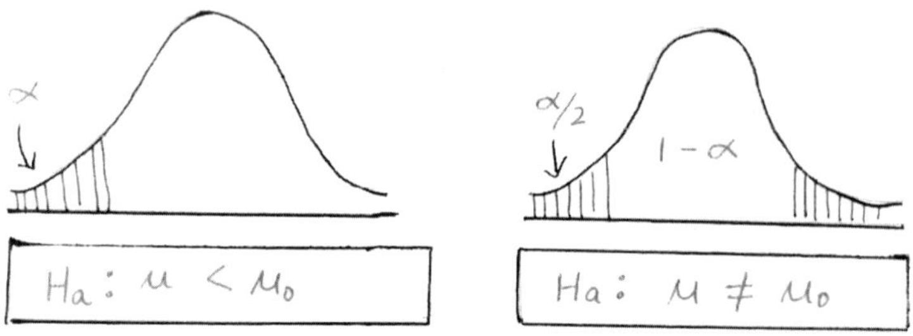


**Figure 4.4:** One and two-tailed tests

E. **Effect Size:** The effect size could be explained as the magnitude of difference which the researcher wants to test and broadly the effect size could be classified as small, medium and large. A small difference to be detected requires a larger sample size and vice-versa. Effect size could be determined using the mean and standard deviation of treatment and control groups and this is called Cohen's D given by

   Cohen's d = $|m_1 - m_2|$ / average SD

   Where $m_1$ and $m_2$ represent the mean in treatment and control groups.

F. **Power of test:** The power of the test is its ability to provide the true effect, that is the probability of rejecting a hypothesis when there is actually a significant difference in the population. Statistical power (1-β) is defined as the probability of rejecting the null hypothesis while the alternative hypothesis is true. Very few studies report the power of their test. More than 70 per cent of the studies giving negative results and did not reach the required power of at least 80 per cent (Barkan, 2015). This means that if the sample size was taken care of to attain the minimum power of 80 per cent, these results could have shown a significant effect for the treatment.

Thus, the estimation of a smaller difference between groups (effect size), a smaller value of the level of significance (type I error), a two-tailed test and a greater variance of measurement within a group would increase the sample size required. The greater the power of a test, the greater the sample size required.

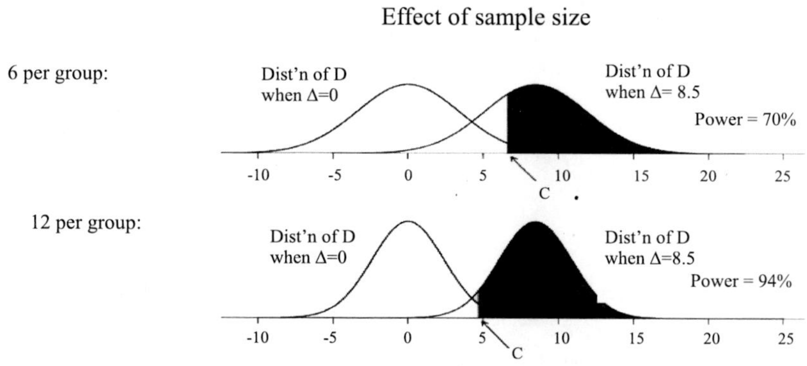


**Figure 4.5:** Power of a test, note the change in power with change in sample size (Browman, http://www.biostat.jhsph.edu/~kbroman)

To determine an appropriate sample size for a mean you must first declare an acceptable margin of error *d*. The margin of error *d* is the wiggle room around the point estimate. This is equal to half the confidence interval width.

$n=4s^2/d^2$

For eg. To obtain a margin of error of 5 for a variable with a standard deviation of 15,

$n = (4)\ (15^2)/\ (5^2) = 36.$

For an experiment, the best way to determine sample size would be based on the power of the experiment. For each statistical test, it is possible to obtain the power and sample size using the inputs on the type of test, level of significance, hypothesis, effect size and power expected. This is easily done using software such as Gpower.

G * Power is free software and available for Mac OS X and Windows XP/ Vista/7/8. G*Power is a tool to compute statistical power analyses for many different t-tests, F tests, ?2 tests, z-tests and some exact tests. G*Power can also be used to compute effect sizes and to display graphically the results of power analyses.

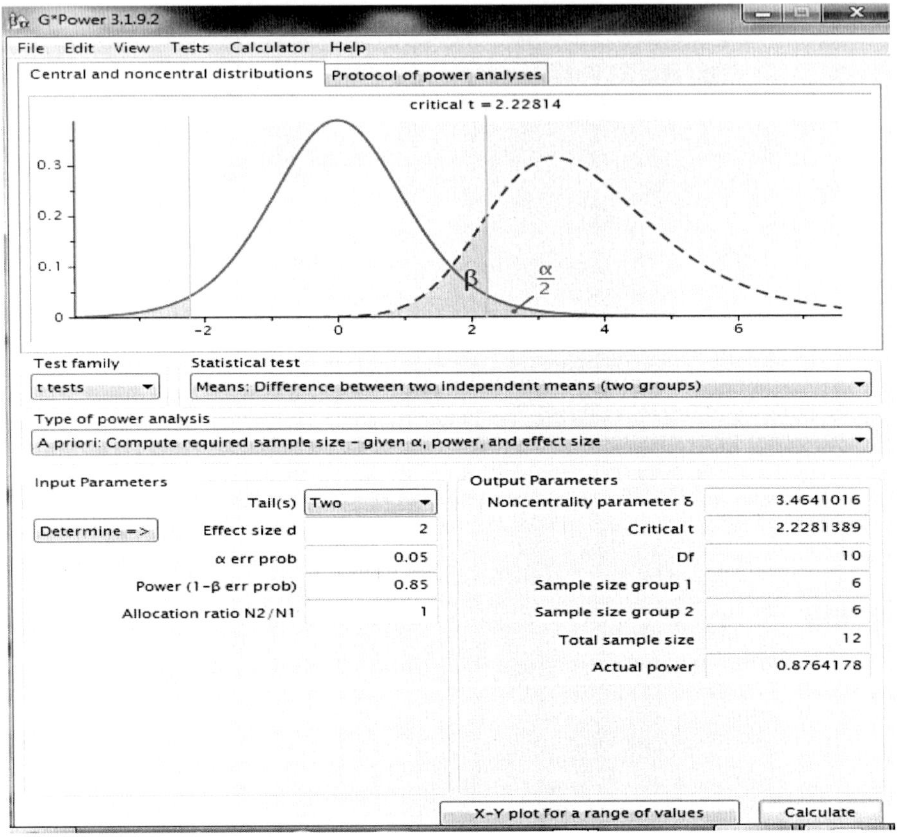


**Figure 4.6:** Calculation of power using G*Power software

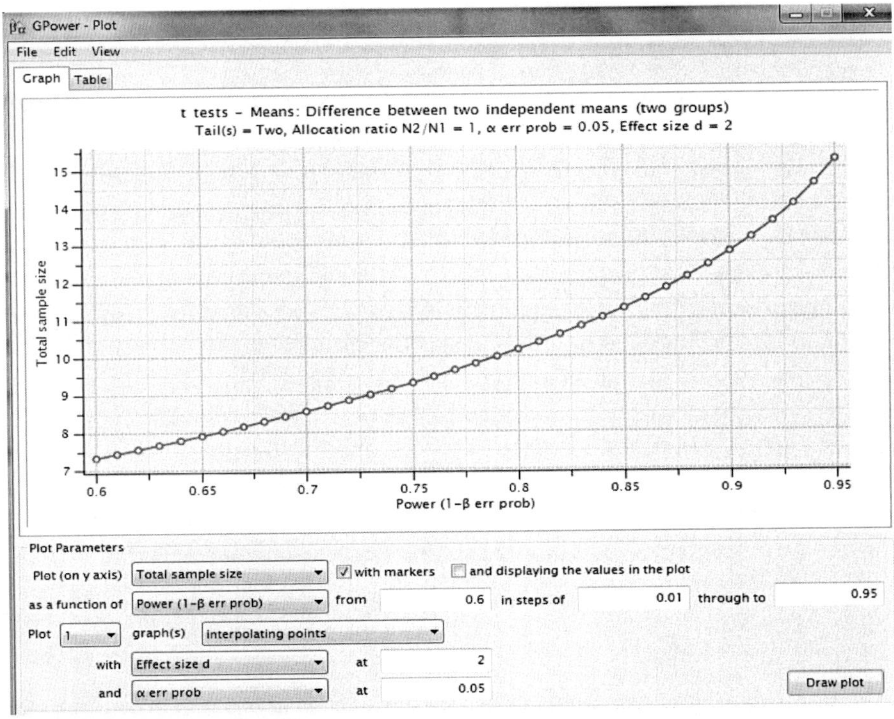


**Figure 4.7:** The graph equating power with sample size as obtained through G*Power

## 2. Randomisation

Randomisation, the second important principle of experimental design is important for the statistical test to be valid. All the experimental units are to be given an equal chance of being in the treatment or control. Some of the methods commonly used for randomization are lottery, random number table or the =rand () function in excel.

## 3. Local control

When the availability of uniform homogenous animals is a problem then the third principle of local control is used wherein the cause of variation such as sex, age or strain is blocked through randomization within the groups. This is important or the effect of significance could be masked or enhanced because of heterogeneity existing.

Some of the commonly used experimental designs are completely randomized design (One-way ANOVA), Randomised block design (two-way ANOVA), and Latin square design (three-way ANOVA). Factorial experiments help in understanding the main and interaction effects with minimal sample size. Numerous methods suitable for specific circumstances have been developed by statisticians. Appropriate use of these methods in analysis of research data will improve efficiency (through reliability) with less sample size and save cost and labour involved in a trial. Experimental designs have been designed to suit the specific needs of researchers and a basic knowledge of statistics can go a long way in determining the best way to obtain valid results from the optimal use of resources. However experimental designs for animal breeding experiments are more complex as the number of factors, the type of data, the period of data, the geographical distribution and the models involved are highly varied and more commonly existing data over a long period of time are utilised for animal breeding data analysis.

## Descriptive Analysis

The first step of any data analysis is a descriptive analysis which will provide several details on measures of central tendency and dispersion, such as the mean, variance, standard error, count, range, minimum, maximum, skewness, kurtosis, etc. This information can be used to decide on the kind of analysis to which the data can be subjected to. The type of analysis will depend on the kind of data and data can be classified as follows.

It is important to describe the data to be analysed and descriptive analysis provides us with several clues regarding the type of analysis to be taken up. In general, data is described statistically using the measures of central tendency and measures of dispersion. A simple descriptive analysis of data using an excel spreadsheet would provide us with the following:

| **Column1** | **Parameter** |
|---|---|
| Mean | 26.082 |
| Standard Error | 2.517 |
| Median | 23.022 |
| Mode | 25 |
| Standard Deviation | 8.324 |
| Sample Variance | 69.301 |
| Kurtosis | -1.030 |
| Skewness | 0.544 |

| Range | 24.57 |
|---|---|
| Minimum | 16.302 |
| Maximum | 40.872 |
| Sum | 286.902 |
| Count | 11 |

The raw mean, variance, standard deviation and standard error are important estimators for any data which will provide us with immediate information about the population under study. The mean will be representative of the population and variance and standard deviation give us an idea of the homogeneity and the standard error the important measure of precision. Other parameters like the skewness and kurtosis tell about the normality of data, which is most important as an assumption for the methods of estimation such as maximum likelihood, least – squares etc.

The minimum and maximum of the data set would give us a hint about the possible range that an economic trait could have. For eg., a value of above 10 for sheep birth weight or a negative value of minimum for a body weight gain could be identified and data checked for correctness. The heterogeneity of the data could be assessed with the standard deviation and most importantly the coefficient of variation, which is standardised with the mean. This standardisation allows comparison among the various traits with different units. For eg., the variability of a trait such as body weight in kg and average daily weight in g is not comparable unless standardised. The total variance of the trait is useful at every stage of the analysis including a meaningful starting value for REML methods

## Exploratory Analysis

As the name indicates exploratory analysis will throw more light on various aspects such as the descriptives, type of data, probability distribution, outliers, normality etc., Before going in to the actual analysis data available may be subjected to exploratory analysis. This will ascertain various features and help in deciding the type of estimation or analysis that will suit the particular type of data. The statistical outliers indicated by the exploratory analysis will show us the extreme values which the researcher could decide whether to include or not. Not all outliers are to be excluded from the analysis. Only those biological outliers which have justification to the fact that it does not fulfil the conditions of a particular subclass may be removed from the analysis. No data point is to be removed just for the sake of extremity in magnitude.

An exploratory analysis with SPSS for birth weight in sheep

**Descriptives**

| | | | Statistic | Std. Error |
|---|---|---|---|---|
| bw | Mean | | 2.6506 | .00925 |
| | 95% Confidence Interval for Mean | Lower Bound | 2.6324 | |
| | | Upper Bound | 2.6687 | |
| | 5% Trimmed Mean | | 2.6549 | |
| | Median | | 2.8000 | |
| | Variance | | .224 | |
| | Std. Deviation | | .47293 | |
| | Minimum | | 1.00 | |
| | Maximum | | 4.00 | |
| | Range | | 3.00 | |
| | Interquartile Range | | .60 | |
| | Skewness | | -.219 | .048 |
| | Kurtosis | | .034 | .096 |

**Percentiles**

| | | Percentiles | | | | |
|---|---|---|---|---|---|---|
| | | 5 | 10 | 25 | 50 | 75 |
| Weighted Average (Definition 1) | bw | 1.8000 | 2.0000 | 2.4000 | 2.8000 | 3.0000 |
| Tukey's Hinges | bw | | | 2.4000 | 2.8000 | 3.0000 |

**Percentiles**

| | | Percentiles | |
|---|---|---|---|
| | | 90 | 95 |
| Weighted Average (Definition 1) | bw | 3.2000 | 3.4000 |
| Tukey's Hinges | bw | | |

**Extreme Values**

| | | | Case Number | Value |
|---|---|---|---|---|
| bw | Highest | 1 | 351 | 4.00 |
| | | 2 | 354 | 4.00 |
| | | 3 | 498 | 4.00 |
| | | 4 | 543 | 4.00 |
| | | 5 | 565 | 4.00[a] |
| | Lowest | 1 | 2390 | 1.00 |
| | | 2 | 2019 | 1.00 |
| | | 3 | 110 | 1.10 |
| | | 4 | 2379 | 1.20 |
| | | 5 | 2316 | 1.20[b] |

a) Only a partial list of cases with the value 4.00 are shown in the table of upper extremes.

b) Only a partial list of cases with the value 1.20 are shown in the table of lower extremes.

**Tests of Normality**

| | Kolmogorov-Smirnov[a] | | | Shapiro-Wilk | | |
|---|---|---|---|---|---|---|
| | **Statistic** | **df** | **Sig.** | **Statistic** | **df** | **Sig.** |
| bw | .125 | 2612 | .000 | .972 | 2612 | .000 |

## a) Lilliefors Significance Correction

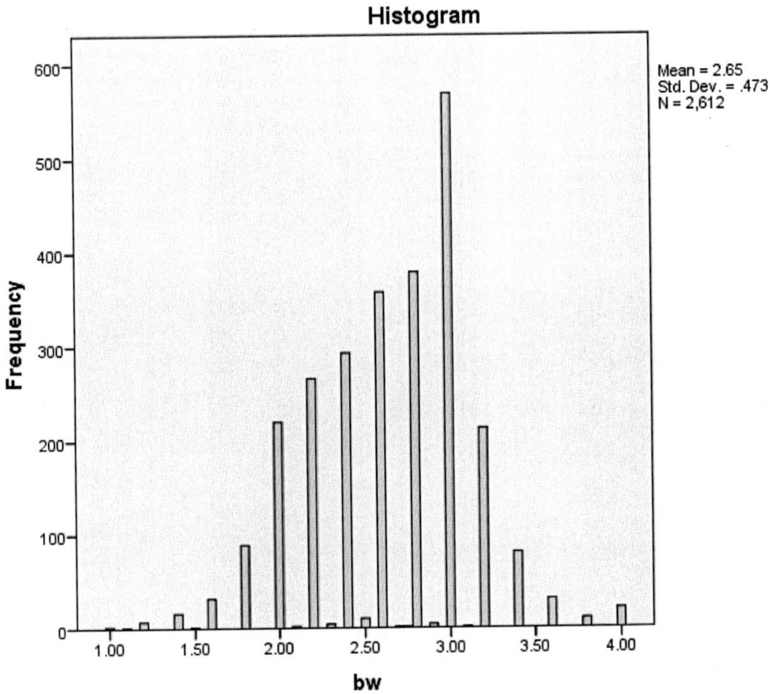


Stem-and-Leaf Plot

Frequency Stem & Leaf

26.00 Extremes (=<1.40)

1.00 15 . &

32.00 16 . 00000

.00 17 .

89.00 18 . 000000000000000

.00 19 .

```
220.00   20 . 0000000000000000000000000000000000000
2.00     21 . &
266.00   22 . 00000000000000000000000000000000000000000000
4.00     23 . 0
293.00   24 . 0000000000000000000000000000000000000000000000000
10.00    25 . 00
358.00   26 . 000000000000000000000000000000000000000000000000000000000000
2.00     27 . &
379.00   28 . 000000000000000000000000000000000000000000000000000000000000000
4.00     29 . 0
569.00   30 . 000000000000000000000000000000000000000000000000000000000000000
              00000000000000000000000000000000
1.00     31 . &
213.00   32 . 00000000000000000000000000000000000
.00      33 .
81.00    34 . 0000000000000
.00      35 .
31.00    36 . 00000
.00      37 .
10.00    38 . 00
21.00    Extremes (>=4.00)
```

Stem width: .10

Each leaf: 6 case(s) & denotes fractional leaves.

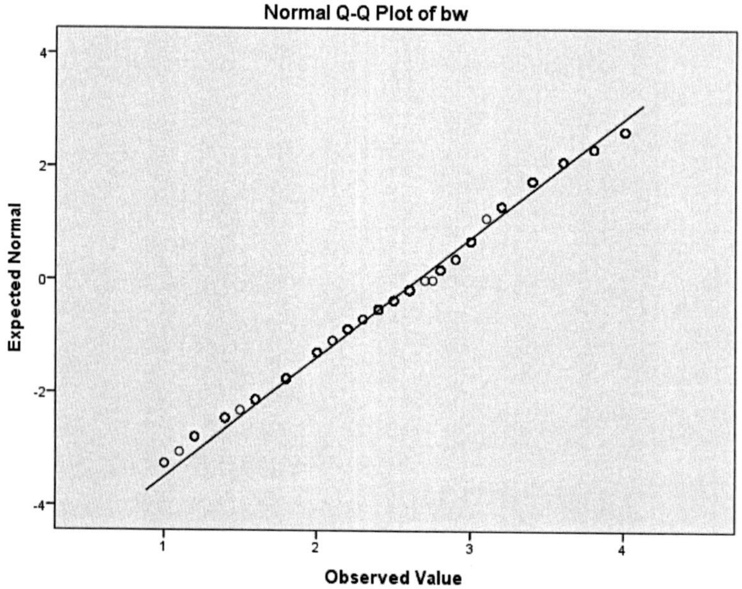

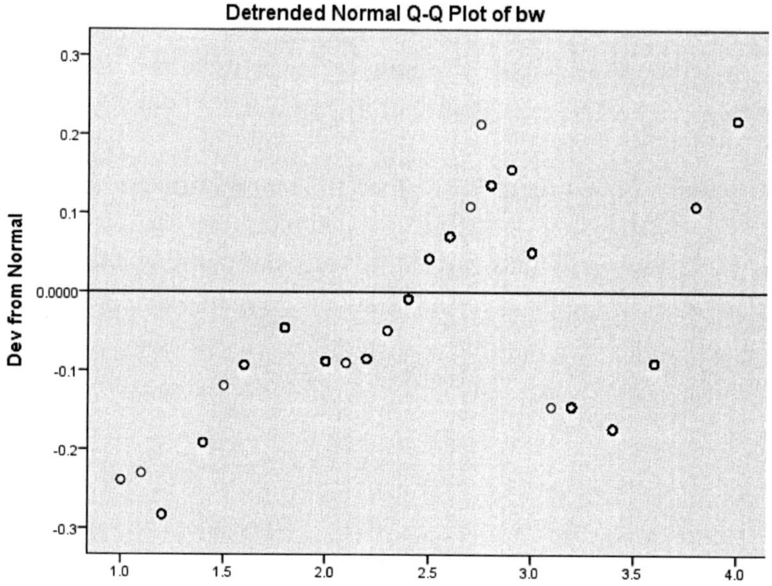


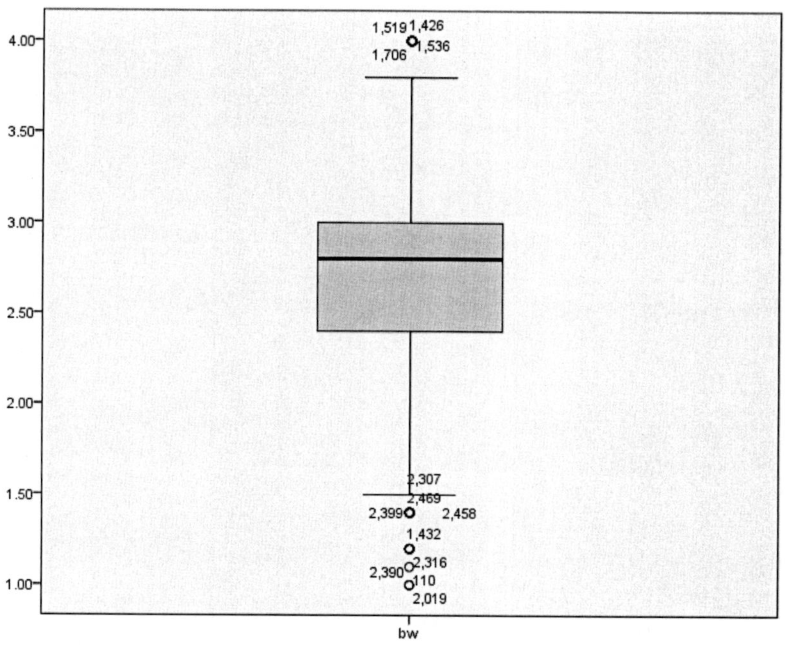


To explain, the data for exploratory analysis was birth weight in sheep. The histogram, Q-Q plot, box plot, stem and leaf plot and Kolmogorov – Smirnov test all prove that data follows a normal distribution. The statistical outliers indicated by the box plot or table all fall within the range of birth weight for sheep and hence are not excluded from the analysis. The percentiles provide valuable information especially when birth weight is used as a factor, this could be used in classifying the population under study into different classes based on birth weight.

Before the actual animal breeding analyses, it is important to understand and describe the data using descriptive and exploratory analysis. These preliminary analyses will help in identifying the suitable method of estimation and models to be used in the actual breeding analyses.

# 5

# Correlation and Regression

Correlations and regression are important components of animal breeding analysis. The genetic correlation is an important genetic parameter that is useful in the planning of breeding programs involving multiple traits. In this chapter, the basic concepts of correlation and regression including method of estimation, assumptions and test of significance are presented. An example using SPSS software is also given at the end for better understanding.

## Correlation

The study related to the characteristics of only one variable such as height, weight, age, marks, wages, etc., is known as *Univariate Analysis*. The statistical Analysis related to the study of the relationship between two variables is known as *Bivariate Analysis*. Sometimes the variables may be interrelated, for example; feed intake and weight of animals, etc. The nature and strength of the relationship may be examined by correlation and regression analysis. Correlation is statistical Analysis that measures and analyses the degree or extent to which the two variables fluctuate with reference to each other. The word relationship is important. It indicates that there is some connection between the variables.

## Correlation and Covariation

When there exists some relationship between two variables, we must measure the degree of the relationship. This measure is called the measure of correlation (or) correlation coefficient and it is denoted by '*r*'. The covariation between the variables *x* and *y* is defined as

$$\text{Cov}(x, y) = \frac{\sum (x - \bar{x})(y - \bar{y})}{n}$$

where $\bar{x}, \bar{y}$ are respectively means of x and y and 'n' is the number of pairs of observations.

## Types of Correlation

Correlation is classified into various types. The most important ones are

i) Positive and negative
ii) Linear and non-linear
iii) Partial and total
iv) Simple and Multiple

### Positive and negative correlation

It depends upon the direction of change of the variables. If the two variables tend to move together in the same direction (ie) an increase in the value of one variable is accompanied by an increase in the value of the other, (or) a decrease in the value of one variable is accompanied by a decrease in the value of other, then the correlation is called *positive* or *direct correlation*. Height and weight, yield and rainfall, are some examples of positive correlations. If the two variables tend to move together in opposite directions so that an increase (or) decrease in the value of one variable is accompanied by a decrease or increase in the value of the other variable, then the correlation is called a *negative* or *inverse correlation*. Milk yield and fat percent is an example of a negative correlation.

### Linear and non-linear correlation

If the ratio of change between the two variables is a constant then there will be linear correlation between them. Consider the following.

X 2 4 6 8 10 12

Y 3 6 9 12 15 18

Here the ratio of change between the two variables is the same. If we plot these points on a graph, we get a straight line and its functional relationship is represented by the relation, $y = a + bx$, where '$a$' and '$b$' are constants. If the amount of change in one variable does not bear a constant ratio of the amount of change in the other. Then the relation is called *Curvilinear* (or) *nonlinear correlation*. The graph will be a curve.

### Simple and Multiple correlations

When we study only two variables, the relationship is a *simple correlation*. For example, feed intake and growth of animals, birth weight and litter size, demand and price. But in a *multiple correlation,* we study more than two variables simultaneously. The relationship of milk yield vs. first lactation period, food supplied, age etc are an example for multiple correlation.

## Partial and total correlation

The study of two variables excluding some other variable is called *Partial correlation*. For example, the correlation between the weight of broiler and feed intake assuming the other factors like area provided, labour used, medicinal cost etc. as constant. If there is no relationship between the two variables, they are said to be independent or uncorrelated. Partial correlation is important in Path Analysis which has been extensively used in conducting pedigree analysis and estimation of the inbreeding coefficient.

## Real and spurious correlation

When there is a real correlation between two variables, it may be that a change in one variable is the cause of the change in the other. There is covariation based on logical relationships and causation. Sometimes, even if two variables are independent of each other, there may be a high degree of correlation between them. Such a correlation indicates a relationship with no logical basis. For e.g., rainfall in Tamil Nadu and milk yield in Karnataka, cattle number and the number of human illiterates. Such a correlation is called *spurious* or *nonsense correlation*.

## Methods of Studying Correlation

1. Scatter diagram
2. Correlation graph
3. Karl Pearson's coefficient of correlation
4. Concurrent deviation method
5. Rank method

## 1. Scatter diagram

A scatter diagram or scattergram or scatterplot or dot diagram is a chart prepared to represent graphically the relationship between two variables. Take one variable on the horizontal and another on the vertical axis and mark points corresponding to each pair of the given observations after taking suitable scale. Then, the figure which contains the collection of dots or points is called a *scatter diagram*. The way in which the dot lies on the scatter diagram shows the type of correlation. If these dots show some trend either upward or downward the two variables are correlated. If the dots do not show any trend, there is absence of correlation between the two variables.

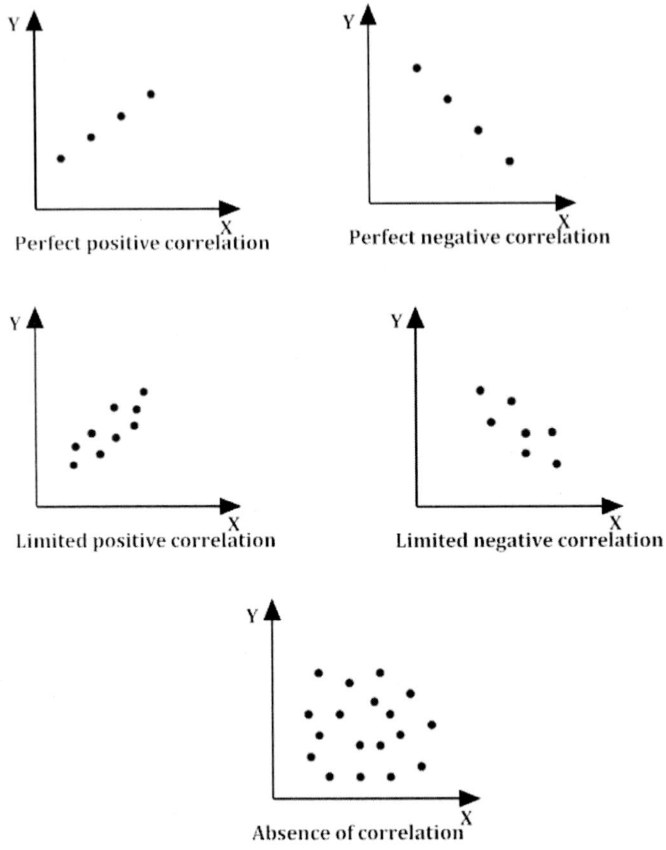


**Figure 5.1:** Scatter diagram for different forms of correlation

Scatter diagram is a simple and attractive method of finding the nature of the correlation between two variables. It is a non-mathematical method of understanding correlation and is easy to understand. The diagram is not affected by extreme items and is the first step in finding out the relation between the two variables. We can have a rough idea at a glance whether there exist a positive or negative correlation.

## 2. Correlation graph

In this method, curves are plotted for the data on two variables. By examining the direction and closeness of the two curves so drawn, we can infer whether or not the variables are related. If both the curves drawn on the graph are moving in the same direction (either upward or downward), the correlation is said to be positive. On the other hand, if the curves are moving in the opposite direction, the correlation is said to be negative.

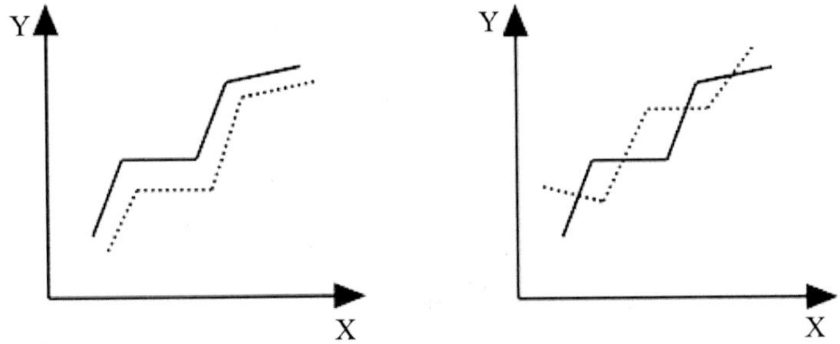


**Figure 5.2:** Correlation graph indicating positive correlation, the parallel lines are more closely related than the zigzag ones

This method is normally used for time series data. However, like a scatter diagram, this method also does not offer any numerical value for the coefficient of correlation.

### 3. Karl Pearson's coefficient of correlation

Karl Pearson, a great biometrician and statistician, suggested a mathematical method for measuring the magnitude of linear relationships between the two variables. It is the most widely used method in practice and it is known as the pearsonian coefficient of correlation. It is denoted by '*r*'. It is also called the product moment formula. It is given by

$$r = \frac{\text{Cov}(x, y)}{\acute{o}_x \acute{o}_y}$$

Where,

$\sigma_x$, $\sigma_y$ are S.D. of x and y respectively

$$\text{Cov}(x, y) = \frac{\sum (x - \bar{x})(y - \bar{y})}{n}$$

If simplified

$$r = \frac{\sum XY}{\sqrt{\sum X^2 \sum Y^2}}$$

Where $X = (x - \bar{x})$ and $Y = (y - \bar{y})$

### 4. Rank method

It is studied when no assumption about the parameters of the population is made. This method is based on ranks. It is useful to study the qualitative measure of attributes like honesty, colour, beauty, intelligence, character, morality etc. The individuals in the group can be arranged in order and there on, obtaining for each individual a number showing his/her rank in the group. This method was developed by Edward Spearman in 1904. It is defined

$$r = 1 - \frac{6\sum D}{n \ \ - n}$$

$r$ = rank correlation coefficient

'$D$' is the difference in the ranking of the two series $x$ and $y$, and $n$ is the number of paired observations

The value of $r$ lies between $-1$ and $+1$. If $r = +1$, there is complete agreement in the order of ranks and the direction of ranks is also the same. If $r = 1$, then there is complete disagreement in the order of ranks and they are in opposite directions.

## Coefficient of Determination and Non-determination

The square of the correlation coefficient ($r^2$) is defined as the *coefficient of determination*. If $r^2 = 0.85$, it implies that 85% of the variation in the dependent variable is due to the independent variable studied. ($1 - r^2$) is defined as the *coefficient of non-determination*. If $1\text{-}r^2 = 0.24$, we infer that 24% of the variation in the dependent variable is due to the other variables which are not studied. This is called unexplained variations.

## Properties of Correlation Coefficient

1. Correlation coefficient lies between –1 and +1 (i.e) $-1 \leq r \leq +1$
2. '$r$' is independent of change of origin and scale.
3. It is a pure number independent of units of measurement.
4. Independent variables are uncorrelated but the converse is not true.
5. Correlation coefficient is the geometric mean of two regression coefficients.
6. The correlation coefficient of $x$ and y is symmetric. $rxy = ryx$.

## Limitations

1. Correlation coefficient assumes a linear relationship regardless of whether the assumption is correct or not.
2. Extreme items of variables are being unduly operated on the correlation coefficient.
3. Existence of correlation does not necessarily indicate cause-effect relations.

## Testing the Correlation Coefficient

The correlation coefficient is tested using a t-test which tests the hypothesis that the correlation is significantly different from zero. The following rules help in interpreting the value of '*r*' and its degree. The following table 5.1 provides the value of *r* and its degree.

**Table 5.1:** Classification of degree of correlation based on values

| Degree | Value of "r" | |
|---|---|---|
| | **Positive** | **Negative** |
| Perfect | +1 | -1 |
| Strong | 0.75 to 1.00 | -0.75 to -1.00 |
| Moderate | 0.25 to 0.75 | -0.25 to -0.75 |
| Weak | 0 to 0.25 | 0 to -0.25 |
| Absence | 0 | 0 |

## Regression

The meaning of regression is the act of returning or going back. This term was introduced by Francis Galton when he studied the relationship between the heights of fathers and sons. After knowing the relationship between two variables through correlation, we may be interested in estimating (predicting) the value of one variable given the value of another. The variable predicted on the basis of other variables is called the "dependent" or the "explained" variable and cause variables are called the "independent" or the "predicting" variable. The prediction is based on the average relationship derived statistically by regression analysis. The equation, linear or otherwise, is called the regression equation or the explaining equation. In a study where data on the age and weight of animals are available, age could be considered the independent variable, while weight is the dependent variable. It means that weight regresses on age.

## Types of Regression

The regression analysis can be classified into:

a) Simple and Multiple

b) Linear and Non –Linear

c) Total and Partial

## a) Simple and multiple

Simple regression is the measure of the average relationship between two variables in terms of the original units of the data. In simple terms, regression is the change in the dependent variable 'Y' per unit change in the independent variable 'X'. If two variables have a linear relationship then as the independent variable (*X*) changes, the dependent variable (*Y*) also changes. If the different values of *X* and *Y* are plotted, then the straight lines of best fit can be made to pass through the plotted points. The equations are linear and the line is called the slope. For example, the influence of age in days on body weight.

One Dependent variable (Y)

One independent variable (X)

The relationship is linear (or straight line)

The linear regression equation of Y on X is

$Y = a + bx + \text{error}$

The values of a and b are unknown

"a" is called the intercept

"b" – Slope or Regression Coefficient

In the case of multiple regression, more than two variables are involved. While one variable is a dependent variable the remaining variables are independent ones. For example, the weight of the animal (*y*) may depend on age ($x_1$) and the feed intake of the animals ($x_2$). Then the functional relationship can be expressed as $y = f(x_1, x_2)$.

One dependent variable

One or more independent variables, some may be qualitative (called Dummy variable)

$Y = a + b_1X_1 + b_2X_2 + \ldots + b_pX_p + \text{error}$

Where a, $b_1$, $b_2$, …, $b_p$ are unknown and

E(error) = 0; Var (error) = $\sigma^2_e$; Errors are independently distributed

## b) Linear and non-linear

The linear relationships are based on a straight-line trend, the equation of which has no power higher than one. But, remember a linear relationship can be both simple and multiple. Normally a linear relationship is taken into account because, besides its simplicity, it has a better predictive value; a linear trend can be easily projected into the future. In the case of a non-linear relationship curved trend lines are derived. The equations of these are parabolic.

### c) Total and partial

In the case of total relationships, all the important variables are considered. Normally, they take the form of multiple relationships because most economic and business phenomena are affected by a multiplicity of cases. In the case of a partial relationship, one or more variables are considered, but not all, thus excluding the influence of those not found relevant for a given purpose.

## Methods of Regression Analysis

A line fitted by the method of least squares is known as the line of best fit.

*(i) Regression Equation*

The two regression equations

for $X$ on $Y$; $X = a + bY$

And for $Y$ on $X$; $Y = a + bX$

Where $X$, $Y$ are variables, and $a$, $b$ are constants whose values are to be determined

For the equation, $X = a + bY$

The Normal equations are

$\sum X = na + b\sum Y$ and

$\sum XY = a\sum Y + b\sum Y^2$

For the equation, $Y = a + bX$, the normal equations are

$\sum Y = na + b\sum X$ and

$\sum XY = a\sum X + b\sum X^2$

From these normal equations the values of a and b can be determined.

*(ii) Regression Co-efficient*

The regression Co-efficient of Y on X is $b_1 = b_{yx} = r\frac{\sigma_y}{\sigma_x}$

The regression Co-efficient of X on Y is $b_2 = b_{xy} = r\frac{\sigma_x}{\sigma_y}$

If the deviation are taken from respective means of x and y.

$$b_1 = b_{yx} = \frac{\sum(X - \bar{X})(Y - \bar{Y})}{\sum(X - \bar{X})^2} = \frac{\sum xy}{\sum x^2} \text{ and}$$

$$b_2 = b_{xy} = \frac{\sum (X - \bar{X})(Y - \bar{Y})}{\sum (Y - \bar{Y})^2} = \frac{\sum xy}{\sum y^2}$$

Where $x = (X - \bar{X}), y = (Y - \bar{Y})$

## Testing the Regression Coefficient

As in correlation, a t-test is used to test the significance of the individual regression coefficient in a simple regression, which tests the hypothesis that regression is significantly different from zero. In the case of multiple regression, an ANOVA is used to test the significance of the overall regression sum of squares.

## Assumptions and Regression Diagnostics

- Errors are independent
- Errors have constant variance
- Errors are normally distributed
- The relationship between Y and X's are linear

Checking the assumptions required calculation of residual values and residual plots. Residuals are the deviation if individual value of the dependent variable from the predicted value using the regression equation.

**Inference:** Linearity Assumption is valid and , error variances are homogenous

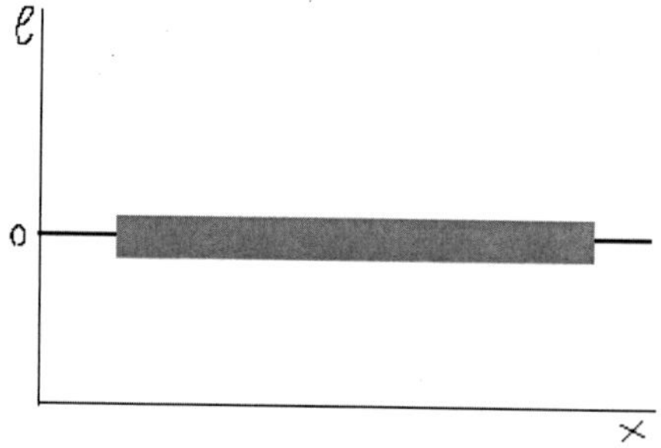


**Inference** - Linearity Assumption is not valid

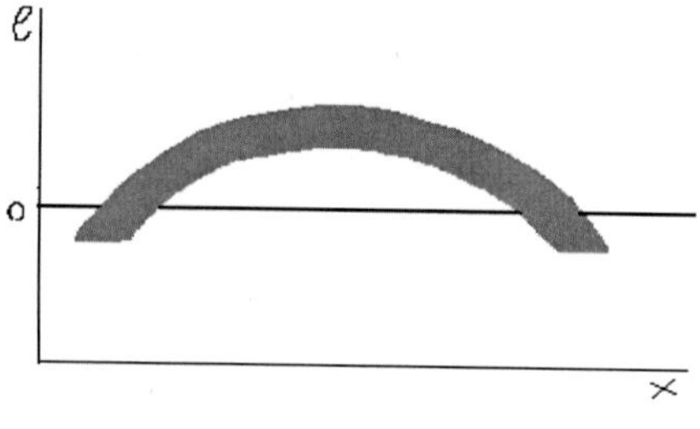

**Inference:** Most of the observation are within a band; no systematic variation seen Linear Relationship holds good

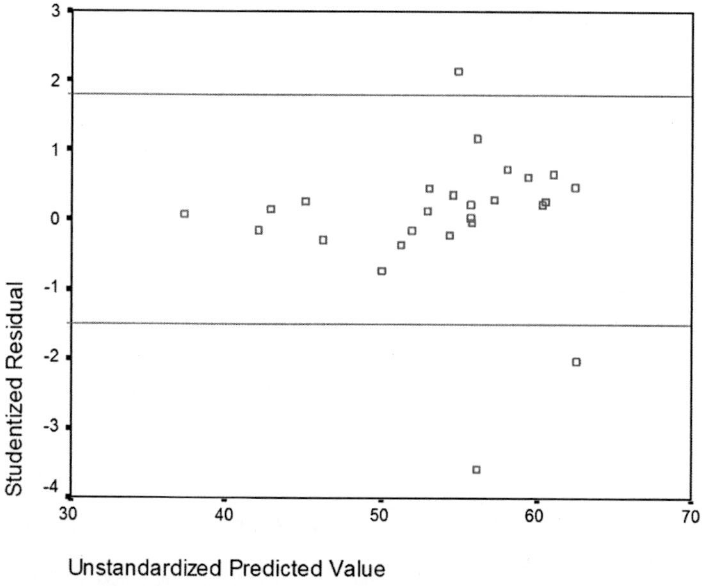


Inference: Error variances are not constant; Here they increase as X increases

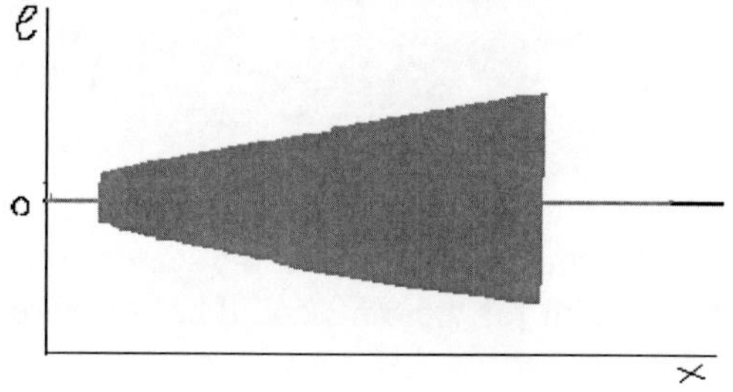


**Inference:** Errors are not independent

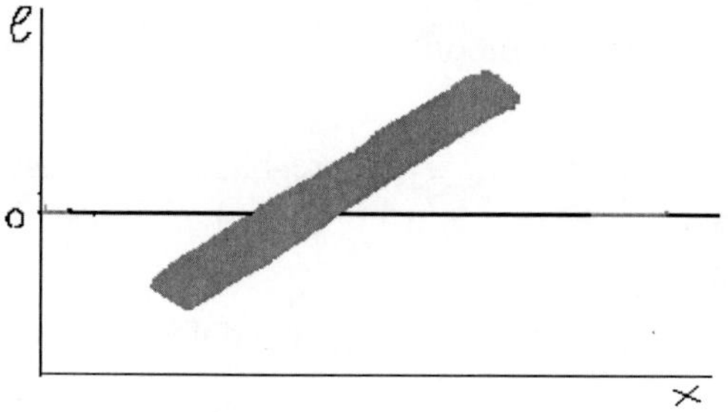


**Figure 5.3:** A plot obtained by fitting the residuals against the predicted values will throw light on the assumption of linearity

The normality of errors could be evaluated using a QQ-plot or Kolmogorov – Smirnov test of the calculated residuals. Software packages such as the SPSS have provisions for saving residuals of individual data points.

The assumption of independence of errors could be tested using Durbin -Watson test (DW value ranges from 0 to 4). A D=W value near 2 indicates the absence of autocorrelation; a value near 0 indicates positive autocorrelation and a value near 4 indicates negative autocorrelation

## Multicollinearity

- Another Important assumption about independent variables in multiple regression is there should not be any correlation between independent variables themselves
- If there is a strong correlation among independent variables, the fitted model may be unstable, leading to multi-collinearity
- Use Collinearity Diagnostics in SPSS Regression to study multi-collinearity
- If multicollinearity is present, remove one or more variables showing strong collinearity from the model
- Some of the statistics used to detect multicollinearity: Strong correlation; Variance inflation factors; eigenvalues of X'X (nearer to zero indicate multicollinearity).

## Properties of Regression

The value of regression varies from 0 to infinity and has a unit. Hence it is not meaningful to compare two regression coefficients. However, the standardized regression coefficient (per standard deviation for the trait) could be compared between traits.

## Uses of Regression Analysis

- Regression analysis helps in establishing a functional relationship between two or more variables.
- Since most of the problems of economic analysis are based on cause-and-effect relationships, regression analysis is a highly valuable tool in economic and business research.
- Regression analysis predicts the values of dependent variables from the values of independent variables.
- We can calculate the coefficient of correlation ($r$) and coefficient of determination ($r^2$) with the help of regression coefficients.

- In statistical analysis of demand curves, supply curves, production functions, cost functions, consumption functions, etc., regression analysis is widely used.

**Table 5.4:** Difference between Correlation and Regression

| S.No. | Correlation | Regression |
|---|---|---|
| 1. | Correlation is the relationship between two or more variables, which vary in sympathy with the other in the same or the opposite direction. | Regression means going back and it is a mathematical measure showing the average relationship between two variables |
| 2 | Both the variables X and Y are random variables | Here X is a random variable and Y is a fixed variable. Sometimes both variables may be random variables. |
| 3 | It finds out the degree of relationship between two variables and not the cause and effect of the variables. | It indicates the causes and effect relationship between the variables and establishes a functional relationship. |
| 4 | It is used for testing and verifying the relation between two variables and gives limited information. | Besides verification, it is used for the prediction of one value, in relationship to the other given value. |
| 5 | The coefficient of correlation is a relative measure. The range of relationship lies between -1 and +1 | The regression coefficient is an absolute figure. If we know the value of the independent variable, we can find the value of the dependent variable. |
| 6 | There may be spurious correction between the two variables. | In regression, there is no such spurious regression. |
| 7 | It has limited application because it is confined only to a linear relationship between the variables. | It has a wider application, as it studies the linear and nonlinear relationship between the variables. |

## Example 5.1

Correlation between age and feed conversion ratio of chicken

**Correlations**

| | | age | fcr2 |
|---|---|---|---|
| age | Pearson Correlation | 1 | .944** |
| | Sig. (2-tailed) | | .000 |
| | N | 96 | 96 |
| fcr2 | Pearson Correlation | .944** | 1 |
| | Sig. (2-tailed) | .000 | |
| | N | 96 | 96 |

**. Correlation is significant at the 0.01 level (2-tailed).

Regression of age on feed conversion ratio

**Model Summary**[b]

| Model | R | R Square | Adjusted R Square | Std. Error of the Estimate | Durbin-Watson |
|---|---|---|---|---|---|
| 1 | .944[a] | .890 | .889 | 1.71409 | .601 |

a. Predictors: (Constant), age
b. Dependent Variable: fcr2

**ANOVA**[a]

| Model | | Sum of Squares | df | Mean Square | F | Sig. |
|---|---|---|---|---|---|---|
| 1 | Regression | 2239.553 | 1 | 2239.553 | 762.240 | .000[b] |
| | Residual | 276.183 | 94 | 2.938 | | |
| | Total | 2515.736 | 95 | | | |

a. Dependent Variable: fcr2
b. Predictors: (Constant), age

**Coefficients**[a]

| Model | | Unstandardized Coefficients | | Standardized Coefficients | t | Sig. |
|---|---|---|---|---|---|---|
| | | B | Std. Error | Beta | | |
| 1 | (Constant) | -1.859 | .373 | | -4.985 | .000 |
| | age | .700 | .025 | .944 | 27.609 | .000 |

**Coefficients**[a]

| Model | | 95.0% Confidence Interval for B | | Collinearity Statistics | |
|---|---|---|---|---|---|
| | | Lower Bound | Upper Bound | Tolerance | VIF |
| 1 | (Constant) | -2.600 | -1.119 | | |
| | age | .649 | .750 | 1.000 | 1.000 |

a. Dependent Variable: fcr2

**Collinearity Diagnostics**[a]

| Model | Dimension | Eigenvalue | Condition Index | Variance Proportions | |
|---|---|---|---|---|---|
| | | | | (Constant) | age |
| 1 | 1 | 1.883 | 1.000 | .06 | .06 |
| | 2 | .117 | 4.015 | .94 | .94 |

a. Dependent Variable: fcr2

**Casewise Diagnostics**[a]

| Case Number | Std. Residual | fcr2 | Predicted Value | Residual |
|---|---|---|---|---|
| 83 | 3.074 | 18.80 | 13.5314 | 5.26857 |
| 92 | 3.436 | 20.82 | 14.9306 | 5.88941 |

a. Dependent Variable: fcr2

**Residuals Statistics**[a]

| | Minimum | Maximum | Mean | Std. Deviation | N |
|---|---|---|---|---|---|
| Predicted Value | -.4602 | 14.9306 | 7.2352 | 4.85533 | 96 |
| Residual | -3.59395 | 5.88941 | .00000 | 1.70505 | 96 |
| Std. Predicted Value | -1.585 | 1.585 | .000 | 1.000 | 96 |
| Std. Residual | -2.097 | 3.436 | .000 | .995 | 96 |

a. Dependent Variable: fcr2

# 6

# Correction of Data

It is known that the phenotype of an individual is a combination of genotype and environment. Animal breeding analysis is mainly done to partition the genetic part from the environmental part so as to assess the actual genetic worth of the animal. In this process correction for the known environmental part is integral to any animal breeding analysis. In this chapter, a list of common factors affecting important economic traits are described. The analytical part for these effects will be explained in later chapters.

Correction or standardization of data is very important in any animal breeding analysis. Unless the candidates under selection are placed on a common platform, various factors affecting the trait will lead to bias in assessing the performance of the individual with respect to a particular trait. For eg. a lamb born during a favorable season, a lactating cow in its third parity, first lactation yield of a cow with longer age at first calving.

Before the estimation of variance components and genetic parameters or prediction of breeding value, all the records are to be corrected for known non-genetic factors. In this regard, record maintenance should also include various factors that are expected to influence the particular economic trait for which selection is proposed.

The simplest form of correction is to estimate the effect size for each factor on the trait under question and correct the raw data so that this effect is nullified. The least squares method of fitting constant is one of the most commonly used statistical techniques to quantify the effect size. The General Linear Model using least squares estimation also provides a list of significant factors affecting a particular trait. For animal breeding analyses, especially the estimation of variance components the use of mixed models with these significant factors as fixed effects and other sources of variation as random effect provides the estimates of variance components corrected for these significant factors.

## Common Factors for Correction

**Period:** Period is a factor with years grouped into different periods. This is one factor that corrects for changes in management, climate, the infrastructure of the farm, etc. Most of the studies use each year as one level or years grouped into a single period as a level. Care is to be taken to group the years in such a way that there is more similarity within the period and greater difference between periods. The period of the year is taken either at birth, calving, or measurement of a particular trait. For age at first calving, the period of birth is taken; for growth traits, it is meaningful to take the period of measurement and for lactation yield, the period of calving is considered.

**Season:** Season is another important factor that affects almost every trait of economic importance. Traits like growth are better during the lush rain season and animals lose weight during the lean season. Especially in an extensive system of management, this difference is more explicit as grazing is the only source of nutrition for these animals. Similarly, a cow calving in a favourable season will have better lactation milk yield compared to that in its peak of lactation during the dry season.

**Contemporary groups:** Contemporaries are animals that are born during the same season and year. Especially in sheep, with seasonal breeding in practice, animals born during a particular year and season are grouped as contemporaries. It is almost like an interaction between year and season. In situations where we have animals from different locations an interaction of Herd x Year x Season is taken as contemporaries.

**Parity:** Certain traits like milk yield, birth weight of lamb and litter size are known to vary with parity. The parity of the dam is an important known physiological factor to be corrected for analysing such traits.

**Age at first calving:** Age at first calving is another important physiological factor affecting first lactation milk yield. The factor measured in days is included as a covariate for first lactation traits.

**Table 6.1:** Common factors for correction

| **Factor** | **Levels** |
|---|---|
| Location/Herd | Number of locations for all traits |
| Period/year | Year or years grouped into period for all traits |
| Season | Season based on the region for most of the traits |
| Parity | 1,2,3,4,5 and later parities are pooled together for milk yield |
| Sex | Male, Female for growth and survivability |
| Birth type | Single, Twin, and Triplet for growth, reproduction and mortality |
| Litter size at birth in pigs | 1 to 12 for growth and reproduction traits |
| Dam age at lambing/ Parity | Age in years, months or days for growth |
| Order of ejaculate | One and two for semen traits |
| Collection interval | $\leq 2$ days, 3 days, 4 days, $\geq 5$ days for semen traits |

| Season of breeding | Season depending on the region for fertility |
|---|---|
| Age of bull | 1 to 8 for semen traits and fertility |
| Birth weight | As an effect for survivability |
| Age at marketing | In days for market weight |
| Age at the measurement of weight | In days for body weight traits |

**Sex:** Any trait which is expected to differ between sexes is to be corrected for the factor. For eg. Males always weigh heavier and analysing a trait like market weight or six months' body weight could result in all males getting selected. The effect of sex is important even in laboratory experiments as correction is to be made for the effect if the experimental design had to be compromised with a different number of males and females. Growth traits are mainly affected by sex, while wool yield, mortality, and disease incidence may also vary with sex.

**Age at the measurement of weight**: This is an important criterion to be adjusted for. For traits such as six months' weight or yearling weight it is expected that all the animals are weighed at the same age, i.e the day they reach the particular weight. However, this is not possible due to constraints like non-availability of labor, animals are usually weighed on a particular day of the month as a routine. This leads to variation in the age of the animal at measurement of weight. For eg., the age for animal's 180-day weight could range from 165 to 205 and this difference could bring a lot of significant variation in the body weight. The adjustment for such differences must be based on the average daily gain of the individual animal that too for the nearest available period.

The formula for such correction could be given as follows:

The animals at a sheep farm are weighed on the fifth day of every month. Animal no. 55 was born on 01/05/2022 and the expected date of the animal reaching 180 days is 28/10/2022. Thus the nearest weight available for the animal as of 05/11/2022 is for 188 days and the weight on 188 days is to be corrected by subtracting the average daily gain in kg for the month from 05/10/2022 to 05/11/2022 multiplied by 8.

Adjusted 180 day body weight = (Actual weight) – [(age at measurement-180) ADG)]

ADG = Latest weight available -previous weight/interval

---

**Birth type/Litter size at birth:** This is an important factor affecting birth weight, pre-weaning mortality, weaning weight and sometimes the effect could prolong even after weaning. Birth type in sheep and goats has fewer classes while in polytocous species such as pigs and rabbits, the effect is more significant. The competition starts right in the uterus for space and until weaning the stronger piglets or bunnies grow at a faster rate. Some weak young ones become unthrifty and are called runts too. Hence litter size is to be included as an important factor for correction.

**Dam age at lambing/kidding/farrowing:** This is another important factor similar to the parity of a cow but could be included as a covariate when measured in days for more sensitive traits. In general traits like growth are expected to increase with the increase in age of dam up to a certain age and hence is to be corrected for during animal breeding analysis. Twins and triplets weigh low at birth however are superior in terms of litter size as a trait for selection. Similarly, the age of the bull at semen collection has been found to affect the semen evaluation traits

A simple code for calculation of age of dam in foxpro.

```
USE growthfinal
SET TALK OFF
DO WHILE .NOT. EOF()
STORE DAM TO MDAM
STORE RECNO() TO MREC
STORE DOB TO MDATE
LOCATE FOR ANi=MDAM
STORE DOB TO MS
GO MREC
REPLACE AGEdam WITH MDATE-MS
SKIP
ENDDO
```

**Order of ejaculate:** An important factor affecting semen traits such as volume, concentration and motility. While analysing semen traits the ejaculate number is also recorded as in most of the frozen semen stations, collection of semen is done two times a day.

**Collection interval:** The period between two collections (not ejaculate) is again an important factor affecting semen traits such as concentration and live and dead sperms. It is usual practice to do semen collection twice in a week and when there is a change in such interval the factor has to be corrected for.

**Time of collection:** Semen is usually collected early in the morning as lower temperatures are ideal for collection freezing. However, the time of collection could be a factor for correction in analyzing semen traits.

**Semen collector:** Semen collector has also been found to influence semen volume and other semen traits. However, this is usually included as a random effect, the explanation for which is given in a later chapter on linear models.

**Birth weight:** Birth weight though a dependent trait by itself, has been included as a factor for correction especially in survivability analysis where the birth weight is classified into an ordinal low, medium and high animals for correction of this factor.

The stars (Table 6.2) indicate the significance of a particular factor and the superscripts indicate pairwise comparisons for the factors with more than two levels. The overall mean is the estimate of the particular growth trait corrected for all the factors included in the model.

**Table 6.2:** A GLM analysis for birth, 6-month and yearling weight providing marginal means for different fixed classes of factors to be corrected

| Effects | Birth weight | | 6-month weight | | 12-month weight | |
|---|---|---|---|---|---|---|
| | n | Mean ± S.E. | N | Mean ± S.E. | n | Mean ± S.E. |
| **Overall mean** | 2612 | 2.64 ± 0.02 | 1878 | 13.71 ± 0.13 | 924 | 20.46 ± 0.21 |
| **CG at birth** | | ** | | ** | | ** |
| Lowest | - | 2.15 ± 0.05 | | 9.18 ± 2.27 | - | 17.79 ± 1.37 |
| Highest | - | 3.01 ± 0.08 | | 17.22 ± 0.46 | - | 28.91 ± 1.20 |
| **Sex** | | ** | | ** | | ** |
| Male | 1317 | 2.72 ± 0.02 | 882 | 14.43 ± 0.14 | 385 | 21.73 ± 0.23 |
| Female | 1295 | 2.57 ± 0.02 | 996 | 13.01 ± 0.14 | 539 | 19.19 ± 0.22 |
| **Age of dam at lambing** | | ** | | ** | | NS |
| Below 2 years | 228 | $2.41^{d} \pm 0.03$ | 155 | $13.38^{bc} \pm 0.22$ | 69 | 20.57 ± 0.38 |
| 2-3 years | 603 | $2.52^{c} \pm 0.03$ | 407 | $13.69^{a} \pm 0.17$ | 208 | 20.40 ± 0.27 |
| 3-4 years | 581 | $2.72^{b} \pm 0.03$ | 436 | $13.99^{a} \pm 0.16$ | 234 | 20.32 ± 0.26 |
| 4-5 years | 467 | $2.73^{ab} \pm 0.03$ | 354 | $13.54^{ab} \pm 0.18$ | 171 | 20.29 ± 0.29 |
| 5-6 years | 362 | $2.78^{a} \pm 0.03$ | 263 | $14.09^{a} \pm 0.19$ | 117 | 20.57 ± 0.32 |
| Above 6 years | 371 | $2.71^{b} \pm 0.03$ | 263 | $13.63^{c} \pm 0.19$ | 125 | 20.62 ± 0.31 |

** P<0.01; NS – Not significant; Means with at least one common superscript within classes do not differ significantly; n - Number of observations; S.E. - Standard Error.

# 7

# Genetic Parameters

| The key genetic parameters available with the animal breeder to attain improvement are heritability, repeatability and genetic correlation. This chapter will mainly deal with the theoretical considerations of these parameters. |
|---|

The goal of an animal breeder is to bring about permanent improvement in different economic traits, either individually (univariate) or simultaneously in multiple traits (multitrait). The phenotypic value available from the animal is a combination of genotypic value and environmental deviation. By permanent improvement in a trait, we mean the improvement in genotypic value, which could be carried over to future generations. The environmental deviations are spatially and temporally specific, and thus will not be the same over generations. The genotypic value, itself is made up of additive effect, dominance deviation and interaction deviation. The additive effect is a value of genes (the sum of the average effect of genes) and hence is more important for the breeder as only the genes are passed on to the next generation. The dominance deviation is caused due to the dominance of alleles within a locus and genotypes as such are not transmitted for these effects to be permanent. Similarly, the interaction deviations are also altered due to crossing over and sampling during inheritance. Thus the animal breeder is always interested in the additive part of the genotype, also called breeding value.

The theoretical derivations of breeding value, dominance deviation and interaction deviation based on the genotypic value 'a', degree of dominance 'd' and gene frequencies (p and q) in a population are impractical because the underlying assumptions of uniform environment and identical genotypes will never be available under practical conditions (Falconer and Mackay, 1996). Most of the genetic problems especially in quantitative genetics are addressed through variances and the success of any animal breeding programme depends entirely on the accurate estimation of variance components. Like the values described above, the total phenotypic variance ($V_P$) can also be partitioned into genetic variance ($V_G$) and environmental variance ($V_E$). The genetic variance can further be partitioned into additive genetic variance ($V_A$), variance due to dominance deviation ($V_D$) and variation due to interaction deviation ($V_I$). The environmental variation is further partitioned into permanent environmental variance ($V_{PE}$) and temporary environmental variance ($V_{TE}$) specific to a particular measurement. The presence of maternal genetic influence could further include variation due to direct genetic, maternal genetic ($V_M$) and maternal permanent environmental ($V_{MPE}$) variances

$$V_P=V_G+V_E$$

$$V_P = V_A + V_D + V_I + V_{PE} + V_{TE}$$

Certain circumstances may also lead to additional sources of variation to those described above. There may exist a correlation between the genotype and environment (eg. better feeding for superior genotypes) and if present then the value of $V_P$ will increase by twice the covariance between genotypic and environmental values. Similarly, there could also be situations when the additional source of variation in the form of genotype x environment interaction (comparison of different genotypes in different environments) might add to the total variance.

The three primary objectives of the animal breeder are:

i. To assess whether the traits of concern have any genetic basis.

ii. Inference of genetic merit from phenotypic data. The data available with the breeder are traits like body weight, litter size, etc. and appropriate statistical methods are necessary to evaluate the genetic merit from available data.

iii. To design suitable mating programs for improvement in production and at the same time sustain genetic variability and prevent loss from inbreeding depression.

## Heritability, Repeatability and Genetic Correlation

The key genetic parameters available to the breeder to attain these goals are heritability, repeatability and genetic correlation.

Heritability is the fraction of total variation which is heritable and heritability in the broad sense ($H^2$), also called as the degree of genetic determination is defined as the ratio of total genetic variance ($V_G$) to phenotypic variance ($V_P$). However, the additive genetic variation ($V_A$) is more important and heritability in the narrow sense ($h^2$) hereinafter called as heritability is defined as the ratio of $V_A$ to $V_P$. The estimates of heritability are important in understanding the proportion of total variance that is due to the additive action of genes and is useful in the prediction of breeding values, calculation of response to selection and determining the accuracy of selection. Being a proportion, the value of heritability is always between 0 and 1. Heritability can be classified as low, medium and high (Turner and Young, 1969). The values are considered high when greater than 0.3, medium when the values are between 0.1 and 0.3 and low when the values are less than 0.1 (Turner and Young, 1969). Heritability values estimated are specific for a population at a particular time.

## Estimation of Heritability

The basis of methods for estimating heritability is the resemblance between relatives. The resemblance between relatives depends upon the extent to which relatives have 1) genes in common, 2) genotypes in common, 3) environment in common. Heritability is associated with resemblance due to genes in common, which is the actual additive relationship. The measurement of the degree of resemblance between relatives rests on the partitioning of the phenotypic variance in a different way, into components corresponding to the grouping of individuals into families. For eg., when individuals are grouped as full sibs, by using ANOVA the variance can be partitioned into between and within groups. The resemblance can be looked at as the similarity of individuals within the group of full sibs or differences between groups. It can be expressed as the proportion of between-group component on the total variance, called as intraclass correlation coefficient.

$$t = \frac{\sigma_B^2}{\sigma_B^2 + \sigma_W^2}$$

In the case of offspring and parent, the grouping of offspring is into pairs; one parent or the mean of two parents, paired with one offspring or the mean of several offspring and the degree of resemblance is expressed as the regression of offspring on parents. The resemblance between relatives, be it intraclass correlation or offspring-parent regression can be deduced in the form of covariance of related individuals. Depending on the type of relationship, the causal components of covariance will vary. The commonest and most useful relationships are offspring with parents, half-sibs, full-sibs and twins. In sheep, paternal half-sib correlation has been the most commonly used method for the estimation of heritability. The composition of phenotypic variances under different groups of relatives is as follows.

**Table7.1.** Coefficients of additive variance component in the covariances of relatives (Falconer and Mackay, 1996)

| **Relationship** | **Coefficient of $V_A$** |
|---|---|
| Monozygotic twins | 1 |
| Offspring-parent | ½ |
| Half sib | ¼ |
| Offspring-grandparent | ¼ |
| Offspring-great-grandparent | ⅛ |

The derivations for these causal components are described in detail by Falconer and Mackay (1996). Recently, with the advent of better computing ability, the individual animal as the source of random variation for estimation of variance components is commonly used as the animal model (explained in later chapters) and this also gives scope for additional random effects in the model. The precision of heritability estimates are indicated by the standard error.

Approximate sampling errors for the parameters and covariance components estimated are calculated from the inverse of the respective average information matrices. The sampling errors of heritability estimates are estimated by the approximations as described by Meyer (2007).

Repeatability is the correlation between records of the same animal and hence can be calculated only for repeatable traits which can be measured more than once in the lifetime of the animal. Some of the repeatable traits are milk yield, greasy fleece weight, fibre diameter and litter size. Repeatability is calculated as the ratio of variance due to permanent differences between individuals sum of genetic ($V_G$) and permanent environmental ($V_{EP}$) variance) to $V_P$. Repeatability is considered an upper limit to heritability and indicates the gain in accuracy expected from multiple measurements. When repeatability is high then the gain in accuracy due to multiple measurements is less. Repeatability estimates are said to be high when the values are greater than 0.6, medium when the values are between 0.3 and 0.6 and low when the values are less than 0.3 (Turner and Young, 1969). Repeatability is also estimated as the intraclass correlation of repeated measurements between animals.

Genetic correlation between two traits is the correlation between breeding values and is usually attributed to pleiotropy and linkage. The genetic correlation between two traits X and Y is given as the ratio of additive covariance between the traits to the square root of the product of additive variances. Estimates of genetic correlation are important in the calculation of response to selection. Estimates of (co) variance between different traits are obtained through multivariate analyses. The estimates of correlations are grouped as high (above 0.60), medium (0.4 to 0.60) and low (less than 0.4).

Correlations less than 0.2 usually are considered negligible. The details of testing a correlation coefficient are given in detail in the chapter on correlation and regressions.

multivar - Notepad

File Edit View

```
COM Example 3 from DFREML; analyse as multi-trait NILAGIRI GROWTH

ANAL MUV 6

PEDS NILPED.D

DATA MULTITR.D GRP
  TRN 1 2 3 4 5 6
  traitno 6
  animal
  sire |
  dam
  gmdam
  pedam
  subject 8000
  period 4
  season 2
  sex 2
  ls 2
  agedam 6
  inbr 5
  fcov
  af
  damage
  NAM BW1 BW2 BW3 BW4 BW5 BW6
END

MODEL
  FIX period
  FIX season
  FIX sex
  FIX ls
  FIX agedam
  FIX inbr
  RAN animal  nrm
  tr BW1 1
  tr BW2 2
  tr BW3 3
  tr BW4 4
  tr BW5 5
  tr BW6 6
END MOD

VAR animal 6
 1 1 1 1 1 1 3 1 1 1 1 2 1 1 1 4 1 1 5 1 13
VAR residual 6
 1 1 1 1 1 1 4 1 1 1 1 7 1 1 1 8 1 1 12 1 18
```

**Figure 7.1:** Parameter file in WOMBAT software for a multivariate analysis using traits

MULTITR - Notepad

File Edit View

```
1 1471 1230 1302 1302 1302 1471  2  1  1 1  5  3   0.06250   0.03276 1831  2.40
2 1471 1230 1302 1302 1302 1471  2  1  1 1  5  3   0.06250   0.03276 1831  6.00
1 1732    0 1482 1482 1482 1732  1  1  2 1  2  1   0.00000   0.00000 1033  3.50
2 1732    0 1482 1482 1482 1732  1  1  2 1  2  1   0.00000   0.00000 1033 16.80
3 1732    0 1482 1482 1482 1732  1  1  2 1  2  1   0.00000   0.00000 1033 19.50
4 1732    0 1482 1482 1482 1732  1  1  2 1  2  1   0.00000   0.00000 1033 22.00
5 1732    0 1482 1482 1482 1732  1  1  2 1  2  1   0.00000   0.00000 1033 24.00
6 1732    0 1482 1482 1482 1732  1  1  2 1  2  1   0.00000   0.00000 1033 38.00
1 1733    0 1205 1205 1205 1733  1  1  2 1  4  1   0.00000   0.00000 1788  3.00
2 1733    0 1205 1205 1205 1733  1  1  2 1  4  1   0.00000   0.00000 1788 17.00
3 1733    0 1205 1205 1205 1733  1  1  2 1  4  1   0.00000   0.00000 1788 20.00
4 1733    0 1205 1205 1205 1733  1  1  2 1  4  1   0.00000   0.00000 1788 25.00
5 1733    0 1205 1205 1205 1733  1  1  2 1  4  1   0.00000   0.00000 1788 26.00
6 1733    0 1205 1205 1205 1733  1  1  2 1  4  1   0.00000   0.00000 1788 33.00
1 1734    0 1334 1334 1334 1734  1  1  2 1  1  1   0.00000   0.00000 1507  3.20
2 1734    0 1334 1334 1334 1734  1  1  2 1  1  1   0.00000   0.00000 1507 14.50
3 1734    0 1334 1334 1334 1734  1  1  2 1  1  1   0.00000   0.00000 1507 17.00
4 1734    0 1334 1334 1334 1734  1  1  2 1  1  1   0.00000   0.00000 1507 19.50
5 1734    0 1334 1334 1334 1734  1  1  2 1  1  1   0.00000   0.00000 1507 22.00
6 1734    0 1334 1334 1334 1734  1  1  2 1  1  1   0.00000   0.00000 1507 29.50
1 1735    0 1393 1393 1393 1735  1  1  2 1  3  1   0.00000   0.00000 1264  2.10
2 1735    0 1393 1393 1393 1735  1  1  2 1  3  1   0.00000   0.00000 1264 10.70
3 1735    0 1393 1393 1393 1735  1  1  2 1  3  1   0.00000   0.00000 1264 11.40
4 1735    0 1393 1393 1393 1735  1  1  2 1  3  1   0.00000   0.00000 1264 13.00
1 1736 1444 1249 1249 1249 1736  1  1  1 2  4  1   0.00000   0.00000 1507  1.20
1 1737 1488 1403 1403 1403 1737  1  1  2 1  2  1   0.00000   0.00000 1093  2.40
2 1737 1488 1403 1403 1403 1737  1  1  2 1  2  1   0.00000   0.00000 1093  9.30
3 1737 1488 1403 1403 1403 1737  1  1  2 1  2  1   0.00000   0.00000 1093 10.00
4 1737 1488 1403 1403 1403 1737  1  1  2 1  2  1   0.00000   0.00000 1093 14.00
5 1737 1488 1403 1403 1403 1737  1  1  2 1  2  1   0.00000   0.00000 1093 16.20
6 1737 1488 1403 1403 1403 1737  1  1  2 1  2  1   0.00000   0.00000 1093 24.00
1 1738 1406 1274 1274 1274 1738  1  1  2 1  1  3   0.07177   0.01934 1507  3.00
2 1738 1406 1274 1274 1274 1738  1  1  2 1  1  3   0.07177   0.01934 1507 11.70
```

**Figure 7.2:** Structure of data file for multivariate analysis

```
SumEstimates - Notepad
File   Edit   View

***** Estimates for RE  1   "animal"    ***************************************
        No. of levels          =    3483
        Covariance structure =     NRM
        Order of fit           =       6
 Covariance matrix
   1    0.94114E-01
   2    0.25188        1.3842
   3    0.21444        1.4381        2.0021
   4    0.25053        1.8174        2.3719        3.5081
   5    0.30732        1.6712        2.2778        3.3394        3.3869
   6    0.36939        1.6952        2.2505        2.8978        3.1368        4.4173
 Eigenvalues of covariance matrix
 Value          12.68          1.28           0.53           0.21           0.09           0.00
   (%)          85.69          8.64           3.59           1.44           0.64           0.00
 Trace          14.79
 Matrix of correlations and variance ratios
   1      0.3970
   2      0.6978    0.2506
   3      0.4940    0.8639    0.2576
   4      0.4360    0.8247    0.8950    0.3212
   5      0.5443    0.7718    0.8747    0.9688    0.2547
   6      0.5729    0.6855    0.7568    0.7361    0.8110    0.2211
 Covariances & correlations with approximate sampling errors
  22  COVS A 1 1        0.941145E-01    0.101113E-01    vrat      0.397    0.035
  23  COVS A 1 2        0.251877        0.360495E-01    corr      0.698    0.060
  24  COVS A 1 3        0.214441        0.432709E-01    corr      0.494    0.079
  25  COVS A 1 4        0.250530        0.548630E-01    corr      0.436    0.079
  26  COVS A 1 5        0.307322        0.592281E-01    corr      0.544    0.081
  27  COVS A 1 6        0.369395        0.754025E-01    corr      0.573    0.096
  28  COVS A 2 2         1.38422        0.204192        vrat      0.251    0.033
  29  COVS A 2 3         1.43811        0.229260        corr      0.864    0.037
  30  COVS A 2 4         1.81741        0.284285        corr      0.825    0.048
  31  COVS A 2 5         1.67122        0.288051        corr      0.772    0.063
  32  COVS A 2 6         1.69519        0.349488        corr      0.686    0.092
  33  COVS A 3 3         2.00215        0.323453        vrat      0.258    0.037
  34  COVS A 3 4         2.37189        0.374780        corr      0.895    0.034
  35  COVS A 3 5         2.27785        0.383419        corr      0.875    0.045
  36  COVS A 3 6         2.25054        0.447750        corr      0.757    0.086
  37  COVS A 4 4         3.50806        0.541180        vrat      0.321    0.043
  38  COVS A 4 5         3.33939        0.539084        corr      0.969    0.017
  39  COVS A 4 6         2.89784        0.604353        corr      0.736    0.077
  40  COVS A 5 5         3.38694        0.598890        vrat      0.255    0.041
  41  COVS A 5 6         3.13680        0.651464        corr      0.811    0.067
  42  COVS A 6 6         4.41727        0.990693        vrat      0.221    0.046
```

**Figure 7.3**: The output from WOMBAT providing estimates of heritability and correlation with standard errors

## Precision and bias of genetic parameters

The genetic parameters are ratios of variance components and the method of estimation/partitioning of the variance components could influence precision and bias. The accuracy of the estimate (reliability) is given by the precision and can be quantified by the Standard error. The larger the sample size and the more information from relatives, the standard error would be less indicating better precision of the estimate. The biasedness of the estimate tells us about the additional components included with the expected variance component. For eg., a full-sib model is able to partition the additive genetic variance component along with a lesser fraction of dominance variance also and thus is biased compared to the half-sib model in which we are able to filter out the additive variance component alone.

## Breeding Value

The breeding value is the sum of the average effect of all the genes affecting the trait. In other terms, it is given as twice the mean deviation of the progeny from the population mean.

The mixed model equation (MME) described in Henderson (1973) created a revolution in animal breeding history. The MME algorithm has been used worldwide for the genetic evaluation of livestock, using models where components of 'u' the breeding value have a genetic meaning. Arguably, it may be the most important technical contribution of statistics to animal breeding (Gianola, 2000). In contrast to simpler techniques typically used to estimate heritability estimates in breeding such as parent–offspring regression or sib analyses, these models incorporate, multigenerational information from complex pedigrees and allow estimation of a range of causal components of variance. Furthermore, they are not bound by assumptions of non-assortative mating, inbreeding or selection, and allow for unbalanced datasets. The animal model has a well-established history in the quantitative genetics of plant and animal breeding, based on a series of key papers by Henderson (1950, 1975, 1984), and significantly advanced by the application of maximum likelihood techniques (Thompson 1973; Shaw 1987).

## Best Linear Unbiased Prediction (BLUP)

The use of a selection index for genetic evaluation has certain disadvantages. Firstly, records may have to be pre-adjusted for fixed or environmental factors and these are assumed to be known, but these are usually not assumed to be known. Henderson (1975) developed a methodology called best linear unbiased prediction (BLUP), by which fixed effects and breeding values can be simultaneously estimated.

**Best:** maximizes the correlation between true (a) and predicted breeding value (a') or minimizes prediction error variance (PEV)

**Linear**: Predictors are linear functions of observations

**Unbiased**: Estimation of realized values for a random variable such as animal breeding values and of estimable functions of fixed effects are unbiased (E(a/a')=a'

**Prediction:** involves the prediction of true breeding value.

BLUP has found widespread usage in the genetic evaluation of domestic animals because of its desirable properties. This has evolved from simple models such as the sire model in its early years to more complex models such as the animal, maternal and multivariate models. The MME for BLUP could be represented as

$Y = Xb + Z_a a + e$ ----------------------------- Animal model

$Y = Xb + Z_s s + e$ ----------------------------- Sire model

Where, 'Y' is a N x 1 vector of records, 'b' denotes the fixed effects in the model with association matrix X, 'a' is the vector of animal genetic effects with the association matrix $Z_a$, 's' is the vector of sire effects with the association matrix $Z_s$, and 'e' denotes the vector of residual (temporary environment) effect. The fixed effects included in the model are those found to have a significant effect. The assumed variance structure is as follows:

$$V\begin{pmatrix} a \\ s \\ e \end{pmatrix} = \begin{pmatrix} A\sigma^2_a & 0 & 0 \\ 0 & I_s\sigma^2_s & 0 \\ 0 & 0 & I_n\sigma^2_e \end{pmatrix}$$

The animal genetic effect, 'a' are assumed to be normally distributed with mean 0 and variance $A\sigma^2_a$ where A is the additive numerator relationship matrix and $\sigma^2_a$ additive genetic variance. Sire and residual effects are assumed to be normally distributed with mean 0 and variances $I_s\sigma^2_s$ and $I_n\sigma^2_e$, respectively, where $I_s$ and $I_n$ are identity matrices with orders equal to the number of sires and individual records, respectively and $\sigma^2_s$ and $\sigma^2_e$ are sire and residual variances, respectively.

The BLUP mixed model method is a combination of the best features of the selection index and least squares estimation. Thus the fixed effects (B) are estimated as BLUE, while the random effects (u) are predicted as BLUP. The estimation of fixed effects required construction of phenotypic variance-covariance matrix (V) and obtaining its inverse for formation of generalised least squares equation.

$$E(B) = (X^TV^{-1}X)^{-1}X^TV^{-1}Y$$

$$E(U) = GV^{-1}(Y\text{-}XB)\ A\sigma^2_a(A\sigma^2_a + I\sigma^2_e)^{-1}(Y\text{-}XB)$$

With field data, obtaining the V was not always practical and Henderson (1959) showed that the BLUE and BLUP could be simultaneously done with the following Mixed Model Equations (MME). The simultaneous estimation of fixed and random effects helps in the comparison of random effects corrected for the fixed effects. Moreover, the shrinkage in breeding value due to corrections depends on the number of progeny available for the sire.

| | | | | | |
|---|---|---|---|---|---|
| X'X | X'Z | | b | = | X'Y |
| X'Z | $Z'Z+A^{-1}\lambda$ | | u | | Z'Y |

Where, $\lambda = \sigma^2_e / \sigma^2_a$

A question is to how to invert A when the order of u is in the millions, as in routine genetic evaluation of sheep. Henderson (1976) made a breakthrough. He discovered that $A^{-1}$ could be written directly from a list of parents of the animals, enabling the use of all available relationships in genetic evaluation. This gave more precise inferences about genetic values and allowed accounting for biases due to ignoring many relationships in naive variance component analyses (Gianola, 2000).

BLUP under the Animal model can be done by using existing variance estimates or REML estimates obtained from data. Under normality and in the absence of prior knowledge on variance components BLUP methodology with unknown variances replaced by REML estimates from the same data should be used for predicting the breeding values (Gianola *et al.,* 1986). The main purpose of the exhaustive review of genetic parameters of sheep by Fogarty (1995) and that of Safary *et al.* (2005) was to develop appropriate estimates of variance-covariance matrices for the estimation of breeding values. Thus the actual need for variance component estimates in the animal breeding analysis is for the value of variances to obtain G and V in the mixed model equations described.

The solutions to the MME give the Best Linear Unbiased Estimate (BLUE) of xb and the BLUP of breeding value (a) under certain assumptions as follows

i. Distributions of y, u and e are assumed to be multivariate normal, implying that traits are determined by many additive genes of infinitesimal effects at many unlinked loci.

ii. The variances and covariances (R and G) for the base population are assumed to be known or at least known to proportionality. In practice, variances and covariances of the base population are never known exactly but, assuming the infinitesimal model, these can be estimated by restricted maximum likelihood (REML) if data include information on which selection was based.

iii. The MME can take selection into account if they are based on the linear function of y and there is no selection on information not included in the data.

Nicholas (1982) and Mrode (1996) have described the steps involved in using these MME of Henderson (1975) for the prediction of breeding values.

In genetic applications mixed model with both fixed and random effects is more common and can be described as follows

$y = X\beta + Zu + e$

Where,

y = Vector of observations (No. of records x 1) with mean Xβ and variance V

X = Known design matrix relating fixed effects to Y (No. of records x No. of levels of fixed effect).

B = Vector of unknown fixed effects (BLUE) (No. of levels of fixed effect x 1)

Z = Known design matrix relating animals to Y (No. of records x No of animals)

u = Vector of unknown breeding values (BLUP of EBV) (No. of animals x 1)

'e' = Vector of unknown random residual effects (No. of records x 1)

V = $ZGZ^T + R$

G = $A\sigma^2_a$

R = $I\sigma^2_e$

A = Numerator relationship matrix of order (No of animals x No of animals)

I = Identity matrix of order (No of observations x No of observations)

For the simple model, the REML analysis will provide estimates $\sigma^2_a$ and $\sigma^2_e$, from which the heritability can be estimated as $h^2 = \sigma^2_a / \sigma^2_a + \sigma^2_e$. The estimates of components of variance provided by the animal model are for a base population from which all other individuals in the population are descended. However, because the information in any pedigree rarely dates back to a true base population, the usual assumption is that the first generation of animals with data forms the base population. One important advantage of the animal model is that, because it corrects for the flow of genetic information across subsequent generations, estimates of variance components are unbiased by any effects of finite population size, assortative mating, selection or inbreeding in subsequent generations (Thompson 1973; Sorenson & Kennedy 1984; vander Werf & de Boer, 1990). Garrick (2010) has given a detailed explanation of the mixed model equation with an example, in which the principle of BLUP, the importance of the number of progenies, absorption of fixed effect and translational invariance proven with REML have been described.

## Property of BLUP to avoid bias because of selection

Most of the animal breeding data available for genetic analysis are usually from populations under selection. The selection changes the proportionality of the elements of A and tends to reduce $\sigma^2_a$. Further, u and e may become correlated. This would seem to imply that G and R should be estimated periodically to utilize a prediction of u. This would be a most difficult task because of the alteration of A. Henderson (1975) showed that this is not necessarily provided that the distributions in the base populations are multivariate normal, the variances and co-variances are known to proportionality, the selection decisions are based on translation-invariant linear functions of the data, and all the data used in the selection decisions are used in the mixed model equations. Under these conditions, BLUE of fixed effects and BLUP of random solutions can be obtained from MME that ignore selection and use the base population variances and co-variances. However, using the base population data alone would lead to a large portion of data being unutilised. Meyer and Thompson (1984) suggest that ML and REML have the remarkable property of estimating the base population parameters free of bias due to selection and can be used for data arising from selection. Several authors have shown that use of complete pedigree will provide better variance estimates, when the population undergo selection.

Reliability estimation for breeding values

The reliability of the obtained breeding values can be calculated as

$$\text{Reliability} = 1 - \frac{\text{PEV}}{\sigma^2_a}$$

The diagonal elements of the inverse of the left-hand-sided matrix i.e. prediction error variance (PEV) is used for the purpose. The standard error (SE) of the breeding values can be squared to get the PEV (Masuda et al., 2014). $\sigma^2_a$ is the additive genetic variance obtained for the trait.

## Genetic and Phenotypic Trends

The genetic and phenotypic trends are depicted using the breeding values and phenotypic values for different semen traits respectively. Breeding values predicted from the best model are fitted in a univariate fixed model with the year of birth as the only fixed effect. The least-squares solutions of breeding values for different years are plotted against the year of birth to depict the genetic trend for semen traits at different ages. Similarly, the least-squares means of phenotypic values for different years are plotted against the year of birth to depict the phenotypic trends. Estimates of genetic and phenotypic trends could be obtained from the slope of the trend line.

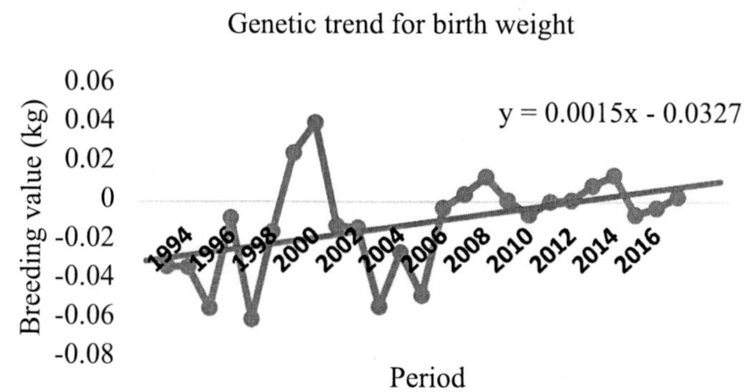


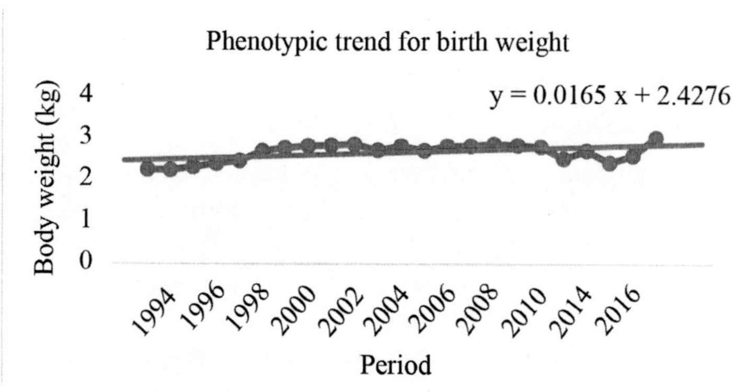


**Figure 7.4:** Genetic and phenotypic trend for birth weight in sheep obtained using the breeding values and phenotypic mean over year of birth

## Response to Selection

The change in the mean performance of progenies obtained from the selected parents is the response to selection and a knowledge of expected response is essential to formulate a breeding programme. The expected direct and correlated response for single trait selection is estimated following the procedure described by Falconer and Mackay (1996).

## Direct response

$$\mathbf{R} = ih\sigma_a / L$$

Where,

R = Expected response in the selected trait per year

i = Intensity of selection

h = Square-root of heritability of the trait

$\sigma_a$ = Square-root of additive genetic variance

L = Generation interval

## Correlated response

$$CR_y = ih_x r_g \sigma_{ay} / L$$

Where,

$CR_y$ = Correlated response in trait 'y' per year when trait 'x' was Selected

i = Intensity of selection

$h_x$ = Square-root of heritability of the trait 'x'

$\sigma_{ay}$ = Square-root of additive genetic variance of the trait 'y'

L = Generation interval

Once the genetic parameters and variance components are available, the intensity of selection could be obtained from the proportion selected and generation interval calculated from pedigree information (Details are provided in chapter on Inbreeding). Thus the quality of variance component estimates obtained is going to determine the accuracy of predicting the response to selection. The chapter on Estimation of Variance components gives a detailed description on the various methods of estimation of variance components.

# 8

# Estimation of Variance Components

Estimation of variance is primary for any breeding program as all the genetic parameters are dependent on these estimates. The properties of an estimate, their assumptions, type of data, availability of data, and computational requirement make it important to understand the method of estimation of variance components so as to make a wise choice that would suit the breeder's requirement. This chapter explains the methods of estimation of variance with merits and demerits of each and the reader could use these as a guide to choose the right method of estimation.

The genetic parameters are the basis for any animal breeding program and the important parameters such as heritability, repeatability and genetic correlation are ratios of (co)variances and their reliability depends on the accurate estimation of variance components. Estimates of variance components are used extensively in animal breeding. To list some the construction of selection indexes, mixed model BLUP, estimation ofheritability, repeatability and genetic correlation, calculation of response to selection, estimation of genetic trend, planning of breeding programmes, interpretation of the genetic mechanism of quantitative traits etc., require Variance components. The choice of method of estimation of variance components depends on the use for which they are estimated, computational feasibility, source of data and type of data.

## ANOVA

Fisher's (1918) paper and (1925) book made a major contribution to the variance components model in what has come to be known as the Analysis of Variance (ANOVA) method of estimation. The sums of squares from an ANOVA are equated to the expected values and thereby obtain a set of equations that are linear in the variance components to be estimated. For the one-way model with balanced data the expectations can be obtained as follows.

The model equation for describing a one-way analysis of variance with one treatment can be represented as

$$y_{ij} = \mu + \alpha_i + e_{ij}$$

Where $y_{ij}$ is the $j^{th}$ observation for the $i^{th}$ treatment, $\mu$ represents the general mean and $\alpha_i$ is the effect of $i^{th}$ treatment and $e_{ij}$ is a random error defined as $e_{ij} =$

$y_{ij} - E(y_{ij})$ for $E(y_{ij}) = \mu + \alpha_i$ where E represents the expectation over repeated randomization. Thus, $e_{ij}$ is taken as a random variable, with $E(e_{ij}) = 0$.

Further assumptions attributed to the error terms are normality, that the variance of $e_{ij}$ is the same for all 'i' and 'j' and that the covariance between any two error terms is zero.

The variance components are estimated by solving a set of linear equations, which are obtained by equating the expected values of sums of squares obtained through ANOVA.

The method of Eisenhart (1947) was similar to ANOVA except that besides the mean all other factors were considered random. Eisenhart (1947) saw the need for describing and distinguishing between what we call fixed, random and mixed models in the estimation of variance through ANOVA. The details of the fixed, random and mixed models are explained in the chapter on Linear Models in Animal Breeding

Searle (1989) and Becker (1992) have given a detailed description of expectations under various models and designs. However, these methods are effective only under one-way classification with nested designs or factorial classification with equal subclass numbers. **ANOVA has the best properties of an estimate when data is balanced, but in animal breeding never can we expect balanced data sets**. Analysis of breeding data involves multiple classifications with unequal subclass numbers (non-orthogonal with unequal subclass numbers). Because the datasets are large and unbalanced, and the models have a large number of nuisance parameters, simple ANOVA-type estimation methods seldom work well (Gianola, 2000).

## Henderson's Methods (Least squares method of estimation)

The **method of least squares** estimates the estimator that gives the least sum of squares between the y and the expected value of y. This method requires an assumption about the distribution of response variables only for expected value and possibly their variance-covariance structure (Dobson and Barnett, 2008).

Henderson (1953) described three methods for unbalanced data (Searle, 1989).

Method 1 is simply an analog of the analysis of variance method used with balanced data and is a combination of standard ANOVA and Eisenhart's model II as described above;

Method 2 is designed to correct a deficiency of Method 1 that arises with mixed models. In method II, least squares estimate of fixed effects are obtained and these estimates are used to correct the data. The corrected data are analysed for the estimation of variance components as in method I;

Method 3 is based on the method of fitting constants so often used in fixed effects models. It involves the computation of mean squares by a conventional least squares analysis of non-orthogonal data (method of fitting constants or weighted squares of means) and then equating these mean squares to their expectations and solving the unknown variances.

The first method gave biased estimates because even the fixed effects were considered random. The second method could not account for the correlation between fixed and random effects. The third method was the best method, but computationally very demanding for data with a large number of random effects. These unbiased, translational invariant, quadratic methods including methods I, II or III may provide negative estimates of variances.

**Translation Invariant**

Estimates are translation invariant, when the values do not change if for example any constant is added to all the observations in a particular cohort, *i.e.,* A function f(y) is said to be translation invariant if f(y) =f(y+Xb) for any vector b (location invariance))

The ordinary least-squares solutions remain the best linear unbiased estimate only when the assumptions regarding the error terms (independent and homogenous) as described above hold good (Henderson, 1976).

The least squares method in Henderson's method III could be represented as follows.

The conventional model of least squares (Ordinary least squares) is

$y = XB + e$

Where y is the observation vector of records. X is a known incidence matrix relating the observation to the fixed effects. B is an unknown vector of fixed effects and *e* is a non-observable random vector with mean, a vector of zeros and a variance-covariance matrix equal to V $\sigma^2_e$. V= I is an identity matrix and elements of *e* are independent. When the matrixV is not equal to I, generalised least squares/weighted least squares is used for best linear unbiased estimation. Weighted least squares is usually used when V is a diagonal matrix but not I. The combination of the selection index methodology of Lush and the least squares method resulted in the mixed model equations of Henderson (1973) and this would be discussed in a separate chapter on Genetic parameters. Harvey (1960) implemented method 3 in software for variance and covariance component estimation in animal breeding. Some of the disadvantages of generalization of ANOVA to unbalanced data were that it was difficult to study the effect of different degrees of unbalancedness on sampling variances of ANOVA, negative estimates could not be prevented and choice of different quadratics (the sums of squares in simple ANOVA or other forms as used by

Henderson) was very difficult.

**Example 8.1**: Estimation of heritability from sire variance for birth weight of sheep using MIXED MODEL LEAST-SQUARES AND MAXIMUM LIKELIHOOD COMPUTER PROGRAM PC-2 – Harvey (1990). The software uses method III of Henderson and estimation is by the least-squares method

## The input data file for Harvey (1990)

File Edit View

```
821   270   0   821   2   1   1   1   200
822   270   0   822   2   1   2   1   200
823   270   0   823   2   1   1   1   200
824   265   0   824   2   1   1   1   180
825   265   0   825   2   1   1   1   200
826   266   0   826   2   1   2   1   200
827   265   0   827   2   1   1   1   180
828   265   0   828   2   1   1   1   220
829   265   0   829   2   1   1   1   160
830   265   0   830   2   1   1   1   180
831   266   0   831   2   1   2   1   200
832   269   0   832   2   1   1   1   160
833   269   0   833   2   1   1   1   200
834   269   0   834   2   1   1   1   200
835   269   0   835   2   1   2   1   200
836   270   0   836   2   1   1   1   200
837   270   0   837   2   1   1   1   230
838   270   0   838   2   1   2   1   220
839   270   0   839   2   1   1   1   230
840   270   0   840   2   1   1   1   200
841   270   0   841   2   1   2   1   200
842   271   0   842   2   1   2   1   180
843   266   0   843   2   1   2   1   180
844   269   0   844   2   1   1   1   210
845   270   0   845   2   1   1   1   220
846   270   0   846   2   1   1   1   200
847   270   0   847   2   1   1   1   260
848   270   0   848   2   1   1   1   210
849   271   0   849   2   1   1   1   180
850   265   0   850   2   1   2   1   200
851   265   0   851   2   1   1   1   250
852   267   0   852   2   1   2   1   280
853   268   0   853   2   1   2   1   200
```

## The control or parameter file indicating the model in Harvey (1990)

```
TITLE VENKATARAMANAN PHD ANAL GROWTH HERITABILITY HALFSIB SANDYNO/ CENTER;

INPUT AN 7-10 SIRE 17-20 DAM 30 SUBJ 37-40 CENTRE 48 PERIOD 56 SEX 64

SEASON 72 WT 77-80 2;

CLASSES SIRE CENTRE PERIOD SEX SEASON;

MODEL2 WT = SIRE CENTRE PERIOD SEX SEASON/BETWEEN=.25 WITHIN=.75;
```

The output file showing Analysis of Variance

WT

| SOURCE | D.F. | SUM OF SQUARES | MEAN SQUARES | F | PROB |
|---|---|---|---|---|---|
| SIRE | 523 | 207.791584 | .397307 | 5.159 | .0000 |
| CENTRE | 2 | .301830 | .150915 | 1.960 | .1409 |
| PERIOD | 4 | 108.058555 | 27.014639 | 350.802 | .0000 |
| SEX | 1 | 42.501325 | 42.501325 | 551.907 | .0000 |
| SEASON | 2 | 35.216479 | 17.608239 | 228.654 | .0000 |
| REMAINDER | 25841 | 1989.968754 | .077008 | | |

Genetic parameters & constants for fixed effects in output file

ESTIMATES OF HERITABILITIES, GENETIC, PHENOTYPIC, ENVIRONMENTAL CORRELATIONS

| JOB | ROW | COL | RHM | RHM | HERITABILITY OR GENETIC R | STANDARD ERRORS | PHENOTYPIC CORRELATION | ENVIRONMENTAL CORRELATION | NEG | VARIANCE OR COV COMPONENTS AMONG | WITHIN |
|---|---|---|---|---|---|---|---|---|---|---|---|
| 2 | 1 | 1 | WT | WT | .309 | .022 | 1.000 | 1.000 | 0 | .00644622 | .07700819 |

LISTING OF CONSTANTS, LEAST-SQUARES MEANS AND STANDARD ERRORS FOR PROBLEM NO. 2

| RHM NAME | ROW CODE | INDEPENDENT VARIABLE | | NO. OBS. | EFFECTIVE NO. | CONSTANT ESTIMATE | STANDARD ERROR OF CONSTANT | LEAST-SQUARES MEAN | STANDARD ERROR OF LS MEAN |
|---|---|---|---|---|---|---|---|---|---|
| WT | 1 | MU | | 26374 | 763.3 | 2.60619428 | .03042354 | 2.60619428 | .03042354 |
| WT | 2 | CENTRE | 1 | 12323 | 110.9 | .05481355 | .02831562 | 2.66100783 | .03897784 |
| WT | 3 | CENTRE | 2 | 13959 | 112.4 | .05573439 | .02817453 | 2.66192867 | .03885955 |
| WT | 0 | CENTRE | 3 | 92 | 21.0 | -.11054793 | .05604581 | 2.49564635 | .06696380 |
| WT | 4 | PERIOD | 1 | 2074 | 268.6 | -.24464822 | .01276784 | 2.36154606 | .03333755 |
| WT | 5 | PERIOD | 2 | 7669 | 318.1 | .05287859 | .01134685 | 2.65907288 | .03266218 |
| WT | 6 | PERIOD | 3 | 9659 | 307.7 | .14219452 | .01178811 | 2.74838880 | .03278734 |
| WT | 7 | PERIOD | 4 | 6578 | 284.5 | .04246613 | .01251226 | 2.64866042 | .03309715 |
| WT | 0 | PERIOD | 6 | 394 | 44.2 | .00710898 | .04121590 | 2.61330326 | .05064932 |
| WT | 8 | SEX | 1 | 12658 | 743.5 | .04095848 | .00174346 | 2.64715276 | .03046757 |
| WT | 0 | SEX | 2 | 13716 | 738.4 | -.04095848 | .00174346 | 2.56523581 | .03047935 |
| WT | 9 | SEASON | 1 | 7405 | 656.1 | -.08383051 | .00393016 | 2.52236377 | .03069311 |
| WT | 10 | SEASON | 2 | 5463 | 665.9 | .05753235 | .00347011 | 2.66372663 | .03066514 |
| WT | 0 | SEASON | 3 | 13506 | 735.0 | .02629816 | .00276164 | 2.63249245 | .03048725 |

## Maximum likelihood (ML) and Restricted maximum likelihood (REML) method

In 1967, the second revolution with respect to estimation was published by Hartley and Rao, in which they applied Fischer's maximum likelihood theory for the estimation of variance components in mixed models. ML estimates are never negative. Kruuk (2004) has described the use of ML and REML in Animal models. ML estimation is based on a simple yet powerful logic that can be applied to any form of statistical inference. For a given set of parameters defining a statistical model, their likelihood is defined as the probability of observing the actual data in hand if those parameter estimates were true: parameter estimates with low likelihoods are therefore those under which observing the actual data would be a rare event, and so forth. Probability is calculated based on assumptions about the statistical probability distribution of the data, usually that it is multivariate normal. An ML analysis then simply identifies the set of parameters that maximizes the likelihood of observing the actual data (Fisher, 1921). Maximum likelihood under assumptions of normality were extensively used for variance estimation. All ML estimates have the undesirable property of being statistically biased because they fail to account for the degrees of freedom lost in estimating fixed effects (Patterson & Thompson, 1971; Shaw, 1987). This generates bias even when the only fixed effect being considered is the mean, but the bias can be considerable for larger numbers of fixed effects (Meyer, 1989). As a result, an ML approach will underestimate the residual variance. The bias of the ML estimate of the residual variance led to great interest in a method called "restricted" maximum likelihood (REML), in which only the likelihood of the part of the data that does not depend on the fixed effects is considered (Patterson & Thompson 1971). The likelihood functions and basis of ML and REML methods are described under the mixed model later in this chapter. The probability of a solution outside the parameter space is zero for ML and REML estimates. Thus solutions can be obtained only when it lies within the parameter space.

For the animal model, the likelihood function for the ML estimates (Kruuk, 2004) is given as

$$L = c - 1/2 \ln|V| (y - X\beta)^T V^{-1} (y - X\beta)$$

where c is a constant and can be ignored and the remaining symbols are as described above. This expression is then used to find the values of β and V (or, in the simplest case, $\sigma^2_a$ and $\sigma^2_e$), by differentiating with respect to each parameter and solving for zero to give ML estimates.

To obtain REML estimators rather than just ML for the mixed model equation, the likelihood is maximized for a transformed vector $\boldsymbol{y^*}$, where $\boldsymbol{y^*}$ contains the data corrected by a particular transformation matrix $\boldsymbol{K}$ (so $\boldsymbol{y^*=Ky}$), and $\boldsymbol{K}$ depends on the design matrix $\boldsymbol{X}$ such that $\boldsymbol{KX} = 0$. The equation becomes

$$\boldsymbol{Y^* = KZu + Ke}$$

and the REML estimates are essentially the ML estimates for these transformed variables. Note that because $\boldsymbol{K}$ is determined entirely by $\boldsymbol{X}$, we are no longer considering estimates of β, but only of the variance components.

## Algorithms for solutions to REML

In practice, ML and REML require an iterative solving procedure, which can make the process computationally highly intensive. The algorithms used in obtaining solutions have been reviewed by Hofer, 1998 and has been grouped according to the order of derivative used. Among the derivative free REML (DFREML), Simplex and Quasi – Newton algorithm have been used. However, in such methods the solutions are difficult especially when number of parameters increase. The algorithm based on first-order derivatives is the expectation maximization (EM) algorithm and this has the property of solutions within parameter space, when starting values are >0. The convergence for EM algorithm is slow but acceleration techniques or reparameterization help in faster convergence. Sparse matrix and transformation reparameterisation are techniques to improve convergence rate as well as finding out solutions outside parameter size. The Newton-Raphson (NR), Method of scoring

(MSC) and Average Information (AI) algorithm are based on first and second derivatives. AI has the advantage of less computation compared to NR and MSC. AI algorithm apart from having the property of faster convergence, also has the advantage that at convergence sampling (co)variances of parameters are available. Software like ASREML and WOMBAT use AI algorithm by default, while other options are also available.

## Example 8.2

Data file for REML estimation for WOMBAT (Meyer, 2007) software

File Edit View

```
1471 1230 1302 2 1 1 1 5 3 1302 1302 2.4
1732 0    1482 1 1 2 1 2 1 1482 1482 3.5
1733 0    1205 1 1 2 1 4 1 1205 1205 3
1734 0    1334 1 1 2 1 1 1 1334 1334 3.2
1735 0    1393 1 1 2 1 3 1 1393 1393 2.1
1736 1444 1249 1 1 1 2 4 1 1249 1249 1.2
1737 1488 1403 1 1 2 1 2 1 1403 1403 2.4
1738 1406 1274 1 1 2 1 1 3 1274 1274 3
1739 1444 1249 1 1 1 2 4 1 1249 1249 1.7
1740 1444 1390 1 1 1 2 3 1 1390 1390 1.4
1741 1444 1390 1 1 1 2 3 1 1390 1390 2.1
1742 0    1251 1 1 2 1 1 1 1251 1251 3.1
1743 1464 1530 1 1 2 1 1 1 1530 1530 2.2
1744 1419 1254 1 1 1 2 4 1 1254 1254 2.6
1745 1419 1254 1 1 1 2 4 1 1254 1254 2.6
1746 1406 1425 1 1 1 1 2 1 1425 1425 2.4
1747 0    1362 1 1 2 1 3 1 1362 1362 2.4
1748 0    1412 1 1 2 1 1 1 1412 1412 2.4
1749 1464 1358 1 1 2 1 1 1 1358 1358 2.5
1750 1419 1450 1 1 1 1 2 1 1450 1450 2.1
1751 0    1411 1 1 2 1 2 1 1411 1411 2.4
1752 1444 1285 1 1 2 1 3 2 1285 1285 3.2
1753 1498 1184 1 1 2 1 6 2 1184 1184 3.8
1754 1406 1326 1 1 2 1 1 3 1326 1326 2.8
1755 1419 1418 1 1 1 1 2 1 1418 1418 3.2
1756 1405 1270 1 1 1 1 4 1 1270 1270 2
1757 1495 1479 1 1 1 1 2 1 1479 1479 2.9
1758 0    1510 1 1 2 1 2 1 1510 1510 2.4
1759 1495 1518 1 1 1 1 2 1 1518 1518 2.4
1760 1464 1208 1 1 2 2 1 1 1208 1208 2.4
1761 1464 1208 1 1 2 2 1 1 1208 1208 2.6
1762 1419 1470 1 1 1 1 2 1 1470 1470 2.5
1763 1464 1241 1 1 1 1 4 1 1241 1241 3.4
```

Parameter file with starting values for REML estimation of variance using

WOMBAT

File Edit View

```
COM BW NILAGIRI : Simple univariate analysis
PED NILPED.D
DAT BW.D
  animal 0
  sire
  dam
  pedam 4444
  gmdam 4444
  period 4
  season 2
  sex 2
  ls 2
  agedam 6
  inbr 5
  fcov
  afcov
  damage
  bwt
end
ANAL UNI
MODEL
 RAN animal NRM
 FIX period
 FIX season
 FIX sex
 FIX ls
 FIX agedam
 FIX inbr
 TR bwt
END
VAR animal 1
.14
VAR error 1
.22
```

The output file with variance components and estimates of the genetic parameter from WOMBAT

```
Convergence criteria for last 3 iterates
Change in log likelihood      =     8.546065      0.020103      0.000000
Change in parameter vector    =     0.043012      0.002167      0.000009
Norm of gradient vector       =     261.1615       12.3060        0.0287
Newton decrement              =     -16.5641       -0.0401       -0.0000

***** Estimates of residual covariances     ************************************
      Order of fit           =        1
 Covariance matrix
   1     0.14218
 Matrix of correlations and variance ratios
   1       0.5990
 Covariances & correlations with approximate sampling errors
   1  COVS Z 1 1         0.142181        0.700498E-02    vrat      0.599    0.035

***** Estimates for RE  1    "animal"    ***************************************
      No. of levels          =     3484
      Covariance structure =      NRM
      Order of fit           =        1
 Covariance matrix
   1     0.95197E-01
 Matrix of correlations and variance ratios
   1       0.4010
 Covariances & correlations with approximate sampling errors
   2  COVS A 1 1         0.951973E-01   0.102687E-01    vrat      0.401    0.035

***** Estimates of phenotypic covariances   ***********************************
 Covariance matrix
   1     0.23738
 Covariances & correlations with approximate sampling errors
   3  COVS T 1 1         0.237378        0.718836E-02
======== end of file ===========================19-02-2013==========18:56====
```

## MINQUE and MIVQUE

In the 1970s C.R. Rao created a procedure known as MINQUE (Minimum norm quadratic unbiased estimation) from which other practical estimation procedures like the MIVQUE (minimum variance quadratic unbiased estimation) were developed. These estimates were quadratic in y, unbiased and translational invariant, but for optimality, these estimators require prior knowledge of true parameters. Even though they are not entirely dependent on the underlying distribution, minimal sampling variances are obtained only when the distribution is multivariate normal. These methods cannot be used when the true parameter is not known.

### Simulation of Data

As defined earlier, a Model can be described as 'a physical, mathematical or otherwise logical representation of a system, entity, phenomenon, or process.' A Simulation is 'the implementation or exercise of a Model over time'. Hence, the simulation, utilizing models, becomes the dynamic representation of a real-world activity or entity. Simulation is done in order to get numerous subsets of data with different circumstances so as to enable prediction and forecasting. Simulation helps in obtaining data with more volume, greater detail and accuracy. Real data can have some disadvantages like false positive significance, lack of power or absence of true signal, which can be overcome by simulation. Simulation has been used in new method development and genetic models for disease. However, simulated data is much cleaner and can never replace real data.

## Bayesian Method of Estimation

The distribution-dependent properties of ML and REML can be overcome by the Bayesian approach. This methodology is more useful when the assumptions of normality or other distributions are not fulfilled in the case of the maximum likelihood distribution. Bayesian inference is a form of inference, which consider the parameters as random variables possessed of prior distributions reflecting the state of accumulated knowledge. Bayes estimation uses the method of inverse probability. The main basis of this method is **Bayes' theorem**. This theorem is based on the fact that there is a prior probability that gets updated when more and more information is added to it to give a posterior conditional probability. Bayes' theorem was named after Thomas Bayes (1702-1761), an English mathematician who wrote "An Essay towards solving a Problem in the Doctrine of Chances" and divided the statistical community into Frequentists and Bayesians forever. The Bayesian theory boomed after its rebirth in the 1950s and now it has been used in several scientific fields (Gianola and Fernando, 1986; wright et al., 2000). Unlike the frequentists, Bayesians believe in the idea that there may be more to a process than what the data tells us. So, when there is a reliable prior, Bayesian methods can be used to obtain better estimates, especially in biological systems where the data is continuously getting updated.

Bayes' theorem for conditional probabilities can be denoted as:

$$P(A \mid B) = \frac{P(B \mid A) \times P(A)}{P(B)}$$

In this method, the available knowledge about the parameter estimate could be incorporated as the prior distribution. Flat priors (non-informative or vague priors) used for data analysis indicate that all the values of the parameter had equal likelihood which implied that all the estimates are obtained from the available data.

In particular, variance components can be estimated using a Bayesian framework (Gianola & Fernando 1986; Sorensen et al., 1994), which may have advantages in certain situations (Blasco, 2001). Gianola and Fernando (1986) and Gianola et al. (1990) emphasized that Bayesian methodology offers a general framework for the estimation of breeding values when variances are not known. For mixed model, Bayesian inference about unknown variance components σ should be based on the marginal posterior density f(σ/y), i.e.

$f(\sigma/y) = \int_b f(b,\sigma/y)db$

with the joint posterior density

$f(b,\sigma/y) \propto f(y/b,\sigma)*f(b,\sigma)$

Where f(y/b,σ) corresponds to the likelihood and f(b,σ) is the joint prior density of b and σ. The prior density may be based on information contained in past data, theoretical considerations or personal beliefs (Gianola and Fernando, 1986). The posterior inference is affected by the specified prior density unless the information in the data analyzed (likelihood) overwhelms the prior. Initially, the Bayesian approach did not gain popularity due to the difficulty in obtaining solutions to the complex integrals involved in the analysis. However, the simulation and sampling methods of MCMC (Markov Chain Monte Carlo) led to a revolution in the application of these in the estimation of variance components. The Metropolis Hasting algorithm and Gibbs sampling are the two main sampling methods to generate the posterior distribution of parameters in the MCMC method. The Gibbs sampling is extensively used in the animal breeding analysis. Ambike (2022) has explained the use of MCMC in animal breeding analysis.

## MCMC (Markov Chain Monte Carlo) and Gibbs sampling

MCMC or Markov Chain Monte Carlo is a procedure that is used to obtain random samples from the marginal posterior distribution which results in the formation of chains for all the parameters of interest. The average of each chain gives the estimate for that parameter. This algorithm generates random samples from the probability distribution and fits the statistical model to the data. One of the most popular algorithms of MCMC which is the Gibbs sampler (Gelfand and Smith, 1990) was used for generating these samples and building a Markov chain where the next sample is dependent only on its penultimate sample. Gibbs sampler draws each sample conditional to the most recently generated values of other components of the parameter vector and the data.

The Gibbs sampling (GS) algorithm enables the estimation of random samples of parameter estimates based on a given data set, by generating posterior distributions of parameter values that are proportional to the product of the parameter probabilities and the observation probabilities. In one round, the Gibbs sampler solves the mixed model equations with the current variance components and adds a small random number (noise) to each solution. Then the sampler generates a covariance estimate as a random number based on the solutions. The samples of solutions and variance components in each round are not informative. Having many samples from many rounds repeated, we can figure the posterior distribution of a variance component as a histogram out of the samples.

Burn-in is the practice of discarding a few iterations at the beginning of the MCMC chain. This also helps to obtain better values for the first iteration or the starting values which will be included in the analysis. There are several chains with different starting values where a few starting values may be better than others. Thus, the burn-in period helps to stabilize the chain so that it is not drifting up or down eventually. Thinning is a process of discarding all the observations obtained from the Markov chain except every $k^{th}$ observation. MCMC produces a Markov chain of all the estimates where the next value is obtained from its previous value which leads to auto-correlations between the samples. If an algorithm is generating highly correlated samples, then it will need more iterations to cover the entire parameter space and converge. For this thinning was done to reduce the auto-correlation. The average of samples (posterior mean) as a point estimator of a variance component is calculated. The standard deviation of samples (posterior SD), which is corresponding to the standard error in a frequentist approach (e.g., REML) gives the confidence interval. The Credibility intervals for the estimates so obtained suggest that when the experiment will be repeated an infinite number of times then, 95% of those infinite intervals obtained will contain the true estimate (Blasco, 2005). The highest posterior density interval gives the smallest interval with a 95% probability of containing the true estimate where the estimate does not need to be symmetrical, unlike the frequentist approach.

## The length of the chain and the number of samples

Depending upon the model the number of iterations and sample size would differ and there are several ways to decide upon the length of the chain, the burn-in and thinning interval for Gibbs sampling. Geweke's convergence diagnostic (Geweke, 1992) is used to infer whether the number of samples drawn is sufficient to obtain the desirable convergence. Convergence is not a single point but a posterior distribution obtained from a prior distribution when the Bayesian framework is used for estimation. To study whether the models have converged, different convergence statistics are used. Convergence occurs when the Markov chain has reached a stationary posterior distribution. Estimates of parameters obtained are also examined using trace plots (Figure) which plotted the parameter value against the iteration number. The absence of directionality indicated that the convergence is reached and the number of iterations and burn-in period is sufficient. Some authors have used the Raftery and Lewis method (1991) to decide upon the length of the chain for Gibbs sampling.

**Table 8.1:** Example Output from PostgibbsF90 which has the mean, median, mode and other diagnostics of the Gibb's Sampling.

| Random effect | MCE | Mean | Median | Mode | Eff. sample size | Geweke diagnostic | Autocorrelations | | |
|---|---|---|---|---|---|---|---|---|---|
| | | | | | | | Lag1 | Lag10 | lag50 |
| Direct Additive | 4.12E-02 | 0.45932 | 0.39170 | 0.31256 | 51.2 | 0.45 | 0.836 | 0.190 | 0.049 |
| Common litter | 7.69E-03 | 0.61481 | 0.59670 | 0.55558 | 402.2 | 0.44 | 0.100 | 0.023 | 0.048 |
| Residual | 8.72E-04 | 0.99961 | 0.99940 | 0.99766 | 784.9 | 0.08 | -0.025 | -0.005 | -0.035 |

BLUPF90 family of software (Misztal et al, 2018) include several programs for generating Gibbs samples. Post-Gibbs analyses with POSTGIBBSF90 give the posterior estimates and diagnostics as in Table 8.1.

Trace plots obtained to ascertain the stability of the MCMC chains for the parameters of the model as illustrated one of our earlier studies (Ambike, 2022) are presented in figures 8.1 and 8.2. The analysis was for variance components estimation of the semen trait, ejaculate volume. The number of samples, burn-in and thinning interval used for the analyses were 200,000, 20,000 and 50 and this was finalized based on the trace plots and earlier studies conducted. The random distribution without any directionality or trend indicated convergence.

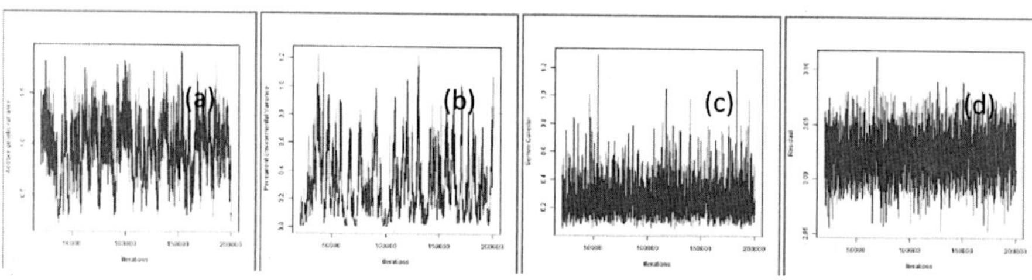


**Figure 8.1 :** Trace plot for additive effect **(a)**, permanent environmental effect **(b)**, effect of the semen collector **(c)** and residual effect **(d)** for ejaculate volume in HF purebred bulls (Ambike, 2022)

For estimation of genetic and phenotypic correlation estimates in bivariate analyses (Figure) The number of iterations was increased from 2,00,000 to 5,00,000 with a burn-in of 50,000 when stability was achieved. The need for additional burn-in is explicit from the trace plots which indicates stability after 50,000 iterations of the cycle and as a result, the burn-in period was increased to 1,00,000 iterations after which chains were stable for all the bivariate analyses.

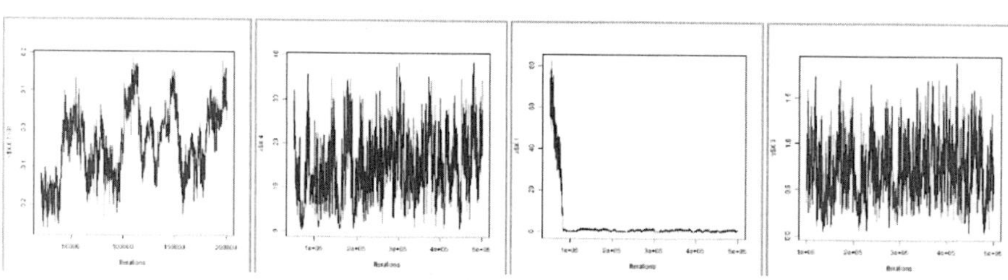

**Figure 8.2:** Trace plot for bivariate analysis (Ambike, 2022)

## Model selection in Gibbs sampling

The most parsimonious model for a Bayesian analysis is deduced based on the lowest DIC (Deviance Information Criterion) as proposed by Spiegelhalter et al. (2002). This is a Bayesian measure that helps to determine the model fit while penalizing for the model complexity similar to BIC (Bayesian

Information Criterion). According to Misztal et al. (2014), deviance (D) is a measure of the overall fit of a model from which DIC can be calculated by subtracting posterior deviance from twice the expectation of D.

$$D(\bar{\theta}) = -2\log L(\hat{\theta})$$

$$DIC = 2(\bar{D}) - D(\bar{\theta})$$

The DIC values obtained for different semen production traits have been summarized in Table 8.2 where the selected models have been highlighted in bold. Model 2 was found to be best with the lowest DIC value.

**Table 8.2:** DIC values of different models analyzed for semen production traits

| Model No. | EV | SC | ISM | PTM | TNS | TNSD |
|---|---|---|---|---|---|---|
| 1 | 637187 | 205465 | 1242360 | 716991 | 864733 | 1934684 |
| 2 | **635944** | **204267** | **1240600** | **715632** | **863662** | **1933803** |
| 3 | 636307 | 204928 | 1241951 | 716764 | 864326 | 1934320 |

DIC: Deviance Information Criteria, EV: Ejaculate volume (ml), SC: Sperm concentration ($10^9$/ml), ISM: Initial sperm motility (%), PTM: Post-thaw motility (%), TNS: Total number of spermatozoa per ejaculate ($10^9$/ejaculate), TNSD: Theoretical number of doses produced (doses/ejaculate)

## Comparison of Different Methods of Estimation of Variance Components

ANOVA is the best method when data is balanced. For unbalanced data, ML, REML or MINQUE methods must be used. The disadvantage of MINQUE is that the estimated variance component varies with the prior value provided for the parameter. However, MINQUE can be iterated to get convergence (I-MINQUE), but negative estimates are always a problem. Thus, ML and REML are superior to MINQUE. The REML estimates for balanced data are the same as that of ANOVA. Compared to ML, REML has another advantage in that it takes into account the degrees of freedom for estimation of fixed effects and hence provides variance components unaffected by the fixed effects However to get estimates of fixed effects in a mixed model methodology, ML has to be resorted to. Both ML and REML methods rely on normality assumptions and an important advantage is a positive estimate. Another disadvantage of ML is that the estimates are strictly restricted to parameter space, precluding solutions outside parameter space, which might have higher values of likelihood. The use of REML (variance components ignoring the number of fixed effects estimated) does not lose any information obtained in ML and moreover the estimates are unbiased. REML has become the method of choice for estimation of variance components, especially when data is multivariate normal and by virtue of its desirable properties, has been extensively used in sheep breeding analysis.(Meyer, 1989; Hofer, 1998; Kruuk, 2004).

# 9

# Linear Models in Animal Breeding

Linear models have been extensively used in animal breeding. This chapter explains the basics of linear models including description; fixed, random and mixed models; model diagnostics and covariates. The concept of linear models in animal breeding is explained with representation and actual examples of use in different types of livestock.

## Introduction to Linear Models

A model can be defined as a physical, mathematical or otherwise logical representation of a system, entity, phenomenon, or process. Linear models are a way of describing response variables in terms of a linear combination of the predictor variable. They provide a framework for a large set of models whose common goal is to explain or predict a quantitative dependent variable by a set of independent variables that can be categorical or quantitative.

When an effect of various levels of a factor could be depicted in a straight line then it is called a linear model. The left-hand side is otherwise called the dependent variable and the right-hand side has the predictor or independent variables which may vary from 1 to many. The unaccounted part denoted as 'e' is the error that has no source of information. The dependent and independent variables are known by different names as given in the table.

**Table 9.1:** Description of a linear model

| **Left Hand Side (LHS)** | **Right Hand Side (RHS)** |
|---|---|
| **Y=** | **X1 +X2 +—+ e** |
| Response variable | Explanatory variable |
| Dependent variable | Independent variable |
| Effect | Cause |
| Effect | Treatment |
| Predictand | Predictor |

As described in earlier chapters the dependent and independent variables could be quantitative or qualitative and follow different probability distributions and the estimation methods would vary. Similarly depending on the objective and available source of data different designs such as half-sib, full-sib, offspring-parent, maternal effect, animal model, sire model, threshold model, random regression model, etc could be designed. The factors or right-hand side again could be included in the form of a fixed class (sex) or covariate (age at first calving). Such representations with a continuous dependent variable, linear relationship and a combination of classes and covariates are called General Linear Models. The linearity when not direct but is brought through a link function such as probit, logit makes the general linear model into a generalized linear model. The fixed classes are initially included as a main effect, but certain factors such as season x year or combination of herd x season could lead to an interaction (synergistic effect) which also could be modeled through a general linear model. The assumptions, type of data and other features are discussed in the chapter on methods of estimation.

**Fixed class and covariate**

Fixed class is a classification of the dependent variable into different levels of the fixed factor. For eg. First parity is a level of the factor, parity in which all the milk yields recorded of first calving will be included. Similarly, sex, season, period, etc., are examples of fixed classes.

Fixed covariate is a dependent continuous variable that varies with an individual case of the dependent variable and is usually included to study the effect as a regression coefficient. For eg. age at first calving is a covariate for the individual first lactation milk yield

## Fixed, Random and Mixed Models

In general, as described by Searle (1989) when we want to make inferences only to the effects of a factor that occurs in the data, then those effects are considered fixed effects, but when inferences are going to be made to a set of effects that is larger than just those that occur in the data, then the effects will be taken as random effects. The fixed effects could be included as a fixed class or covariate. In a fixed model all the independent variables are fixed, except for the error component that is always random. In a random model, all the factors are random except for the mean. In addition to the mean $\mu$, if the randam model has other fixed effects, the model is called a mixed model. The mixed model is one which has both fixed and random effects and has been the most successful model used in the animal breeding analysis.

For the simple linear model

$$y_{ij} = \mu + \alpha_i + e_{ij}$$

In the equation, the parameters of interest are the mean $\mu$ and $\alpha_i$s, the effects of different levels of the treatment 'i' using linear functions. The best linear unbiased estimators (BLUE) for these fixed effects are given as $\alpha$

$$\text{BLUE}(\mu + \alpha_i) = \bar{y}_i = \sum_{j=1}^{n} y_{ij} / n \text{ and}$$

$$\text{BLUE}(\alpha_i - \alpha_h) = \bar{y}_{i.} - \bar{y}_h$$

The estimates obtained are fixed constants and hence called **fixed effects**. Let us consider an example for effect of sex on lamb weight. They are deemed to be constants representing the effect of sex. If we consider the effect on body weight of lamb sired by sire 'i' then $\alpha_i$ would represent the genetic contribution of sire 'i' to the body weight, $y_{ij}$. Genetically, the $\alpha_i$s are treated as random variables and in this context the effects are called as **random effects**. The distributional properties of zero mean and the same variance to $\alpha_i$ are attributed to the random effect. In the case of a random model, E $(\alpha_i)$ and covariance between each pair of $\alpha_i$s equals zero. The variance among $\alpha_i$s is given by $V(\alpha)$. Thus $E(y_{ij}) = \mu$ and $e_{ij} = y_{ij} - E(y_{ij}/ \alpha_i)$ where $E(y_{ij}/ \alpha_i)$ is the conditional expected value of $y_{ij}$ for given $\alpha_i$. When the $\alpha_i$s are considered as random effects and with there being no other terms except $\mu$ and $e_{ij}$ in the model, it is called as a random effects model. As in the present example the sires are no longer the $\alpha$s of sole interest, as they are when they are fixed effects like in the case of sex. There is no reason for estimating $\alpha_i$s of all the sires or difference between them; the parameter of interest so far as they are concerned is now the variance of random effect $V(\alpha_i)$. In general, as described by Searle (1989) when we want to make inferences only to the effects of a factor that occur in the data, then those effects are considered as fixed effects, but when inferences are going to be made to a set of effects that is larger than just those that occur in the data, then the effects will be taken as random effects. In a random model, in addition to the mean $\mu$, if the model has other fixed effects, the model is called a mixed model.

**Table 9.2** The fixed and random model

| **Fixed Model** | **Random Model** |
|---|---|
| $Yi = \mu + fi + ei$ | $Yi - \mu + ri + ei$ |
| Yi - observation | Yi - observation |
| $\mu$ - overall mean | $\mu$ - mean |
| fi - fixed effect | ri - random effect |
| ei - error | ei - error |
| All the independent variables including mean are fixed except the error component which is random. | All the independent variables except the mean are random. |
| By fixed we mean that all the levels of the factor are exhausted in predicting the dependent variable. | By random we mean a random sample from an infinite set of levels. |
| Sex is a fixed factor with male and female as levels | Sire is a random effect representing the numerous sires available in the population |
| Fixed effect affects the mean and hence also called location effect | Random effects affect only the variance and are usually assumed to follow a normal distribution with 0 mean and variance |
| The number of levels is usually less and the effect remains constant in different samples | The number of levels is infinite and the effect varies with sample size as the representation of the whole set of levels increases with an increase in sample size. |
| Also called as the location effect | Also called as the frailty effect |

**A fixed model to analyse age at first service and calving in dairy cattle. Note the error term alone is random. All the factors are used as fixed classes**

$$Y_{ijk} = \mu + p_i + s_j + e_{ijk}$$

Where,

$Y_{ijk}$ = age at first service and calving of $k^{th}$ heifer / cow, born / calved in the $i^{th}$ period and $j^{th}$ season

$\mu$ = overall mean when equal subclass frequencies exist

$p_i$ = fixed effect of $i^{th}$ period (i=1 to 5)

$s_j$ = fixed effect of $j^{th}$ season (j=1 to 4)

$e_{ijk}$ = random errors normally and independently distributed with mean zero and variance $\sigma^2_e$ [NID $(0, \sigma^2_e)$]

**Fixed model with age at first lactation as covariate for first lactation traits**

$$Y_{ijk} = \mu + p_i + s_j + b\,(A_{ijk}) + e_{ijk}$$

Where,

$Y_{ijk}$ = first lactation character of the $k^{th}$ cow that calved in the $i^{th}$ period and $j^{th}$ season

$\mu$ = overall mean when equal subclass frequencies exist

$p_i$ = effect of $i^{th}$ period (i=1 to 5)

$s_j$ = effect of $j^{th}$ season (j=1 to 4)

b = partial regression of the first lactation trait (Y) on age at first calving (A)

$A_{ijk}$ = age at first calving for the corresponding $Y_{ijk}$ observation

$e_{ijk}$ = random errors NID $(0, \sigma^2_e)$

**A mixed model used for Semen production traits is presented below**

$$Y_{ijklmnopqrs} = \mu + L_i + O_j + C_k + T_l + B_m + A_n + S_o + R_p + W_q + U_r + e_{ijklmnopqrs}$$

$Y_{ijklmnopqrs}$ = Semen production trait record

$\mu$ = Overall mean

$L_i$ = Fixed effect of $i^{th}$ location

$O_j$ = Fixed effect of $j^{th}$ order of ejaculate

$C_k$ = Fixed effect of $k^{th}$ collection interval

$T_l$ = Fixed effect of $l^{th}$ collection time

$B_m$ = Fixed effect of $m^{th}$ breed of the bull

$A_n$ = Fixed effect of $n^{th}$ age class for EV, SV, ISM and PTM and age taken as a quadratic covariate for TNS and TNSD

$S_o$ = Fixed effect of $o^{th}$ season of semen collection

$R_p$ = Fixed effect of $p^{th}$ year of semen collection

$W_q$ = Random effect of $q^{th}$ semen collector

$U_r$ = Random effect of $r^{th}$ bull

$e_{ijklmnopqrs}$ = Random error associated with each record, NID $(0, \sigma^2_s)$

## Building a Linear Model

Once the dependent and independent variables are identified, the building of the linear model could be done in various ways. A complete model with all the effects including interactions is called the saturated model. However, a parsimonious model is preferred to a saturated model as even though a saturated model could account for more variability in the dependent variable, non-significant effects can cause bias due to loss of degrees of freedom and also reduce the precision due to an increase in the error of estimates. The model diagnostics help in identifying the best model.

## Model Diagnostics help in identifying the most suitable one

The model diagnostics such as root mean sum of squares, loglikelihood and its functions in the form of BIC, AIC, AICC, the deviation information criteria

(DIC) etc., all are more reliable than the coefficient of determination, $R^2$ which indicates the proportion of variability explained by the independent variables included in the model. Nevertheless, the adjusted $R^2$ is a better means to rely as it takes into consideration the number of parameters estimated. In general, the estimates of genetic parameters are said to be different from zero when the estimate is greater than twice the standard error of the estimate. When additional random effects are included, the statistical significance can be assessed via a likelihood ratio test (LRT), as twice the difference in log-likelihood between two nested models will approximate to a Chi-square distribution (with degrees of freedom equal to the difference in the number of variance components estimated). Information criteria are also considered in selecting the best model. They are the Akaike Information Criteria (AIC), the finite-sample corrected Akaike Information Criteria (AICC) and Schwarz's Bayesian Information Criteria (BIC). The value of information criteria closest to zero indicates a better model fit to the data. As its name implies, AICC is a finite-sample corrected AIC for small samples, and it reduces the bias that results from AIC. With large samples, the AICC converges to the AIC. In general, AICC is preferred to AIC. The BIC tends to choose a simpler model than AIC because it increases the penalties, as the number of parameters required in the model increases. As suggested above, when the model becomes too simple, it tends to inflate the Type I error rate. Therefore, when Type I error control is critical in the study, AICC should be used. On the other hand, if test power is a major concern, then BIC may be preferable (Wang and Goonewardane, 2004).

**Table 9.3:** An illustration for combination of factors included in eight different models for semen production traits

| Model No. | L | OE | CI | TC | A | A (L/Q) | B | S | Y | B×A | S×Y | SC | U | E |
|---|---|---|---|---|---|---|---|---|---|---|---|---|---|---|
| 1 | ✓ | ✓ | ✓ | ✓ | ✓ | | ✓ | ✓ | ✓ | | | ✓ | ✓ | ✓ |
| 2 | ✓ | ✓ | ✓ | ✓ | ✓ | | ✓ | ✓ | ✓ | ✓ | ✓ | ✓ | ✓ | ✓ |
| 3 | ✓ | ✓ | ✓ | ✓ | ✓ | | ✓ | ✓ | ✓ | ✓ | | ✓ | ✓ | ✓ |
| 4 | ✓ | ✓ | ✓ | ✓ | ✓ | | ✓ | ✓ | ✓ | | ✓ | ✓ | ✓ | ✓ |
| 5 | ✓ | ✓ | ✓ | ✓ | | ✓(L) | ✓ | ✓ | ✓ | | | ✓ | ✓ | ✓ |
| 6 | ✓ | ✓ | ✓ | ✓ | | ✓(Q) | ✓ | ✓ | ✓ | | | ✓ | ✓ | ✓ |
| 7 | ✓ | ✓ | ✓ | ✓ | | ✓(L) | ✓ | ✓ | ✓ | | ✓ | ✓ | ✓ | ✓ |
| 8 | ✓ | ✓ | ✓ | ✓ | | ✓(Q) | ✓ | ✓ | ✓ | | ✓ | ✓ | ✓ | ✓ |

L: Location, OE: Order of ejaculate, CI: Collection interval, TC: Time of collection, A: Age in years included as a fixed effect, A (L/Q): Age in days included as a covariate (L: linear, Q: quadratic), B: Breed, Y: Year of collection, S: Season of collection, B×A: interaction of breed and age, S×Y: interaction of season and year, SC: Semen collector's effect, U: Bull's effect and E: Random error

From the above combination as shown in Table 9.3 the final model selected for studying the effect of factors affecting semen production traits and estimation of genetic parameters based on DIC was as follows :

$$Y_{ijklmnopqrs} = \mu + L_i + O_j + C_k + T_l + B_m + A_n + S_o + R_p + (B \times A)_{mn} + (S \times R)_{op} + W_s + U_t + e_{ijklmnopqrs}$$

## Solution to Linear Models

The various methods used to solve the linear models can be broadly divided into:

1. Direct inversion
2. Iteration on the MME: Done by Jacobi or Gauss-Seidel iteration
3. Iteration on the data is done by setting up of equations for each level of the effect and solution is through any one of the iterations.

The methods of estimation are explained in detail in the chapter on the estimation of variance components.

## Linear Models in Animal Breeding

Mrode (2014) has described in detail the linear models used in animal breeding. Linear models have been used extensively in animal breeding analysis where the phenotype (available information on an economic trait) is modeled based on various genetic and non-genetic factors so as to obtain a precise and unbiased estimate of the breeding value. The main practical advantage of a linear model is that it can appropriately account for all effects that influence a measurement. This is particularly useful when the data is unbalanced, which is nearly always the case in field data for any model the information that is available in the form of records is the phenotype of the individual. The basic animal model partitions the phenotype into genotype and environment.

The main objective of modeling in animal breeding is to estimate the breeding value of an animal. The breeding value of an individual is represented by the average effect of genes that the individual receives from both parents. Each parent contributes a sample half of its genes to its progeny and the sample half of genes passed on to its progeny is the transmitting ability of the parent.

Phenotype = genetic effects + environmental effects + residual effects

$Y_{ij} = \mu_i + g_i + e_{ij}$

$Y_{ij}$ is the jth record of the ith animal

$\grave{\imath}_i$ refers to the identifiable non-random environmental effects such as herd management, year of birth or sex of the animal

$g_i$ is the sum of the additive, dominance and epistatic genetic values of the genotype of animal i and $e_{ij}$ is the sum of random environmental effects affecting $i^{th}$ animal record.

The additive genetic value in the term g above represents the average additive effects of genes and the individual receives from both parents and is termed the breeding value. Since the additive genetic value is a function of the genes transmitted from parents to progeny, it is the only component that can be selected for and therefore the main component of interest. In most cases, dominance and epistasis, which represent intralocus and interlocus interactions respectively, are assumed to be of little significance and are included in the error ($e_{ij}$) term of the model.

The assumptions for the linear model are

1. Y, the dependent variable follows a multivariate normal distribution, implying that traits are determined by infinitely many additive genes of infinitesimal effect at unlinked loci, the so-called infinitesimal model (Fisher, 1918).
2. Variances $V_a$ and $V_e$ are known, or at least their proportionality is known, and there is no correlation between g and e ($cov(g_i,e_{ij}) = 0$) and no correlation among mates ($cov(e_i,e_{ik}) = 0$). Also, μ, the mean performance of the animals in the same management group is assumed to be known.

## Estimation of Breeding Value (EBV)

The accurate prediction of breeding value constitutes an important component of any breeding programme since genetic improvement through selection depends on correctly identifying individuals with the highest true breeding value. The method employed for the prediction of breeding value depends on the type and amount of information available on the candidate's available information.

### Single record per individual

$EBV=b(y_i - \mu)$

where b is the regression of true breeding value (a) on phenotypic performance (y) and μ, the mean performance of animals in the same management group and is assumed to be known.

$b = cov(a,y)/var(y) = cov(a,a+e)/var(y)$

$= \sigma_a^2/ \sigma_y^2$

$= h^2$

The prediction is simply the adjusted record multiplied by the heritability. The correlation between the selection criterion, in this case, the phenotypic value and the true breeding value is known as the accuracy of selection. It provides the means of evaluating different selection criteria because the higher the correlation, the better the criterion as a predictor of breeding value. This is given as the reliability or repeatability $r_{a,y}$, which is the square root of $h^2$ for selection based on a single measurement per individual.

$$r_{a,y} = h$$

**Repeated records**

When multiple measurements (n) on a single individual are available

$$b = s_a^2/[t + (1 - t/n]\, s_y^2$$

$$= nh^2/[1 + (n-1)t]$$

$$r_{a,y} = \sqrt{b}$$

t is the intraclass correlation between measurement on the same animal

**Breeding value prediction from progeny (n=number of progeny)**

$$b = 2n/n + k, \text{ where } k= (4-h^2)/h^2$$

$$r_{a,y} = \sqrt{n/n + k}$$

**Breeding value prediction from pedigree**

$a_o = (a_s + a_d)/2$ (Average breeding value of sire and dam)

$$r_{a,ao} = 1/2\sqrt{r^2_s + r^2_d}$$

**Selection Index using best linear prediction (BLP)**

After 1940, Lush and Hazel developed the principles of the selection index to optimize artificial selection based on the relationship between individuals and phenotypic trait information. The selection index also called the best linear prediction proved to be a remarkable methodology for practical breeding and it also had the scope to predict selection gains. The different variance components estimated by partitioning are used in the formation of the selection index. The next chapter discusses in detail the methods of estimation of variance components.

In this method, the animal is scored for its merit in each of the traits included in selection. An index is a single numerical value, which is the total of scores given for each trait considered in the selection. Each trait is weighted by a score and the individual scores are summed to a **total score/index value** for each animal which is the selection criterion. The selection index is a method of estimating the breeding value of an animal by combining all information available on the animal and its relatives. It is the best linear prediction of an individual breeding value. The numerical value obtained for each animal is referred to as the index (I) and it is the basis on which animals are ranked for selection. If there are "n" traits under selection the selection index is constructed by multiple regression analysis as:

Selection Index (I) = $b_1X_1 + b_2X_2 + \text{-- - - -} + b_n X_n$

where I = selection index

$X_1, X_2$ - - - $X_n$ are the phenotypic value of the 1,2 - - - - n traits of the individual

$b_1, b_2$ - - - $b_n$ are the corresponding weighing factors of the trait (multiple regression coefficients) by which each measurement / phenotypic value is to be weighed.

The **b's** are estimated by solving a set of normal simultaneous equations whose number is equal to the number of traits under selection.

The equation in matrix form can be written as: **[P] [b] = [G] [a]**

where [P] = is the phenotypic variance – covariance matrix

[b] = is the vector of weighting factors

[G] = is the genotypic variance–covariance matrix

[a] = is the vector of relative economic values

The **b** values are obtained by solving the simultaneous equations and [b] = $[P]^{-1}[G]$ [a] If more than two traits are involved in a selection index the b"s are obtained by following the Matrix algebra procedure.

**Construction of Selection Index**

Information required for the construction of the selection index or calculations of weighing factors are as follows:

1. Phenotypic variance (VP) and additive genetic variance (VA) of all the traits
2. Phenotypic covariance (COVP) and additive genetic covariance (COVA) among the traits
3. Relative/net economic value (ai) of all the traits.

The construction of the selection index for „n" traits (X1,X2.......Xn) are as follows:

**Step: 1**

Using the above information, „n" normal simultaneous equations are formed as

$V_P(X_1)\, b_1 + COV_P(X_1X_2)\, b_2 + \ldots + COV_P(X_1X_n)\, b_n = V_A(X_1)\, a_1 + COV_A(X_1X_2)\, a_2 + \ldots + COV_A(X_1X_n)\, a_n$

$COV_P(X_2X_1)\,b_1 + V_P(X_2)\,b_2 + .... + COVP\,(X2X_n)\,b_n = COV_A(X_2X_1)\,a_1 + V_A(X_2)\,a_2 + .... + COV_A\,(X_2X_n)\,a_n$

$COV_P(X_nX_1)\,b_1 + COV_P\,(X_nX_2)\,b_2 + ... + V_P\,(X_n)\,b_n = COVA\,(X_nX_1)\,a_1 + COV_A\,(X_nX_2)\,a_2 + ... + V_A\,(X_n)\,a_n$

Where:

$a_i$ = relative/ net economic value assigned to traits - $X_i$ ( i = 1,2,...,n)

$b_i$= partial regression coefficient (weighing factor) for traits -$X_i$ (i = 1,2,...,n)

**Step: 2**

The estimated values of genetic and phenotypic variances of the traits, covariances among the traits and net economic values of each trait are substituted and then the values of the weighing factors i.e. bi values are obtained by solving the normal simultaneous equations formed in the step-1

**Step: 3**

The Selection Index (I) = $b_1X_1 + b_2X_2 + \text{-- - - -} + b_n\,X_n$

The bi and Xi values are substituted in the index to obtain the selection index value for each animal.

## Predicting breeding values using Best Linear Unbiased Prediction (BLUP)

An individual's breeding value for a given phenotypic trait is the total additive effect of its genes on that trait (Falconer & Mackay, 1996). Armed with estimates of the variance components that define ***V***, we can return to the equation to make predictions of individual additive genetic effects or breeding values, and estimates of fixed effects. These are known as BLUPs and BLUEs, respectively: best (because they minimize error variance), linear (they are linear functions of the data), unbiased (their expected mean is equal to what they are estimating), predictors (for random effects) or estimates (for fixed effects). The BLUE of fixed effects is simply the least-squares estimator.

Previously, due to computational limitations, sire models were used as random effects with the mean of progeny used in the analysis. Modern evaluations comprise overlapping generations, with some individuals being mildly inbred and many mates being related. Thus, the so-called animal model is used conveniently with one equation for each animal in the pedigree file. Some of the commonly used models in a BLUP analysis are as follows.

## Linear Models for Estimated Breeding Value (EBV) using BLUP

**Animal model**: In this model, the individual or animal is taken as the source of variation and is unbiased. Since it takes into consideration the effect of dams also the animal model can be extended to estimate variance components due to maternal, common environment and permanent environment. However, the number of equations to be solved is more and this model requires more computing power.

**Sire model**: The application of a sire model implies that only sires are evaluated, using progeny records. The main advantage of this model is that the number of equations is reduced compared with an animal model since only sires are evaluated. However, with a sire model, the genetic merit of the mate (dam of progeny) is not accounted for and can result in bias in the predicted breeding value if there is preferential mating.

The sire and animal models could be represented as

$$Y = Xb + Z_a a + e$$

$$Y = Xb + Z_s s + e$$

Where, 'Y' is a N x 1 vector of records, 'b' denotes the fixed effects in the model with association matrix X, 'a' is the vector of animal genetic effects with the association matrix $Z_a$, 's' is the vector of sire effects with the association matrix $Z_s$, and 'e' denotes the vector of residual (temporary environment) effect. The fixed effects included in the model are those found to have a significant effect in the initial least-squares analyses. The assumed variance structure was as follows:

$$V\begin{pmatrix} a \\ s \\ e \end{pmatrix} = \begin{pmatrix} A\sigma^2_a & 0 & 0 \\ 0 & I_s\sigma^2_s & 0 \\ 0 & 0 & I_n\sigma^2_e \end{pmatrix}$$

The animal genetic effect, 'a' are assumed to be normally distributed with mean 0 and variance $A\sigma^2_a$ where A is the additive numerator relationship matrix and $\sigma^2_a$ additive genetic variance. Sire and residual effects are assumed to be normally distributed with mean 0 and variances $I_s\sigma^2_s$ and $I_n\sigma^2_e$, respectively, where $I_s$ and $I_n$ are identity matrices with orders equal to the number of sires and individual records, respectively and $\sigma^2_s$ and $\sigma^2_e$ are sire and residual variances, respectively.

```
COM BW NILAGIRI : Simple univariate analysis
PED NILPED.D
DAT UNIBWN.D
  animal 0
  sire
  dam
  pedam 10000
  gmdam 10000
  SUBJECT 10000
  CG 99
  sex 2
  ls 3
  agedam 6
  inbr 6
  bwt
end
ANAL UNI
MODEL
 Ran animal NRM
 FIX CG
 FIX sex
 FIX ls
 FIX agedam
 TR bwt
END
VAR animal 1
.14
VAR error 1
.22
```

```
Convergence criteria for last 3 iterates
Change in log likelihood    =   15.100990    0.061900    0.000001
Change in parameter vector  =    0.056869    0.003951    0.000016
Norm of gradient vector     =    351.2532     21.5082      0.0964
Newton decrement            =    -29.0060     -0.1234     -0.0000

***** Estimates of residual covariances   ***********************************
      Order of fit           =      1
 Covariance matrix
   1    0.13590
 Matrix of correlations and variance ratios
   1      0.6104
 Covariances & correlations with approximate sampling errors
   1  COVS Z 1 1       0.135902       0.691707E-02   vrat      0.610   0.038

***** Estimates for RE  1   "animal"   **************************************
      No. of levels         =     3483
      Covariance structure =     NRM
      Order of fit          =        1
 Covariance matrix
   1    0.86753E-01
 Matrix of correlations and variance ratios
   1      0.3896
 Covariances & correlations with approximate sampling errors
   2  COVS A 1 1       0.867530E-01   0.101229E-01   vrat      0.390   0.038

***** Estimates of phenotypic covariances  **********************************
 Covariance matrix
   1    0.22266
 Covariances & correlations with approximate sampling errors
   3  COVS T 1 1       0.222655       0.685739E-02
======== end of file ============================14-06-2013==========11:31====
```

**Figure 9.1:** Parameter file and output for an animal model in WOMBAT software (Meyer, 2007)

**Repeatability model:** The repeatability model is appropriate when multiple measurements on the same trait are recorded on an individual, such as litter size in successive pregnancies or milk yield in successive lactations. For an animal, the model always assumes a genetic correlation of unity between all pairs of records, equal variance for all records and equal environmental correlation between all pairs of records. The repeatability model is given by

For individual trait records

$$y = XB + Za + Wpe + e$$

where y = n×1 vector of observations with n = number of records; b= p×1 vector of fixed effects with p as the number of levels for all fixed effects; a = q×1 vector of random animal effect with q as the number of animals including pedigree; pe = r×1 vector of random permanent environmental effects and non-additive genetic effects with r as the number of animals with records; e = n×1 vector of random residual effects; X = design matrix of order n×p which relates records to fixed effects; Z = design matrix of order n×q which relates records to animal direct genetic random effects and W = design matrix of order n×r which relates records to permanent environmental effects. The assumed variance-covariance structure will be

$$V\begin{pmatrix} a \\ pe \\ e \end{pmatrix} = \begin{pmatrix} A\sigma^2_a & 0 & 0 \\ 0 & I\sigma^2_{pe} & 0 \\ 0 & 0 & I\sigma^2_e \end{pmatrix}$$

Animal genetic effect 'a' is assumed to be normally distributed with mean 0 and variance $A\sigma^2_a$ where A is the numerator relationship matrix and $a\sigma^2$ is the additive genetic variance. Permanent environmental and residual effects were assumed to be normally distributed with mean 0 and variances $I\sigma^2_{pe}$ and $I\sigma^2_e$ respectively where I is the identity matrix of the order of the number of records and $\sigma^2_{pe}$ and $\sigma^2_e$ the variances for permanent environmental and residual effects, respectively.

Apart from the resemblance between records of an individual due to permanent environmental conditions, common environmental contributes to the similarity between individuals of a family reared together. This increases the variance between families. Sources of common environmental variance between families may be due to factors such as nutrition and /or climatic conditions. This component must be taken care of in cases of full-sibs or maternal half-sibs etc. Influence of dam also adds to the environmental component of variance in such cases

```
COM  repeatability animal model li

PEDS pedigree.txt

DATA lin.txt
  anid 0
  sireid
  damid
  mat
  mpe
  subject
  brcode
  cg
  seacode
  agecode
  inbcode
  inb
  li

end
ANAL UNI
MODEL
 RAN anid NRM
 RAN subject
 FIX seacode
 FIX agecode
 TR li
END
VAR anid 1
3200
VAR subject 1

VAR error 1
26000

SE+USR
# CALCULATE SUM OF VA AND Vpe
SUM VA+VPE 2 3
# Calculate 'REPEATABILITY', which is Variance component RAtio of 5 and 4
VRA TOTAL 5 4
end
```

```
***** Estimates of residual covariances    ***********************************
      Order of fit            =        1
 Covariance matrix
   1      11066.
 Matrix of correlations and variance ratios
   1        0.9042
 Covariances & correlations with approximate sampling errors
   1  COVS Z 1 1            11066.1          347.385         vrat      0.904   0.021

***** Estimates for RE  1    "anid"    ***************************************
      No. of levels           =      1498
      Covariance structure =          NRM
      Order of fit            =          1
 Covariance matrix
   1     0.70537E-01
 Matrix of correlations and variance ratios
   1        0.0000
 Covariances & correlations with approximate sampling errors
   2  COVS A 1 1           0.705372E-01     241.759         vrat      0.000   0.020

***** Estimates for RE  2    "subject"   ************************************
      No. of levels           =      1201
      Covariance structure =          IDE
      Order of fit            =          1
 Covariance matrix
   1      1172.3
 Matrix of correlations and variance ratios
   1        0.0958
 Covariances & correlations with approximate sampling errors
   3  COVS B 1 1            1172.30          353.705         vrat      0.096   0.029

***** Estimates of phenotypic covariances    *********************************
 Covariance matrix
   1      12238.
 Covariances & correlations with approximate sampling errors
   4  COVS T 1 1            12238.5          306.785

***** User defined functions of covariances**********************************
 Linear functions of covariances
   5  VA+VPE                1172.37          266.380
 Variance ratios and correlations
   1  TOTAL               0.957937E-01   0.212396E-01   vrat
======== end of file ===========================03-06-2016==========15:21====
```

**Figure 9.2:** Parameter file and output for repeatability animal model in WOMBAT software (Meyer, 2007)

**Maternal trait models:** The phenotypic expression of some traits in the progeny, such as weaning weight in beef cattle, is influenced by the ability of the dam to provide a suitable environment in the form of better nourishment. The dam contributes to the progeny in two ways: firstly through her direct genetic effects passed to the progeny and secondly through her ability to provide a suitable environment, for instance in producing milk. Hence the phenotype may be partitioned into the following (Mrode, 2014).

1. Additive genetic effect of the individual, usually termed direct genetic effect.
2. Additive genetic ability of the dam to provide a suitable environment, usually termed indirect or maternal genetic effect.
3. Permanent environmental effects, which include permanent environmental influences on the dam's mothering ability and maternal non-additive genetic effects of the dam.
4. Other random environmental effects, termed residual effects.

## Common statistical models for studying the maternal effect

The following six different single-trait linear models as described by Meyer (1992), which account for the direct and maternal effects, allowing for and ignoring genetic covariances between direct and maternal effects are fitted to evaluate the type of maternal effect on the trait analysed.

$$Y = Xb + Z_a a + e \qquad \text{(Model 1)}$$

$$Y = Xb + Z_a a + Z_p p + e \qquad \text{(Model 2)}$$

$$Y = Xb + Z_a a + Z_m m + e \quad \text{with Cov (a, m)} = 0 \qquad \text{(Model 3)}$$

$$Y = Xb + Z_a a + Z_m m + e \quad \text{with Cov (a, m)} = A\acute{o}_{am} \qquad \text{(Model 4)}$$

$$Y = Xb + Z_a a + Z_m m + Z_p p + e \quad \text{with Cov (a, m)} = 0 \qquad \text{(Model 5)}$$

$$Y = Xb + Z_a a + Z_m m + Z_p p + e \quad \text{with Cov (a, m)} = A\acute{o}_{am} \qquad \text{(Model 6)}$$

Where, 'Y' is a N x 1 vector of records, 'b' denotes the fixed effects in the model with association matrix X, 'a' is the vector of direct genetic effects with the association matrix $Z_a$, 'm' is the vector of maternal genetic effects with the association matrix $Z_m$, 'p' is the vector of permanent maternal environmental effects with the association matrix $Z_p$, and 'e' denotes the vector of residual (temporary environment) effect. Cov (a, m) is the covariance between the direct genetic effect and maternal effect. The fixed effects included in the model are those found to have significant effect in the initial least-squares analyses. The assumed variance and covariance structure is as follows:

$$V\begin{pmatrix} a \\ m \\ c \\ e \end{pmatrix} = \begin{pmatrix} A\sigma_a^2 & A\sigma_{am} & 0 & 0 \\ A\sigma_{am} & A\sigma_a^2 & 0 & 0 \\ 0 & 0 & I_d\sigma_{pe}^2 & 0 \\ 0 & 0 & 0 & I_n\sigma_e^2 \end{pmatrix}$$

Additive direct and maternal genetic effects were assumed to be normally distributed with mean 0 and variance $A\sigma^2_a$ and $A\sigma^2_m$, respectively, where A is the additive numerator relationship matrix and $\sigma^2_a$ and $\sigma^2_m$ are additive direct and maternal genetic variances, respectively. $\sigma_{am}$ is the covariance between direct and maternal genetic effect. Permanent environmental effects of the dam and residual effects were assumed to be normally distributed with mean 0 and variances $I_d\sigma^2_{pe}$ and $I_n\sigma^2_e$, respectively, where $I_d$ and $I_n$ are identity matrices with orders equal to the number of dams and individual records, respectively and $\sigma^2_{pe}$ and $\sigma^2_e$ are maternal permanent environment and residual variances, respectively.

```
COM BW NILAGIRI : Simple univariate analysis
PED NILPED.D
DAT UNIBWN.D
  animal 0
  sire
  dam
  gmdam 10000
  pedam 10000
  SUBJECT 10000
  CG 99
  sex 2
  ls 3
  agedam 6
  inbr 6
  bwt
end
ANAL UNI
MODEL
 Ran animal NRM
 RAN gmdam   nrm
 FIX CG
 FIX sex
 FIX ls
 FIX agedam
 TR bwt
END
VAR animal 1
.9
VAR gmdam 1
.5
VAR error 1
.15
```

```
***** Estimates of residual covariances   ***********************************
      Order of fit            =      1
 Covariance matrix
   1    0.12863
 Matrix of correlations and variance ratios
   1      0.5626
 Covariances & correlations with approximate sampling errors
   1  COVS Z 1 1        0.128630        0.595368E-02   vrat      0.563   0.032

***** Estimates for RE  1    "animal"   **************************************
      No. of levels           =    3483
      Covariance structure =     NRM
      Order of fit            =      1
 Covariance matrix
   1    0.31214E-01
 Matrix of correlations and variance ratios
   1      0.1365
 Covariances & correlations with approximate sampling errors
   2  COVS A 1 1        0.312143E-01   0.779907E-02   vrat      0.137   0.033

***** Estimates for RE  2    "gmdam"   ***************************************
      No. of levels           =    1283
      Covariance structure =     NRM
      Order of fit            =      1
 Covariance matrix
   1    0.68776E-01
 Matrix of correlations and variance ratios
   1      0.3008
 Covariances & correlations with approximate sampling errors
   3  COVS B 1 1        0.687760E-01   0.745877E-02   vrat      0.301   0.026

***** Estimates of phenotypic covariances  **********************************
 Covariance matrix
   1    0.22862
 Covariances & correlations with approximate sampling errors
   4  COVS T 1 1        0.228621        0.779481E-02
======== end of file ==========================14-06-2013==========16:42====
```

**Figure 9.3:** Parameter file and output in WOMBAT for direct genetic and maternal effect

```
DAT UNIBWN.D
  animal 0
  sire
  dam
  gmdam 10000
  pedam 10000
  SUBJECT 10000
  CG 99
  sex 2
  ls 3
  agedam 6
  inbr 6
  bwt
end
ANAL UNI
MODEL
 Ran animal NRM
 RAN gmdam   nrm
 RAN pedam   ide
 FIX CG
 FIX sex
 FIX ls
 FIX agedam
 TR bwt
END
VAR animal+gmdam 2
.03 -.025 .05
VAR pedam 1
.015
VAR error 1
.13

# calculate total heritability
SE+VAR
 SUM sigPhen  1 2 3 4 5
 SUM sigGtotal 2(1) 3(1.5) 4(0.5)
 VRA hsqTotal 10 9
END
```

```
***** Estimates of residual covariances   ************************************
      Order of fit           =        1
 Covariance matrix
   1    0.12505
 Matrix of correlations and variance ratios
   1       0.5668
 Covariances & correlations with approximate sampling errors
   1  COVS Z 1 1          0.125053          0.644055E-02    vrat       0.567    0.034

***** Estimates for RE  1   "animal+gmdam"   *********************************
      No. of levels          =       3547
      Covariance structure =       NRM
      Order of fit           =          2
 Covariance matrix
   1    0.33727E-01
   2   -0.62388E-02  0.50329E-01
 Eigenvalues of covariance matrix
 Value            0.05           0.03
  (%)            62.35          37.65
 Trace            0.08
 Matrix of correlations and variance ratios
   1       0.1529
   2      -0.1514     0.2281
 Covariances & correlations with approximate sampling errors
   2  COVS A 1 1          0.337266E-01    0.893071E-02    vrat       0.153    0.039
   3  COVS A 1 2         -0.623878E-02    0.700018E-02    corr      -0.151    0.154
   4  COVS A 2 2          0.503288E-01    0.112173E-01    vrat       0.228    0.048

***** Estimates for RE  2    "pedam"    ****************************************
      No. of levels          =        913
      Covariance structure =       IDE
      Order of fit           =          1
 Covariance matrix
   1    0.17747E-01
 Matrix of correlations and variance ratios
   1       0.0804
 Covariances & correlations with approximate sampling errors
   5  COVS B 1 1          0.177468E-01    0.682707E-02    vrat       0.080    0.031

***** Estimates of phenotypic covariances   ***********************************
 Covariance matrix
   1    0.22062
 Covariances & correlations with approximate sampling errors
   6  COVS T 1 1          0.220616          0.739022E-02

***** User defined functions of covariances***********************************
 Linear functions of covariances
   9  sigPhen             0.220616          0.739022E-02
  10  sigGtotal           0.495328E-01      0.937378E-02
 Variance ratios and correlations
   1  hsqTotal            0.224520          0.388801E-01    vrat
======== end of file ===========================14-06-2013==========17:21====
```

**Figure 9.4:** Parameter file and output in WOMBAT for maternal effect with non-zero covariance with direct genetic effect

The table shows the result of the analysis for maternal effects. Log Likelihood Ratio test (LRT) indicated a difference in the significance of models for birth and weaning weight. The correlation between direct genetic and maternal effect was significant for the weaning weight. It is important to include maternal effects for traits expected to be affected by maternal effect and ignoring such effect could lead to bias in the heritability estimated thus leading change in breeding value and ranking of animals to be selected.

**Sire-maternal grandsire model** (MGS)**:** The sire model can estimate breeding value only for the sires and thus the maternal effects cannot be estimated. In this case when the usual animal model as described is not computationally feasible, a sire–maternal grandsire model could be of use. The pedigree file for such an analysis comprises the sire, sire of sire and maternal grandsire.

$$\mathbf{y = Xb + Zs + Pmgs + Wpe + e}$$

where y = vector of observations, s = vector of random service sire (direct) effects, mgs = vector of random MGS (indirect) genetic effects and other terms defined as in but Z and P are now incidence matrices relating records to service sire and MGS genetic effects, respectively. Note that if only the first lactation data is being analysed, then the pe can be omitted from the model.

**Reduced animal model**: In order to reduce the total number of equations to be solved, the equations are set for parents alone and the breeding value for progeny can be obtained from the breeding value of the parents.

**Animal models with groups**: In the usual animal model, the breeding value of animals in subsequent generations are usually expressed relative to those of base animals. If the base population differs in mean, for eg. the animals in the base population are from different countries, this must then be accounted for in the model. The sires are grouped based on the time period and country of origin. Within the country, the four selection paths: sire of sires, sire of dams, dam of sires and dam of dams, are usually assumed to be of different genetic merit and this is accounted for in the grouping strategy.

**Other random effects:** In some circumstances, environmental factors constitute an important component of the covariance between individuals such as members of a family reared together (common environment), or between the records of an individual (permanent environmental effects). Such effects are included in the model to ensure accurate prediction of breeding value.

**Time series analysis:** Models using time series analysis are used to analyse data that change over time. The data from the past and current are used to form prediction models. The components of such data are classified as Trend, seasonal fluctuation, cyclical fluctuation and random error. The model is analysed as an additive or multiplicative model.

**Survival Models:** The time to an event is a unique data which can be analysed using a survival model. The effect of various factors could be analysed using Kaplan Meyer's test and the variable could be modeled using a Cox Proportional Hazards Model or Weibull model. Survival analyses provide possibilities to censor data after a particular time (left and right Censoring). The most popular class of survival models is the class of proportional hazard models, where the hazard of an individual at time *t* is described as the product of the baseline function and of a positive term which is an exponential function of a vector of covariates.

The Proportional hazards model could be represented as (Cox, 1972)

$H(t{:}x)=h_0(t)\ \exp\{x'\beta\}$

Where, $\beta$ is a vector of regression coefficients. $h_0(t)$ is called the baseline hazard function and $\exp\{x'\beta\}$, represents a stress-dependent term specific to the animals with covariates x.

Frailty models are an extension of standard survival analysis models which allows accounting for unobserved random heterogeneity or equivalently, to include random effects. These account for an unobserved environmental or genetic effect affecting the hazard of the individual. When two random effects are included, these can be independent of each other or related to some degree, as seen in the maternal effect leading to the need to estimate correlated random effects.

**Random Regression Model:** The random regression model is used to analyse longitudinal data in which the repeatable data varies with time and the change with time is infinitely multidimensional. For eg. the Growth of animals and milk yield. One good example where this model is used is the test day model, where in the breeding value for daily milk production is estimated. The random regression model is useful in understanding the persistency of milk yield. Such models are useful in deriving a precise growth curve. More importantly, the covariance for each level of the time factor is obtained. The random-regression models are extensively being used to model longitudinal data and is explained in depth as a separate chapter in this book.

## Threshold Model

Traits such as disease resistance, mortality, fertility etc., are studied as binary traits. These traits are called as threshold traits as there is an underlying asset (which usually is in a continuous scale) causing a discrete or qualitative trait in the form of an event such as conception, death, disease incidence, etc. The extension of a linear model in the form of generalised linear model using the logit or probit link function has been used to analyse such traits. Some authors claim that such traits could be analysed as a linear model when the sample size is sufficient enough to make the sampling distribution normal through Central Limit Theorem. Nevertheless, the Threshold model has been appropriate to model such traits. Linear model procedures do not adequately account for the discrete nature of the data. Thompson (1979), Gianola (1980) and Hoeschele (1986) identified and extensively discussed some problems in the analysis of categorical traits by linear models. Some of most critical problems are: 1) variances of categorical traits are heterogeneous, 2) BLUP solutions do not take into consideration the restriction that the sum of response probabilities must be total 1 across all categories of responses, 3) the additive genetic variance in the outward scale depends on the incidence of the trait in the population, 4) it is possible that non-additive genetic effect are present in the outward scale even in the case where all the genetic variation is additive in the underlying scale, and 5) when the conditional expectation of the predictand given the data is not linear, the ranking properties of the best linear predictor appear not to be optimal. The threshold model takes into account the asymmetry and extreme incidence of some categories, as in the case of pig mortality. Bayesian analysis of binary or polychotomous threshold traits via Gibbs sampling is commonly used.

**Multitrait analysis:** Multivariate analyses of more than one trait can be used to obtain estimates of genetic and environmental covariances, from which the respective correlations can be calculated as described earlier. Multiple trait analyses are more accurate and less biased. It is not necessary that all the animals must have measurements on all the traits. Through multitrait analyses genetic correlation among traits obtained is utilised in the form of genetic variance-covariance (VCV) matrix to obtain information on the trait in which no information is available. This also helps in estimating breeding values of sex limited traits, where measurements can be made on only one sex. The genetic correlations estimated also help in calculating the responses to selection, both direct and indirect.

**Table 9.4:** Maternal effects model for birth weight and weaning weight.

| Model | $ó^2_e$ | $ó^2_p$ | $h^2 \pm$ S.E. | $c^2 \pm$ S.E. | $m^2 \pm$ S.E. | $ó_{am} \pm$ S.E. | $r_{am} \pm$ S.E. | log L | $h^2_t$ | $t_m$ |
|---|---|---|---|---|---|---|---|---|---|---|
| Birth weight | | | | | | | | | | |
| 1 | 0.166 | 0.269 | 0.382 ± 0.030 | - | - | - | - | 792.13 | 0.382 | 0.096 |
| 2 | 0.146 | 0.263 | 0.214 ± 0.031 | 0.231 ± 0.019 | - | - | - | 890.64 | 0.214 | 0.285 |
| 3 | 0.156 | 0.269 | 0.148 ± 0.028 | - | 0.286 ± 0.022 | - | - | 901.77 | 0.291 | 0.323 |
| 4 | 0.151 | 0.269 | 0.164 ± 0.029 | - | 0.169 ± 0.034 | 0.0004 ± 0.0074 | 0.007 ± 0.131 | 901.77 | 0.251 | 0.211 |
| **5** | **0.157** | **0.269** | **0.147 ± 0.031** | **0.100 ± 0.027** | **0.285 ± 0.030** | - | - | **909.03** | **0.290** | **0.422** |
| 6 | 0.152 | 0.269 | 0.159 ± 0.032 | 0.100 ± 0.027 | 0.162 ± 0.038 | 0.002 ± 0.007 | 0.056 ± 0.160 | 909.09 | 0.253 | 0.311 |
| Weaning weight | | | | | | | | | | |
| 1 | 4.112 | 5.432 | 0.243 ± 0.032 | - | - | - | - | -4876.50 | 0.243 | 0.061 |
| 2 | 3.785 | 5.365 | 0.141 ± 0.029 | 0.154 ± 0.020 | - | - | - | -4840.68 | 0.141 | 0.189 |
| 3 | 3.960 | 5.518 | 0.118 ± 0.028 | - | 0.164 ± 0.023 | - | - | -4846.58 | 0.200 | 0.194 |
| 4 | 4.012 | 5.529 | 0.107 ± 0.029 | - | 0.140 ± 0.028 | 0.152 ± 0.127 | 0.224 ± 0.211 | -4844.67 | 0.218 | 0.194 |
| **5** | **3.821** | **5.387** | **0.126 ± 0.029** | **0.112 ± 0.027** | **0.052 ± 0.027** | - | - | **-4838.88** | **0.152** | **0.196** |
| 6 | 3.872 | 5.399 | 0.114 ± 0.030 | 0.109 ± 0.026 | 0.035 ± 0.027 | 0.129 ± 0.102 | 0.378 ± 0.386 | -4836.74 | 0.167 | 0.196 |

1. $\sigma^2_e$ - error variance; $\sigma^2_p$ – phenotypic variance; $h^2$ – direct heritability; $c^2$ – maternal permanent environmental variance ratio; $m^2$ – maternal heritability; $\sigma_{am}$ – direct-maternal genetic covariance - $r_{am}$ – direct- maternal genetic correlation; log L – log likelihood; $h^2_t$ – total heritability; $t_m$ - maternal across year repeatability for ewe performance;
2. Best fit model is shown in bold letters

# 10

# Longitudinal Traits and Random Regression Models

> Traits such as growth, lactation test day yield, semen evaluation are longitudinal traits measured repeatedly on the animal and random regression models (RRM) have been found to be suitable for modeling these traits, The methodology used, data requirement, assumptions, validity, software available and application of RRM are explained in this chapter.

Growth, test-day milk yield, and semen traits are examples of longitudinal traits measured repeatedly on the animal and random regression models (RRM) have been found suitable for modeling such traits. RRM is based on a covariance function which could be defined as "a continuous function to give the variance and covariance of traits measured at different points on a trajectory" (van der Werf, 2001). Kirkpatrick *et al.* (1990) showed that variance components for longitudinal data can be modelled through covariance functions. Random regression models (RRM) and the resulting covariance function have been recognized as ideally suited for the analysis of longitudinal data (Hill, 1998; Meyer, 1998). In particular, RRM accommodates repeated records for traits that change gradually and continually, over time, and do not require stringent assumptions about the constancy of variances and correlations. In addition, RRM provides insights into the temporal variation of biological processes and physiological implications underlying the studied traits (Strucken *et al.*, 2015).

In general random regressions have been extensively used for test day records in dairy cattle (Schaeffer and Dekkers, 1994; Jamrozik *et al.*, 1997 ; Prakash *et al.*, 2017). Worldwide, several studies on the use of RRM in modeling growth of various livestock species are available (Venkataramanan, 2015; Arthy *et al.*, 2020; Mahala *et al.*, 2020). RRM has the advantage that, variance components can be estimated for any point in the trajectory of the curve and genetic parameters could be estimated for any age class within the range of ages included in the study. In a country like India small ruminants are reared under small holding systems and field performance recording is done through ICAR network projects. Data from these units are available only on the days of visit to the villages and the age at measurement varies between contemporaries.

Random regression could form a very good tool to analyse such data without the need for correction of ages. RRM allows environmental effects specific to the time of recording to be accounted for and can accommodate genetic differences in the shape of each animal's curve.

## Methodology, Analyses and Software

The detailed methodology of the use of RRM is explained by Van der Werf (2001). The ability of the RRM to model the response is based on the Legendre polynomials (Table 10.1 ). According to Meyer (2005) and Silva *et al.* (2013), orthogonal polynomials are the most appropriate to estimate covariance functions of longitudinal traits, and Legendre Polynomial is the most commonly used one due to the correlation reduction between estimated regression coefficients. The regression on orthogonal polynomials does not require prior assumptions about the shape of curves to be modelled and can be recommended as general-purpose functions, especially if higher orders of fit are feasible. Other function used for modeling was the spline function (Iwaisaki *et al.*, 2005; Zamani *et al.*, 2016; Nemutandani *et al.*, 2018; Scalez *et al.*, 2018).

The RRM is done using the Legendre polynomial and standardized ages as $\phi_i = \Lambda_i(t_{ij})$, where, $\Lambda_i$ are the coefficients of Legendre polynomial, and $t_{ij}$ are the ages standardized between -1 and +1, derived as

$$t_{ij} = (2*(T-T_{min})/(T_{max}-T_{min})) -1$$

Where,

$T_{min}$ is the earliest date (or the youngest age) and $T_{max}$ is the latest date (or oldest age) represented in the data. 'T' is the age in original scale for which $t_{ij}$ is calculated.

A sequence of analyses with different orders of fit for the random effects are carried out to determine the most parsimonious model describing the data.

**Table 10.1:** The legendre polynomials of order four for age from 3 to 48 months

| Age in months | Legendre Polynomial of order four | | | |
|---|---|---|---|---|
| 3 | 0.707107 | -1.22475 | 1.581139 | -1.87083 |
| 6 | 0.707107 | -1.06145 | 0.990847 | -0.61252 |
| 9 | 0.707107 | -0.89815 | 0.484883 | 0.213413 |
| 12 | 0.707107 | -0.73485 | 0.063246 | 0.673498 |
| 18 | 0.707107 | -0.40825 | -0.52705 | 0.762189 |
| 24 | 0.707107 | -0.08165 | -0.78003 | 0.185697 |
| 36 | 0.707107 | 0.571548 | -0.27406 | -0.83425 |
| 48 | 0.707107 | 1.224745 | 1.581139 | 1.870829 |

## Error variances

Another important aspect of the RRM model is that heterogeneity of error variance with the control variable age could be modelled by the use of heterogeneous error variance classes in the model (Table). According to Mota *et al.* (2013) and Menezes *et al.* (2013), assuming homogeneity of residual variance may create considerable distortions in the total variance, *i.e.*, the residual variance can be affected by many factors along the curve. In the RRM, error variances could be modelled as heterogeneous for different age classes. Meyer (2004) used RRM for growth from birth to 730 days in beef cattle and the error variances were modelled as a step function with 19 classes (0, 1-30, . . . , 271–300, 301-360, . . . , 661- 720 and 721-730 days).

In a study done in India (Arthy *et al.*, 2020) error variance was modelled as a step function with four and ten different heterogeneous classes and the model with ten classes was found to have a better fit.

## Method of estimation: Frequentist and Bayesian approaches

Most of the studies using RRM have been analysed using restricted maximum likelihood analyses (REML). Few studies (Nobre *et al.*, 2003; Iwaisaki *et al.*, 2005; Arthy *et al.*, 2020) performed through the Bayesian approach indicate better scope for convergence, especially for higher orders of fit and more no. of parameters to be estimated (Vrindha *et al.*, 2022). Arthy *et al.* (2020) compared both frequentist and Bayesian approaches for modeling growth and similar estimates were obtained. However, certain problems with convergence faced in REML were overcome by the Bayesian Gibb's sampling, which helps in obtaining a smoother curve of variance component estimates as compared to the conventional REML. WOMBAT (Meyer, 2007) was the predominant software used for REML and GIBBSF90 (Misztal *et al.* 2018; Masuda, 2018) for Gibbs sampling.

## Deciding the best model of fit

The best model is decided based on Log-likelihood, Akaike's information criterion (AIC) and the Bayesian information criterion (BIC) for REML estimation and Deviance information criterion (DIC) is used to decide the models analysed using the Bayesian approach. The AIC and BIC can be useful as guides because they adjust for the number of parameters and sample size (Foulley and Robert-Granie, 2002).

The orders for random regression could initially be fixed based on recommendations from previous studies for the trait. The Eigen function values of the random regression matrix will also help identify the required order of fit.

In the study of Arthy *et al.* (2020) more than 97% of the Eigenvalue for sire and individual permanent environmental effect were determined by the first three orders of fit, and thus the order of fit of 4 was regarded sufficient for the data set used. Table 10.2 shows the model diagnostics for different orders of fit and type of error variance used. The model 44B was considered the best on account of best model diagnostic criteria.

**Table 10.2:** AIC, BIC and logL values for various orders of fit of random regression models obtained for growth data in sheep

| Model | Order of fit | | | Information criterion | | |
|---|---|---|---|---|---|---|
| | Sire | Subject | Residual | logL | AIC | BIC |
| 22A | 2 | 2 | 1 | -47326.905 | 94667.810 | 94733.058 |
| 22B | 2 | 2 | 4 | -47280.696 | 94581.392 | 94674.600 |
| 23A | 2 | 3 | 1 | -46138.275 | 92296.550 | 92389.758 |
| 23B | 2 | 3 | 4 | -45869.371 | 91764.742 | 91885.914 |
| 32A | 3 | 2 | 1 | -42929.728 | 85879.456 | 85972.666 |
| 32B | 3 | 2 | 4 | -42625.005 | 85276.010 | 85397.182 |
| 33A | 3 | 3 | 1 | -42346.682 | 84719.364 | 84840.536 |
| 33B | 3 | 3 | 4 | -42006.972 | 84045.944 | 84195.078 |
| 34A | 3 | 4 | 1 | -41980.701 | 83995.402 | 84153.856 |
| 34B | 3 | 4 | 4 | -41980.701 | 84001.402 | 84187.820 |
| 43A | 4 | 3 | 1 | -41487.761 | 83009.522 | 83167.978 |
| 43B | 4 | 3 | 4 | -41082.069 | 82204.138 | 82390.556 |
| 44A | 4 | 4 | 1 | -41062.014 | 82166.028 | 82361.766 |
| 44B | 4 | 4 | 4 | -41062.013 | 82172.026 | 82395.728 |

AIC - Akaike information criterion; BIC - Bayesian information criterion (BIC); logL – Log-likelihood value.

## No. of records per animal

Fischer and Van der Werf (2002) showed that RRM could be useful even when the data structure has very few records per animal. However, according to Meyer (2004), the full potential of RRM could be achieved when more number of repeated records are available. Successful estimation of variances with Legendre polynomials is possible with large data sets, even distribution of data points on the trajectory, and careful modeling of other effects (Druet *et al.,* 2003). Similarly, the no. of records per animal is also important to obtain precise estimates of random regression coefficients. In a study on Madras Red sheep, the period of growth with a lesser no. of observations led to sudden disruption in the shape of the variance estimation curve (Arthy *et al.*, 2020). The study reports that the standard error was high for 12W, which was the endpoint for the range of ages studied, indicating the 'effect of extreme ages'. This difference can also be attributed to the variation in the number of observations, which is usually lower for the later ages. Curves at points of the trajectory with few records are likely to contain artifacts (Misztal *et al.,* 2000; Nobre *et al.,* 2003; Meyer, 2005). More observations per age point for the growth data resulted in a smoother curve for the variance and better estimates of variance components.

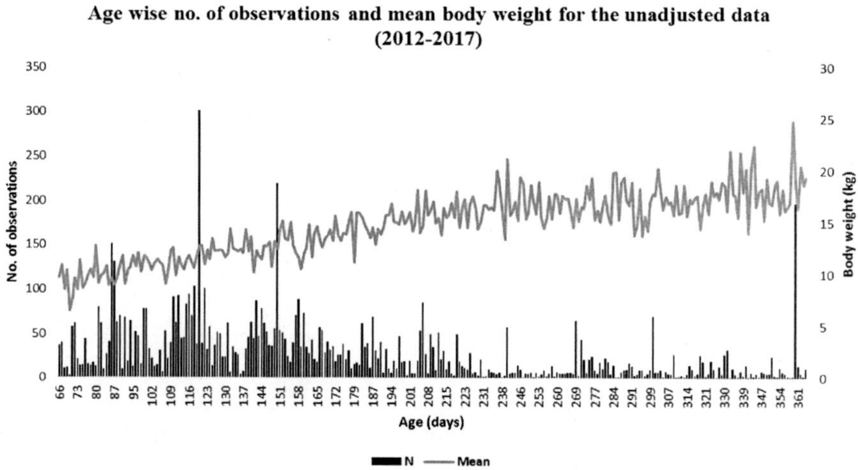


**Figure 10.1:** No. of observations and mean body weights for various ages

## Genetic Parameters from RRM

Estimation of (co)variance components

The genetic (co)variance between time periods were estimated by the general expression

$$G_x = \Phi_{xj} K_{xj} \Phi'_{xj}$$

Where,

$G_x$ is the (co)variance matrix for random effect x which may be the animal, sire or individual permanent environment.

$\Phi_{xj}$ is the vector of Legendre polynomials for the random effect of x and $j^{th}$ age groups. Since this matrix is fixed for a particular age, genetic variance and covariance could be obtained for any age point by using the particular vector and constant random regression matrix. The matrix of genetic variance-covariance thus obtained is then used to estimate the genetic correlation for various ages as the ratio of covariance to the square root of the product of respective variances.

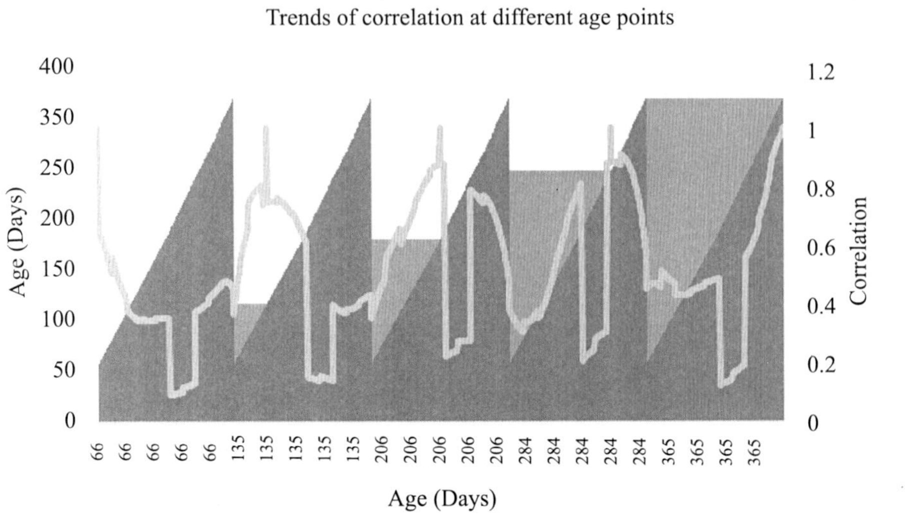


**Figure 10.2:** Correlation between different age points obtained for growth in sheep using RRM

The main advantage of RRM is that variance components and genetic parameters could be obtained for any age point in the trajectory of the trait. This also helps in obtaining the breeding value and genetic trend for bodyweights at various ages. The modeling of the growth curve helps in making decisions for unique selection objectives which could vary for each of the periods. Similarly, breeding values could be obtained for any age point in the trajectory and selection based on multiple traits (weight at different ages) could be done based on weightage given to each trait. Recent papers have attempted use of RRM to study genotype x environment interaction using a reaction norm gradient of the traits over the control variable (Chiala *et al.*, 2015; Mahala *et al.*, 2020).

The genetic (co) variance between ages are estimated by the general expression

$G_{xj} = \Phi_{xj} K_{xj} \Phi'_{xj}$

Where,

$G_x$ is the (co) variance matrix for x = sire or individual permanent environment.

$\Phi_{xj}$ is the vector of Legendre polynomials for the random effect of x and j$^{th}$ age group. The matrix of genetic variance-covariance was used to estimate the genetic correlation for various ages as the ratio of covariance to the square root of the product of respective variances.

Breeding values (EBV) are estimated using RRM for any point 'j' in the age curve between 66 and 365 days were estimated from the $k_i$ random solutions obtained for i$^{th}$ animal and Legendre polynomial corresponding to the j$^{th}$ age group.

$EBV = \Phi_j a'$

Where,

$\Phi_j$ is the Legendre polynomial for the j$^{th}$ age group and $a'_i$ is the transpose of vector of random solutions for the i$^{th}$ animal.

RRM provides breeding value estimates for the entire trajectory and several studies have compared the ranking of animals from the two methods. Compared to the univariate animal model, ranking from RRM is more reliable as information obtained is from the growth curve and not the weight at individual age as is used in the univariate model.

However, RRM suffers from problems associated with polynomials at the ends of the trajectory caused by the absence of constraints at the end (Fischer and Van der Werf, 2002). Nobre *et al.* (2003) reported that parameter estimates obtained by fitting polynomials could be affected by sparse data and extremes of trajectory. Arango *et al.* (2004) reported an inadequacy of RRM to model genetic variability at later ages. Ghafouri-Kesbi *et al.* (2008) in Mehraban sheep, found that the heritability of growth traits especially at later ages was overestimated in RRM. The potential overestimation is possibly due to the 'end effect of polynomials' or "Runge's phenomenon" (Meyer, 2005).

Another important use of RRM has been the ability to use partial records of growth at different age points to obtain information on the complete growth curve. This enables its use for field performance recording, especially in a country like India where the animal holdings are in small number. Group breeding schemes are being implemented and RRM is very much suitable for such recording systems where the growth data will be uneven and for varying age points. Arthy et al (2020) have found the technique very much suitable for such programmes. The study was based on use of RRM in a group breeding scheme involving several farmers for the Madras Red breed of sheep.

## Eigen function

The Eigenvalues ($\lambda_i$) and their associated Eigenvectors of the genetic regression coefficients matrix are used to analyse the patterns of variation existing in the trait over ages (Van der Werf, 2001). Kirkpatrick and Heckman (1989) and Kirkpatrick et al (1990) show that covariance functions can be used to analyze 'patterns of inheritance' in the covariance matrix $\sim G$. For this purpose they determined eigenvalues and eigenfunctions from the coefficient matrix for a given covariance function. The trajectories of these eigenfunctions (Figure 10.3) obtained from the random regression coefficients will give an idea about the possible variation in the function over the entire range of ages.

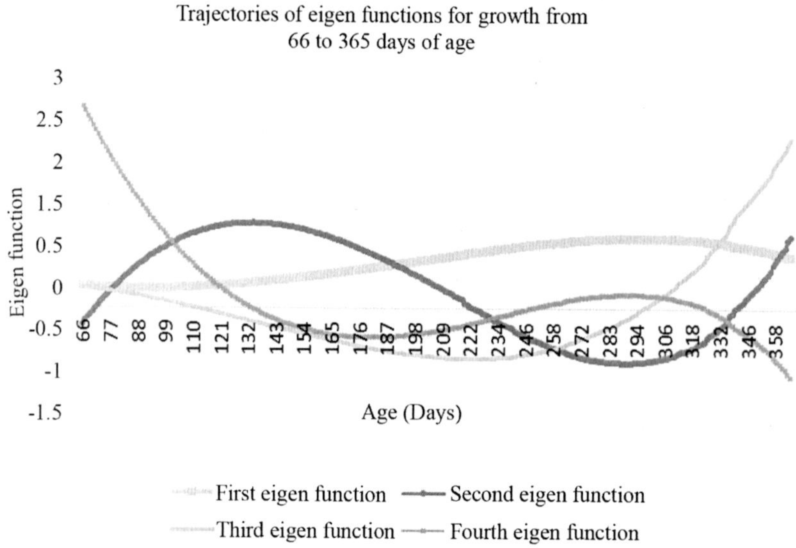


**Figure 10.3:** Eigen function of the random regression covariance matrix of growth from 66 to 365 days of age

Longitudinal traits have been successfully modelled using the RRM and the main utility of the technique is that variance components could be obtained for any point in the trajectory of growth. The heritability estimates obtained through RRM is similar or higher than those obtained through univariate analysis, which is due to the additional information obtained through the growth curve. RRM is able to provide more information for breeding programmes to improve longitudinal traits as that of growth, and additional information from Eigen functions predicts the response to selection based on particular Eigen function.

**Example10.1:** The RRM fitted for growth in sheep using heterogenous error classes.

Could be described as

$k_m^{-1}$

$Y_{ij} = Xb + \Sigma Z_s S_k + \Sigma$

$\kappa = 0$

Where,

$Y_{ij}$ = bodyweight of i[th] animal at j[th] age in days

b = fixed effects of centre, period, sex, season and regression of age of order k=3, associated with the $y_{ij}$, independent of the time scale (age)

X = Known incidence matrix relating fixed effects with Y

$s_k$ is a set of $n_1$ values ($n_1$ = number of sires) and $w_k$ is a set of $n_2$ values ($n_2$ = number of animals), of k random regression coefficients, corresponding to sire and individual permanent environment effects, with order of fit $k_s$ and $k_{w,}$ respectively.

Zs, and $Z_w$ are incidence matrices with dimensions $n_1$ x $k_s$ for $Z_s$, and $n_2$ x $k_w$ for $Z_w$.

'e' is the random residual heterodastic error variance.

The elements of the different Z matrices are $Z_i = \phi_i = \Lambda_i(t_{ij})$, for which $\Lambda_i$ are the coefficients of Legendre polynomial, and $t_{ij}$ are the ages standardized between -1 and +1, derived as

$t_{ij} = (2*(T-T_{min})/(T_{max}-T_{min})) -1$

Where,

$T_{min}$ is the earliest date (or the youngest age) and $T_{max}$ is the latest date (or oldest age) represented in the data. 'T' is the age in original scale for which $t_{ij}$ is calculated.

A sequence of analyses with different orders of fit for the two random effects were carried out to determine the most parsimonious model describing the data. The best model was decided based on LRT, Akaike information criterion (AIC) and the Bayesian information criterion (BIC). The Akaike information criterion (AIC) and the Bayesian information criterion (BIC) can be useful as guides because they adjust for number of parameters and sample size (Foulley and Robert-Granie, 2002). The variance structure for the different random effects fitted was as shown by Turner and Young (1969).

$$V\begin{pmatrix} s \\ w \\ e \end{pmatrix} = \begin{pmatrix} I_s \otimes s & 0 & 0 \\ 0 & I_n \otimes w & 0 \\ 0 & 0 & R \end{pmatrix}$$

Where, S is the variance-covariance matrix of the random regression coefficients for sire of order $k_s$ and W is the individual permanent environment variance-covariance matrix of random regression coefficients of order $k_w$. $I_s$ and $I_n$ are identity matrices of order $n_1$ (no. of sires) and $n_2$ (no. of animals), respectively. R is a diagonal matrix of temporary environment error variances. The error variances were considered independently distributed with heterogenous values varying with age. Mixed model equations for the effects included in these models are

$$\begin{bmatrix} X'X & X'Z_s & X'Z_w \\ Z_sX & Z_sZ_s + I \otimes K_s^{-1} & Z_sZ_w \\ Z_wX & Z_wZ_s & Z_wZ_w + I_w \otimes K_w^{-1} \end{bmatrix} \begin{bmatrix} b \\ s \\ w \end{bmatrix} = \begin{bmatrix} X'y \\ Z'sy \\ Z'wy \end{bmatrix}$$

Where,

'I' is the identity matrix, ⊗ is the Kronecker's product, and $K_i$ is the (co) variance matrix of the random regression coefficients of the effects indicated in subscript.

The eigen values ($\lambda_i$) and their associated eigen vectors of the genetic regression coefficients matrix were used to analyse the patterns of variation existing in growth over ages (Van der Werf, 2001).

For a fourth order random effect each animal receives four regression coefficients, which is used to calculate the EBV of the respective trait.

```
COM  rrm12-17 -

ANAL RR
DATA rrm12-17.dat
  number
  animal
  sire
  dam
  subject
  centre 5
  period 8
  sex 3 2
  season 5
  weight
  age 400
END

MODEL
  FIX centre
  FIX period
  FIX sex
  FIX season
  COV age(3,leg)
  RRC age
  RAN sire (2,leg)
  SUBJ subject
  RAN subject(2,leg)
  trait weight
END MOD

VAR sire 2
   10
   2
   1
VAR subject 3 2
    10
     2
     1
VAR residual 1 Hom
    1
```

**Figure 10.4:** Parameter file for RRM in wombat

```
1    821   270   0   821   2   1   1   1   8.70   90
1    822   270   0   822   2   1   2   1   9.40   90
1    823   270   0   823   2   1   1   1   9.70   90
1    825   265   0   825   2   1   1   1   9.80   90
1    826   266   0   826   2   1   2   1   7.60   90
1    827   265   0   827   2   1   1   1   7.60   90
1    828   265   0   828   2   1   1   1   9.20   90
1    829   265   0   829   2   1   1   1   7.80   90
1    830   265   0   830   2   1   1   1   7.90   90
1    831   266   0   831   2   1   2   1   8.20   90
1    833   269   0   833   2   1   1   1   8.60   90
1    834   269   0   834   2   1   1   1   8.10   90
1    835   269   0   835   2   1   2   1   9.40   90
1    836   270   0   836   2   1   1   1   7.80   90
1    837   270   0   837   2   1   1   1   8.30   90
1    838   270   0   838   2   1   2   1   7.10   90
1    839   270   0   839   2   1   1   1   8.60   90
1    840   270   0   840   2   1   1   1   8.30   90
1    841   270   0   841   2   1   2   1   8.90   90
1    842   271   0   842   2   1   2   1   7.30   90
1    843   266   0   843   2   1   2   1   7.90   90
1    845   270   0   845   2   1   1   1   8.10   90
1    846   270   0   846   2   1   1   1   8.40   90
1    847   270   0   847   2   1   1   1   9.30   90
1    848   270   0   848   2   1   1   1   9.10   90
1    849   271   0   849   2   1   1   1   7.20   90
1    851   265   0   851   2   1   1   1   9.10   90
1    852   267   0   852   2   1   2   1   8.30   90
1    853   268   0   853   2   1   2   1   8.00   90
1    854   269   0   854   2   1   1   1   8.30   90
1    855   269   0   855   2   1   2   1   8.90   90
1    857   269   0   857   2   1   1   1   8.70   90
1    858   270   0   858   2   1   2   1   8.20   90
```

**Figure 10.5:** Data structure for the RRM analysis using WOMBAT

# 11

# Lactation Curve Modelling

Milk yield is one of the most important economic traits and modelling the lactation curve is important with respect to the unique shape with ascending, persistent and descending phases. The non-linear relationship of daily milk yield with days in milk has led to extensive research in modelling the lactation curve. The nature of the lactation curve, different models, identifying the best model of fit, factors affecting the curve parameters and orthogonal polynomials to model the curve are discussed in this chapter.

The lactation curve can be defined as the graphical representation of milk yield against time (Brody *et al.*, 1923). The typical shape of the lactation curve has two characteristic parts i.e. a rapid increase from calving to a peak period in the early stage of lactation and a gradual decline from peak yield to the end of lactation (Leon-Velarde *et al.*, 1995). The persistent phase in between the ascending and descending phases is also sometimes present. Persistency of lactation depends on the duration of this period which helps in the overall increase in the lactation yield of the animal. The data required to fit the lactation curve are the test-day milk yield and the day of lactation. The relationship between the day of lactation and milk yield is not linear and hence the lactation curve modelling requires special mathematical functions to obtain a good fit. Several non-linear/intrinsically linear models have been used by various authors, the details of a few are presented in Table 11.1. The shape of the lactation curve is influenced by several environmental as well as genetic factors.

The term test-day is used under field performance recording the lactation is recorded only on a particular day of the month and monthly test-day records (usually one per month) are recorded from which the lactation yield is estimated. The advantage of a test-day analysis is that correction of yield for environmental factors is better done with the adjustments for factors such as the period and season of particular test-day being used rather than the period and season of calving

There are lots of advantages of evaluating or modelling the lactation curve such as predicting the milk yield of a cow in lactation with minimum error and using it in the process of cow/sire evaluation. It also helps in predicting expected missing values on field records and gives a concise summary of the biological efficiency of dairy cows and the persistency of lactation. Further, the shape of lactation curves in dairy cattle is important for decisions on herd management and selection strategies. Moreover, the lactation curve facilitates visualization of milk yield against days from calving and thus helps in understanding the peak yield and persistency of the lactation.

**Table 11.1:** Lactation curve models

| S.No. | Name of The Model | Model | Reference |
|---|---|---|---|
| 1 | Exponential decline function (EDF) | $Y_t = ae^{-ct}$<br>Log transformation<br>$\ln Y_t = \ln(a) - ct + e$ | Brody *et al.* (1923) |
| 2 | Parabolic exponential model (PEM) | $Y_t = a \exp(bt-ct^2)$<br>Log transformation<br>$\ln Y_t = \ln(a) + bt - ct^2 + e$ | Sikka (1950) |
| 3 | Inverse quadratic polynomial(IQP) | $Y_t = t(a+bt+ct^2)^{-1}$ | Nelder (1966) |
| 4 | IQP Modified Model | $Y_t^{-1} = a + bt^{-1} + ct + e$ | Yadav *et al.* (1977) |
| 5 | Gamma function | $Y_t = at^b e^{-ct}$<br>Log transformation<br>$\ln(Y_t) = \ln(a) + b\ln(t) - ct + e$ | Wood (1967) |
| 6 | Quadratic model | $Y_t = a+bt-ct^2$ | Dave (1971) |
| 7 | Quadratic cum log model | $Y_t = a + bt + ct^2 + d\ln(t) + e$ | Malhotra *et al.* (1980) |
| 8 | Wilmink model (k=0.05) | $Y_t = a + be^{-kt} + ct + e$ | Wilmink (1987) |
| 9 | Wilmink model (k=0.065) | $Y_t = a + be^{-kt} + ct + e$ | Wilmink (1987) |
| 10 | Wilmink model (k=0.61) | $Y_t = a + be^{-kt} + ct + e$ | Wilmink (1987) |
| 11 | Wilmink model (k=0.1) | $Y_t = a + be^{-kt} + ct + e$ | Wilmink (1987) |
| 12 | Ali and Schaeffer model (ALI) | $Y_t = a + bx + cx^2 + d\log(1/x) + f\log(1/x)^2 + e$ | Ali and Schaeffer, (1987) |
| 13 | Mixed log model(ML) | $Y_t = a + bt^{1/2} + c\log(t) + e$ | Guo and Swalve (1995) |
| 14 | Grossman model | $Y_t = at^b e^{-ct}(1 + u\sin(x) + v\cos(x))$<br>Log transformation<br>$\ln Y_t = \ln(a) + b\ln(t) + ct + u\sin x + v\cos x + e$ | Grossman *et al.* (1986) |
| 15 | Cubic model | $Y_t = a + bt + ct^2 + dt^3 + e$ | Dag *et al.* (2005) |

For all the models used, $Y_t$ = Daily milk yield, t = days in milk, e = random error NID $(0, \sigma^2_e)$ a, b, c, d, f, u and v are the regression coefficients according to different models. For Wilmink model k is constant term. For Ali model x = t /305, for Grossman model x = Day of year, ln is natural logarithm to base e.

**Table 11.2:** Classification of the Lactation Curve based on parameters obtained

Macciotta *et al.* (2005) classified the lactation curve based on sign of parameters 'b' and 'c' of Gamma function and Wilmink model as follows.

| Model | Parameter | | Curve shape |
|---|---|---|---|
| | b | c | |
| Gamma Function | + | – | Standard curve |
| | – | – | Continuously decreasing (atypical) curve |
| | – | + | Reversed standard |
| | + | + | Continuously increasing |
| Wilmink Model | – | – | Standard curve |
| | + | – | Continuously decreasing (atypical) curve |
| | + | + | Reversed standard |
| | – | + | Continuously increasing |

## Analysis

Data for lactation curve, the test-day yield and days from lactation collected are subjected to descriptive and exploratory analysis. Individual test day yield is regressed on the day of lactation using the above models. The regressions are fitted using linear or intrinsically linear or non-linear models. Non-linear models like Exponential Decline Function, Grossman Model, Gamma Function and Parabolic Exponential Model are log transformed and used as intrinsic linear models.

## Model of Best Fit

Among the various models used, goodness of fit of the models is evaluated using the following criteria.

Coefficient of determination ($R^2$) and adjusted $R^2$

Coefficient of determination value gives the percentage of variance of monthly yields explained by the model:

$R^2 = [1 - (SSE/SST)] \times 100$

where, SSE is error sum of square and SST is total sum of square.

The adjusted square of correlation coefficient between actual milk yield and predicted milk yield according to model:

$R^2_{adj} = 1 - \{[SSE / (n\text{-}p\text{-}1)] / [SST / (n\text{-}1)]\}$

where, SSE : is error sum of squares,

SST : is total sum of squares,

n : is number of observations, and

p : is number of parameters in each function

$R^2_{adj}$ is used in addition to $R^2$, because $R^2_{adj}$ is adjusted for the number of parameters in the model (p) to make accurate comparison of models.

Root Mean Square Error (RMSE)

RMSE is a kind of generalized standard deviation, which is given as below:

$$RMSE = \sqrt{\frac{\left[\sum_{i=1}^{n}(y_i - \hat{y})^2\right]}{n}}$$

where, n is the number of observations, $y_i$ are the actual values and $\hat{y}$ are values predicted by the regression model. Smaller RMSE indicates better modelling.

Durbin-Watson (DW) Coefficient

The DW coefficient is given by

$$DW = \frac{\sum_{t}^{n}(e_t - e_{t-1})^2}{\sum_{t=1}^{n} e_t^2}$$

where, $e_t$ is residual at time t and $e_{t-1}$ is residual at time t-1.

The Durbin-Watson statistic tests the null hypothesis that the residuals from an ordinary least-square regression are not auto-correlated against the alternative that the residuals follow an auto-regressive process. The Durbin-Watson statistic ranges in value from 0 to 4. A value near two indicates non auto-correlation, a value toward 0 indicates positive auto-correlation and a value toward 4 indicates negative auto-correlation.

### *Identifying the best model using Friedman's test*

The different models are ranked according to mean rank obtained by Friedman's test. The fifteen models were ranked based on each of the above four diagnostic criteria. The ranks obtained are then analysed using Friedman's test to get the mean rank, based on which the model of best fit for each breed were identified.The mean ranks obtained through Friedman's test are then subject to Spearman's rank correlation, in order to understand the similarity of ranking.

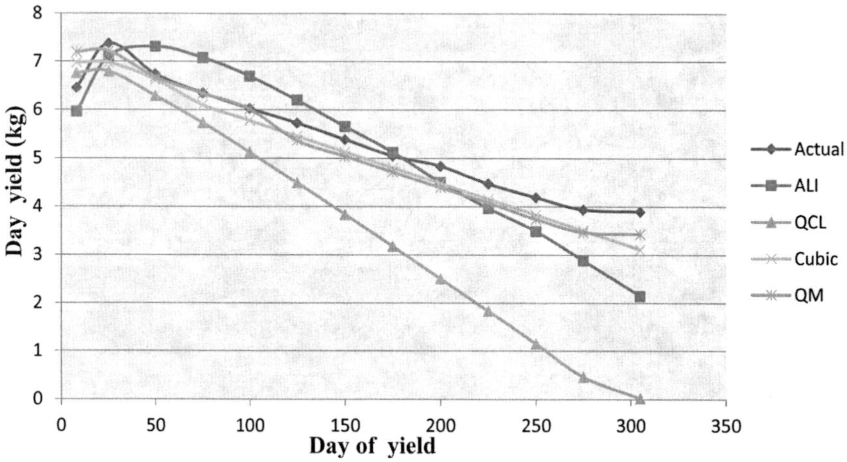


**Figure11.1:** Lactation curve predicted by different models

## Random regressions in test-day model

The random regression models have been described in detail as a separate chapter. The Lactation Curve also could be modelled by considering the test-day yield as a longitudinal trait measured on the same animal and the curves for each animal could be modelled using the orthogonal polynomials such as the Legendre polynomials. The co(variance) components and estimated breeding value could be obtained from the random regression coefficients and Legendre polynomials for the particular test-day. Since the curve extends for 10 test-day yields under field conditions care should be taken to use the correct order of fit. A detailed explanation on analysis of the test-day model could be seen in Miztal (2018).

**Table 11.3:** Example data file for a lactation curve/test-day analysis

| Date | Animal No. | Parity | Morning | Evening | Total | Days |
|---|---|---|---|---|---|---|
| 6/1/2007 | 1 | 1 | 2.5 | 2.5 | 5 | 1 |
| 6/2/2007 | 1 | 1 | 3.5 | 3 | 7.5 | 3 |
| 6/3/2007 | 1 | 1 | 4.5 | 3 | 7.5 | 3 |
| 6/4/2007 | 1 | 1 | 3.5 | 4 | 7.5 | 4 |
| 6/5/2007 | 1 | 1 | 4.5 | 4 | 8.5 | 5 |
| 6/6/2007 | 1 | 1 | 5 | 4 | 9 | 6 |
| 6/7/2007 | 1 | 1 | 5 | 4 | 9 | 6 |
| 6/8/2007 | 1 | 1 | 5 | 4 | 9 | 7 |
| 6/9/2007 | 1 | 1 | 6 | 5 | 11 | 8 |
|  | 1 | 1 | 5 | 4.5 | 9.5 | 9 |

The 'Lactcurves' package in R platform could be used for modeling lactation curve. Examples for lactation parameters, model diagnostics and ranking of models are presented in tables 11.4 to 11.6.

**Table 11.4:** Ascending, persistent and descending parameters under various models of lactation curve analysis.

|  | N | Model | a | b | c |
|---|---|---|---|---|---|
| 1 | 31 | Gamma function | 1.361±0.06 | 0.281±0.042 | -0.007±0.001 |
| 2 | 31 | Wilmink model (k=0.05) | 8.475±0.379 | -2.241±0.615 | -0.022±0.002 |
| 3 | 31 | Wilmink model (k=0.065) | 8.404±0.373 | -2.82±0.688 | -0.02±0.001 |
| 4 | 31 | Wilmink model (k=0.61) | 8.113±0.375 | -224.237±59.011 | -0.019±0.001 |
| 5 | 31 | Wilmink model (k=0.1) | 8.309±0.37 | -3.753±1.002 | -0.02±0.001 |
| 6 | 31 | Cubic model | 7.24±0.476 | 0.006±0.007 | 0±0 |
| 7 | 31 | Grossman model | 4.576±0.629 | 4.369±4.055 | -0.007±0.001 |
| 8 | 31 | IQP modified | 0.012±0.023 | 1.841±0.336 | 0.001±0 |
| 9 | 31 | ML | 3.676±0.919 | -0.831±0.102 | 2.64±0.328 |
| 10 | 31 | ALI | 12.859±3.294 | -14.462±5.627 | 4.085±2.641 |
| 11 | 31 | IQP | 12.503±3.552 | -0.252±0.094 | 0.002±0 |
| 12 | 31 | QM | 7.664±0.425 | -0.012±0.004 | 0±0 |
| 13 | 31 | QCL | 4.515±1.234 | -0.038±0.009 | 0±0 |
| 14 | 31 | EDF | 8.948±0.452 |  | -0.004±0 |
| 15 | 31 | PEM | 7.354±0.421 | 0±0.001 | 0±0 |

**Table 11.5:** Model fit parameters for different models to identify the best fit

| 6/9/2007 | N | Gamma function | Wilmink model (k=0.05) | Wilmink model (k=0.065) | Wilmink model (k=0.61) |
|---|---|---|---|---|---|
| $R^2$ | 259 | 0.69 | 0.70 | 0.73 | 0.66 |
| $R^2_{adj}$ | 259 | 0.69 | 0.69 | 0.68 | 0.65 |
| RMSE | 259 | 0.20 | 0.84 | 0.86 | 0.90 |
| DW | 259 | 0.85 | 0.91 | 0.91 | 0.84 |

**Table 11.6:** Mean ranks of various lactation curve models fitted (Friedman's test)

| Name | Mean Rank |
|---|---|
| ALI | 13.5 |
| Cubic model | 12.25 |
| QCL | 11.25 |
| QM | 9.25 |
| ML | 9 |
| IQP | 8.75 |
| Wilmink model (k=0.05) | 8.25 |
| PEM | 8 |
| Gamma function | 7.88 |
| Wilmink model (k=0.065) | 7.75 |
| Grossman model | 6.25 |
| Wilmink model (k=0.1) | 6.13 |
| IQP modified | 4.75 |
| EDF | 4 |
| Wilmink model (k=0.61) | 3 |

(Chi-Square = (24.067) **, $p<0.05$)

# 12

# Pedigree Analysis and Inbreeding

The aim of the breeder is to improve on various economic traits through selection. However, due to the lesser number of parents used, over a period of time, there creeps in the effect of inbreeding and loss of genetic variability which in turn causes depression and loss of fitness. This is more prominent in finite endangered populations and evaluation for genetic variability also forms an integral part of the animal breeding analysis.

Genetic variability is an integral part of domestic animal populations as fitness is directly related to the variability. Genetic improvement programs look for the genetic variability in important economic traits, while genetic variability with respect to fitness is studied for the existing population as a whole for which pedigree analysis forms an important tool. Several parameters are available from the pedigree analysis to understand the genetic variability of the population from which important inferences could be drawn.

## Generation Interval

Generation Interval is the average age of parents when their progeny used for breeding were born. It is calculated along the 4 gametic pathways; father to son, father to daughter, dam to son and dam to daughter. The evolution of generation interval is studied (Gutierrez (2003)) by calculating the generation interval for individuals who were parents in a block of four years at different times ten years apart.

## Equivalent No. of Generations ($EqG_i$)

Pedigree completeness level is studied as the proportion of parents, grandparents, and great-grand parents known and the complete equivalent number of generations (Boichard *et al.*, 1997). The equivalent number of generations is assessed for each animal (i) in the reference population as follows:

where, '$EqG_i$' is the equivalent complete generation for individual 'i' calculated as

$EqG = \Sigma(1/2)^n$

where 'n' is the number of generations separating the individual from each known ancestor (1= parents, 2 = grandparents, and so on), and the sum is computed across all known ancestors of 'i' (Maignel et al.,1996).

## Rate of Inbreeding and Effective Population Size

Inbreeding results in depression leading to decreased performance in traits related to production, reproduction and health (Falconer 1981). In general, populations with a small number of founders and closed herds have a high level of inbreeding.

Inbreeding is measured as the inbreeding coefficient 'F' defined as the probability that two alleles at a locus from an individual are identical by descent

The inbreeding coefficient only becomes meaningful if we specify some time in the past beyond which ancestries will not be pursued. It is the point at which all genes present in the population are independent, i.e., not identical by descent. This point is the base population and by its definition has an inbreeding coefficient of zero.

The inbreeding coefficient of subsequent generations expresses the amount of dispersive process that has taken place since the formation of the base population. The change in inbreeding over generations or the genetic drift is the most commonly studied parameter for a population in danger of losing variability. The amount of dispersive process expressed in terms of increment of inbreeding or rate of inbreeding is given in terms of the population size as follows:

$\Delta F = 1/2N$

Where, N is the number of breeding individuals in the population.

However, in domestic animals, the sexes are often unequally represented among breeding individuals and, in general, fewer males than females are used. The two sexes, however, contribute equally to the genes in the next generation. Therefore, the sampling variance attributable to the sexes must be calculated separately. For this purpose, a new concept effective population size is introduced. $N_e$, i.e. the number of breeding individuals that would give rise to the same rate of inbreeding if they contribute equally to the next generation, was calculated as per Wright (1931) as below:

$N_e = 1/2\Delta F$

Where, $\Delta F$ is the rate of inbreeding per generation.

Effective population size (Ne) (or) effective number is defined as the size of a standard population equally divided between males and females which would have the same rate of inbreeding as the one in question. In an idealized population, N = Nm+Nf, with an equal number of males and females. When an unequal number of males and females are there then the effective number is twice the harmonic mean of the number of two sexes. It is twice the harmonic mean because the population size is N = Nm + Nf.

The effective population size is related to ΔF in the same way and obtained from calculated ΔF.

$\Delta F = 1/2Ne$

$$\text{The harmonic mean is } \frac{1}{[1/2(1/N_m + 1/N_f)]}$$

$$\text{So } \frac{1}{Ne} = \frac{1}{4N_m} + \frac{1}{4N_f} = \frac{Nm + Nf}{4\,Nm\,Nf}$$

Assuming that a flock has 20 breeding rams and 400 ewes and has the same number in each generation. From the formula given above, the effective number will be 76.

$N_e = 4\ Nf\,Nm/\ Nf + Nm$

$= 4 \times 400 \times 20/420 = 76$

The rate of inbreeding in the above herd in each generation will be equal to that produced by 76 (38 males + 38 females) animals and the major portion of inbreeding is produced by males. The major portion of ΔF is from the less numerous sex ( i.e. male in farm animals).

Rate of inbreeding for the population ΔF = 1/2x76 = 0.006. In general, a rate of inbreeding greater than 1 percent or 0.01 as a proportion is considered endangered with respect to the conservation of domestic animal diversity.

Computation of effective population size (Falconer and Mackay, 1982) is a key not only to understanding genetic diversity but also to further prognosis in terms of conservation. Another important goal in the conservation of endangered breeds is to restrain the rate of inbreeding.

The 50/500 rule i.e. a population with $N_e$ less than 50 is under immediate threat from inbreeding depression, while a minimum $N_e$ of 500 is needed to prevent loss of genetic diversity over centuries, has been used as guidance in conservation schemes (Ryman and Allendorf, 2001).

## Individual Increase in Inbreeding

Coefficients of individual increase in inbreeding were calculated as per Gutierrez et al. (2009). For each animal (i), the individual increase in inbreeding ($\Delta F_i$) was computed as follows:

$$F_i = 1 - \sqrt[EqGi-1]{1 - F_i}$$

Equivalent inbreeding coefficients (EF) were obtained as a product of $\Delta F_i$ and average equivalent number of generations for the pedigree.

## The Inbreeding Coefficient F

The inbreeding coefficient could be obtained from a pedigree using Wright's path coefficient method or Malecot's covariance method. When the pedigrees of the individuals are known the coefficient of inbreeding can be more conveniently deduced directly from pedigrees, instead of indirectly from the population size. This method has several advantages in practice. Information is required of the inbreeding coefficient of the individuals, rather than of the generation. This is what the calculation from pedigree yields. For domestic animals, some individuals often appear as parents in two or more generation and these overlapping generations causes no trouble when the pedigrees are known. Under systems of close inbreeding and when there are overlapping of generations inbreeding is calculated by consideration of pedigrees.

When the coefficient of inbreeding is calculated from the pedigrees of the real population, it is a statement about the pedigree relationship and does not necessarily describe the state of dispersion.

The general expression for the inbreeding coefficient of an individual is

$$F_x = \Sigma\, [\, (1/2)^{n1+n2+1}\, (1+F_A)\, ]$$

$F_x$ = Inbreeding coefficient of the individual: $\Sigma$ = summation

$n_1$ – number of generations between one parent and the common ancestor

$n_2$ – number of generations between the other parent and the common ancestor

$F_A$ – Inbreeding coefficient of the common ancestor

Computation of the inbreeding coefficient requires tracing of the pedigrees back to common ancestors of parents and computing probabilities at each segregation. An individual may have several common ancestors each of which contributes a separate probability that the individual has pairs of genes that are copies of the ancestral genes. These separate probabilities are added to find the total probability of genes identical by descent in the individual. The summation refers not only to each common ancestor but also to each possible connection between the two parents that goes through a particular common ancestor.

Another way to deduce the inbreeding is the Covariance method, where the Numerator Relationship Matrix of all the individuals in the population is deduced and the diagonal elements of this matrix provide the Inbreeding coefficient as the increment over 1, which is the additive relationship of an individual with itself.

The Meuwissen and Luo (1992) algorithm is used to compute the inbreeding coefficients for large pedigrees by computer software.

## Average Relatedness

The average relatedness (AR) could be defined as twice the probability that two random alleles, one from the animal and the other from the population in the pedigree (including the animal), are identical by descent and can then be interpreted as the representation of the animal in the whole pedigree regardless of the knowledge of its own pedigree. This was computed as described in Dunner *et al.* (1998). It is the average of the coefficients in the row corresponding to the individual in the numerator relationship matrix. Higher AR with a lower inbreeding coefficient is indicative of a high degree of relatedness between all individuals of the pedigree. This could lead to difficulties when trying to avoid mating between unrelated or slightly related individuals.

## Founder Equivalent ($f_e$)

The $f_e$, is the number of equally contributing founders that would be expected to produce the same genetic diversity as in the population under study (James *et al.*, 1972; Lacy *et al.*, 1989). This explains the genetic contribution of the founders i.e. the ancestors with unknown parents for the current stock of population.

The effective number of founders is calculated as:

$$f_e = \frac{1}{\sum_{k=1}^{f} q_k^2}$$

where $q_k$ is the probability of gene origin of the $k^{th}$ ancestor.

Effective Number of Ancestors ($f_a$)

The $f_a$, (Boichard *et al.*, 1997) is studied for the reference population. The $f_a$ is the minimum number of ancestors, founders or not, necessary to explain the complete genetic diversity of the population under study. The $f_a$ is less than the $f_e$ and the comparison of both numbers can be used to find the bottlenecks that have occurred from the founders to the present population (Boichard *et al.*, 1997): the greater the $f_e/f_a$ ratio, the more stringent the bottlenecks.

## Genetic Conservation Index

The Genetic Conservation Index (GCI, Alderson, 1992) is calculated for all the individuals in the population under study as the reciprocal of proportion of contribution of all the founders in the pedigree of the animal. This could be used as a scale to use such animals with higher GCI to maintain balanced contributions from the founders.

ENDOG software (Gutierrez and Goyache, 2005) is used to estimate most of the parameters. Tables 12.1 & 12.2 represent results obtained from Endog software for Nilagiri sheep population.

**Table 12.1:** Inbreeding coefficient (F), average relatedness (AR), individual increase in inbreeding (AF) and effective population size ($N_e$) in whole and reference populations for a Nilagiri sheep Population

| **Parameter** | | **Whole Population** | **Reference population (2009-2011)** |
|---|---|---|---|
| F (%) | | 2.17 | 3.16 |
| AR (%) | | 3.45 | 4.23 |
| AF (%) | | 0.65 | 0.50 |
| $N_e$ | Regression over birth date<br>Maximum generations<br>Complete generations<br>Equivalent generations<br>Individual increase in inbreeding | 544.54<br>298.83<br>53.21<br>90.34<br>97.25 | |

**Table 12.2.** Average inbreeding (F), rate of inbreeding (ΔF), proportion inbred, mean inbreeding of inbred population, average relatedness (AR) and effective population size ($N_e$) over complete generations for a Nilagiri sheep population.

| **Generation** | **Number** | **F (%)** | **ΔF** | **Proportion inbred (%)** | **F of Inbred (%)** | **AR (%)** | **$N_e$** |
|---|---|---|---|---|---|---|---|
| 0 | 759 | 0 | 0 | 0 | 0 | 0.52 | |
| 1 | 1148 | 0.34 | 0.34 | 11.32 | 2.97 | 2.63 | 148.6 |
| 2 | 1227 | 2.92 | 2.59 | 62.43 | 4.67 | 4.08 | 19.3 |
| 3 | 994 | 3.59 | 0.69 | 94.67 | 3.79 | 4.68 | 72.1 |
| 4 | 525 | 3.43 | -0.16 | 100.00 | 3.43 | 4.69 | ** |
| 5 | 333 | 3.87 | 0.46 | 100.00 | 3.87 | 4.81 | 170.3 |
| 6 | 65 | 4.95 | 1.11 | 100.00 | 4.93 | 4.87 | 45.1 |

** Negative value for ΔF

# 13

# Meta-Analyses in Animal Breeding

Meta-analyses has been used extensively to combine the results of existing studies and obtain powerful estimates of a parameter. In animal breeding, attempts have been made to obtain meta-analysis estimates for genetic parameters. This tool is more pertinent to animal breeding on account of heterogeneity in terms of location, sample size and other factors in the estimation of genetic parameters. This chapter explains the background, methodology, precautions and implications of meta-analysis with respect to genetic parameters.

A meta-analysis is a powerful tool of statistics that could combine several estimates from different studies for a parameter and the resulting weighted estimate could be used as a representative value for the particular parameter. However, not all the studies are similar with respect to location, sample size, and methodology used and thus various precautions are to be taken right from the selection of studies to incorporating of between-study heterogeneity in the models. In animal breeding, met-analysis is very much useful for obtaining meaningful estimates of genetic parameters and this chapter explains the methodology of meta-analysis in animal breeding.

Genetic parameters are the basis for any breeding programme and precise, unbiased estimates are essential for achieving the expected successful response to selection. However, obtaining such precise estimates requires large populations and reliable pedigree information, which is not available always. However, with the advent of efficient estimation methods several studies on the estimation of genetic parameters in different populations are available. Meta-analyses could be a useful tool that helps in combining the different estimates available from earlier studies to obtain useful estimates of the parameters that could serve as a reference value for the entire region.

Meta-analysis provides reliable genetic parameter estimates as well as helps in understanding the patterns formed by the heterogeneity between studies which cannot be inferred from individual studies or systematic reviews. Meta-analysis is an application of statistical tools to statistics obtained from individual studies and not raw data. It is “The statistical analysis of a large collection of analysis results from individual studies for the purpose of integrating the findings” (Glass, 1976). Pooled estimates can be obtained by giving a weightage to each study based on different criteria of precision such as sample size, sampling variance or standard error. Analyzing the heterogeneity between studies is a vital component of meta-analysis for which a random-effects model could be used (Hedges and Vevea, 1998).

National breeding programmes gaining momentum in the region could benefit from the reliable estimates of genetic parameters obtained from such analyses as it is not possible to have genetic parameter estimates when there is a wide diversity in breeds pertaining to a particular region.

## Steps in conducting a meta-analysis

Methodology of meta-analysis

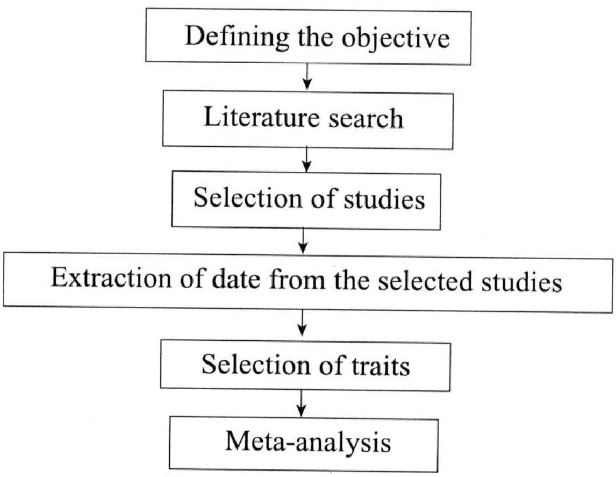


The steps are explained with an actual example of meta-analysis done for the estimates of genetic parameters of growth traits of sheep in the tropics (Ambike et al., 2022)

1. **Defining the objective:** Identify the requirement which should be specific for a purpose so that too much heterogeneity could be avoided and a better estimate for the specific purpose is achieved. For eg. the growth traits of sheep in the tropics.
2. **Literature search:** The search for literature must be complete and ensure that important studies in the field are not missed out. The search engines and scientific databases available are of immense help in completing a thorough search for literature. A search for growth studies for sheep in the tropics, databases like Google, Scopus and Research Gate could be used and the results for our eg. gave 217 articles specific to the broad area.

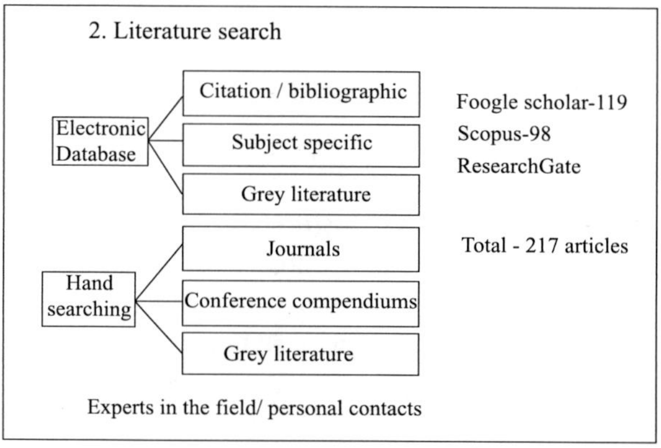


3. **Selection of studies:** From the collected literature the studies to be included in the meta-analysis are to be finalized based on the inclusion and exclusion criteria fixed for the objective. The PRISMA guidelines (Moher *et al.*, 2009) give an idea of forming the inclusion and exclusion criteria. Eg. For the study on growth in sheep, the inclusion criteria were that the articles must be from tropical or sub-tropical countries which lie between latitude 35° North and 35° South and published in English. Duplicate articles or those with incomplete descriptions with the absence of both standard errors and the number of records for the genetic parameters were excluded. Articles using different methodologies for the estimation of these parameters were included like REML, half-sib analysis or Bayesian approach. When genetic parameters for the same traits were estimated in the same population again, only one among them was included to avoid bias caused due to correlation between those estimates. The recent one with a larger sample size was included among such articles and finally, from 217 articles, 68 articles were eligible for inclusion in the analysis.

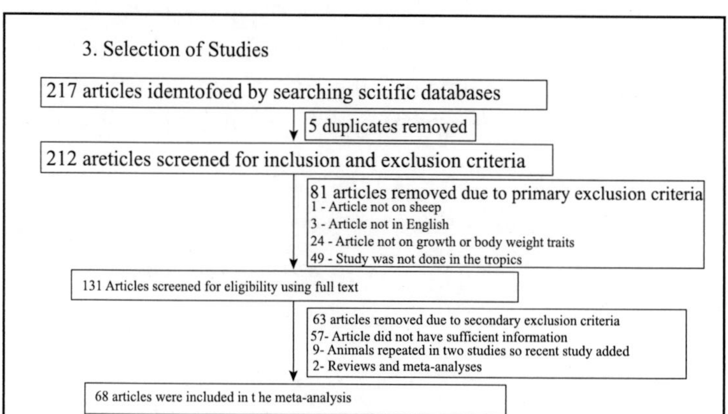

4. **Extraction of data:** The nature of variables to be collected from the selected studies will depend upon the type of meta-analysis. For animal breeding, the meta-analysis is usually done for the genetic parameters, while the descriptives of the traits studied also may be pooled to get weighted estimates.

Data may be tabulated as a spreadsheet in Microsoft Excel which include author, year of publication, duration of data collection, country where the study was conducted, the latitude of the place of study, breed, the utility of the breed, methodology used for estimation of genetic parameters, the origin of data and software used for analysis. Basic descriptive measures of these traits including the number of records, mean, standard error and coefficient of variation and the genetic parameters (direct heritability, maternal heritability, common environmental effects, phenotypic correlation and genetic correlation) with their standard errors obtained are utilized for the meta-analyses. All the traits which are included must have genetic parameter estimates collected from at least two different databases to minimize the possible impact of non-independence among the articles.

In case the standard errors for the parameter estimates are not published the approximate SE could be calculated using the combined variance method (Sutton, 2000) which can be denoted as,

$$SE_{ij} = \left[ \frac{\left( \dfrac{\sum_{k=1}^{k} s_{ik}^2 n_{ik}^2}{\sum_{k=1}^{k} n_{ik}} \right)}{n_{ij}^{'}} \right]^{1/2} \quad (1)$$

where, $SE_{ij}$ is the approximate standard error of the parameter, $s_{ik}$ is the published standard error of the $i^{th}$ trait in the $k^{th}$ article, $n_{ik}$ is the number of records used to obtain a parameter estimate of the $i^{th}$ trait in the $k^{th}$ article, while $n_{ij}$ are the number of records used for predicting the parameter $i^{th}$ trait in the $j^{th}$ article which did not have the standard error for that parameter estimate.

**4. Extraction of data from the selected studies**

- Author
- Year of Publication
- Duration of data collection
- Country
- Latitude
- Breed
- Utility of the breed
- Methodology used for estimation genetic parameters
- Origin of data
- Descriptive statistics of traits with number of records, 303 mean, standard error and CV
- Genetic parameter estimates for 502 heritability (296 direct, 130 material and 76 common environmntal) and 1051 correlation (484 phenotypic and 531 genetic) with standard erros

5. **Selection of traits and quality control:** To obtain reliable weighted estimates through meta-analysis, it is important to ensure that a minimum number of articles have been included for each parameter. This assumption is checked using relative standard error (RSE) given by Zarkovich (1979). The formula for RSE is

$$\text{RSEi}\,(\%) = \frac{S_i \,/\, (n_i)^{1/2}}{\mu_i} \tag{2}$$

where, $S_i$ is the standard deviation of the parameter estimate of i[th] trait, n is the number of articles with the parameter estimate of i[th] trait and $\mu_i$ is the average of parameter estimates of i[th] trait. Parameter estimates of traits beyond 25% are excluded from the analysis as this meant that there was a high sampling error and so the pooled estimate would be biased. For eg., in our study (Ambike et al., 2022) traits like first-month weight and post-weaning average daily gain were excluded from among the fifteen growth traits. Similarly, parameters like phenotypic and genetic correlation had to be eliminated from the analysis as their RSE values were greater than 25%.

6. **Meta-analysis of phenotypic traits:** Weighted means and standard deviations for all the selected traits can be calculated. (package radiant. data from R software). The number of records is used for giving weights to each study while obtaining the pooled estimates. The coefficient of variation for each trait is calculated as

$$CV_i\,(\%) = \frac{S_i}{\mu_i} \times 100 \tag{3}$$

where, $S_i$ is the standard deviation of the i[th] trait, $\mu_i$ is the trait mean.

**Table 13.1:** Weighted mean, standard deviation (SD) and coefficient of variation (CV %) for each trait (Ambike et al., 2022)

| Traits | Unit | N | Records | Mean | SD | SE | CV (%) |
|---|---|---|---|---|---|---|---|
| Birth weight | kg | 58 | 299526 | 3.58 | 0.68 | 0.001 | 19.02 |
| Weight at 3 months | kg | 48 | 222059 | 18.31 | 5.65 | 0.012 | 30.83 |
| Weight at 6 months | kg | 37 | 149625 | 23.95 | 8.47 | 0.022 | 35.37 |

where N is number of articles, SD is standard deviation, SE is standard error and CV is coefficient of variation

7. ***Meta-analysis of genetic parameter estimates:*** Meta-analysis for genetic parameter estimates like heritability and genetic correlation is done using a random-effects model (meta (Schwarzer, 2015) and metafor (Viechtbauer, 2015) packages from the R software). Using a fixed-effect method to combine estimates of genetic parameters makes the assumption that each published estimate is estimating the same underlying true parameter (i.e. no heterogeneity between published estimates) (Barron *et al.*, 2008) and any difference observed is due to chance factors or sampling variation within each study. If this assumption is invalid, as shown by Koots et al. (1994a), then a preferred alternative method would be to fit a random-effects meta-analysis model. A random-effects model assumes that each estimate from the various studies is estimating different underlying true parameters, and takes into account the extra variation implied in making this assumption. This underlying true parameter is assumed to vary at random and its effect is believed to be normally distributed. Hence, this model accounts for the between and within- study sources of variation and has been proposed as a more conservative method of meta-analysis that yields results that can be generalized (Berkey *et al.*, 1995; Barron *et al.*, 2008; Sutton *et al.*, 2000; Safari *et al.*, 2005).

   The model can be represented according to Borenstein *et al.* (2011) as

$$\hat{\theta}_j = \bar{\theta} + d_j + e_j \tag{4}$$

where, $\theta_j$ is the published estimate for a parameter in article j, θ is the weighted average of that parameter obtained from meta-analysis for the population under study, $d_j$ is the between studies deviation with $d_j \sim N(0, \tau^2)$, where where, $\tau^2$ is the variance representing the amount of heterogeneity among studies, and $e_j$ is the within-study component due to sampling error in the parameter estimate in the j$^{th}$ article, assumed as $e_j \sim N(0, \sigma^2_e)$ where, $\sigma^2_e$ is the within-study variance. Inverse-variance method is used to give weights ($w_j$) to each study which was taken from the standard error of the estimate or the sampling variance. Within study variance $v_j = \sigma^2_e/n$ where, n is the number of records and between study variance $\tau^2$ was added to it. Thus, $w_j = 1/( v_j + T^2_j)$. As the inverse of the standard error is taken, it ensures that more weightage is given to studies with a less standard error or more precision. $\tau^2$ is estimated using REML for parameter estimates which are continuous (Viechtbauer, 2005; Jackson *et al.*, 2010; Veroniki *et al.*, 2016). There are other methods as listed by Harrer et al. (2022). All these methods involve intense computations and the R packages provide us with these estimates. The combined estimates were calculated using the equation

$$\overline{\theta} = \frac{\left(\sum_{k=1}^{k} w_j \widehat{\theta_j}\right)}{\sum_{k=1}^{k} w_j} \tag{5}$$

where, $\theta_j$ is the published estimate for a parameter in article j, $\theta$ is the weighted average of that parameter obtained from meta-analysis for the population under study and $w_j$ is the weight of the effect for the parameter estimate in each study. For the traits with fewer than 20 estimates, Knapp-Hartung adjustment (Knapp and Hartung, 2003; IntHout *et al.*, 2014) is used which assumes that the estimates follow a t-distribution instead of a z-distribution and gives larger confidence intervals.

The confidence interval of the weighted average of the parameter estimate at 95% is determined using the equation: IC 95% = $\theta \pm (1.96 \text{ X SE } \theta)$; SE $\theta = [1/\Sigma^{j}_{j=1} wj]^{1/2}$, and the standard error is for the weighted average of the parameter in the population. (6)

**Genetic correlation**

Correlation estimates do not follow a normal distribution and thus cannot be used for fitting of a random-effects model directly. To obtain the weighted estimate of phenotypic and genetic correlations (r), the raw correlations (published values) are first transformed to a normal scale using Fisher's Z transformation (Steel and Torrie, 1960) given in Equation 7. Meta-analysis could be done on these transformed values ($Z_{ij}$) and the results obtained are then back transformed using Equation 8 (Borenstein *et al.*, 2009) to give the weighted estimates (Table 4) of actual correlation.

$$Z_{ij} = 0.5 \, [\text{in}\,(1 + r_{gij}) - \text{in}\,(1 - r_{gij})] \tag{7}$$

$$r^{*}_{gij} = \frac{e^{2z_{ij}} - 1}{e^{2z_{ij}} + 1} \tag{8}$$

where, $Z_{ij}$ is the Fisher's Z transformation, $r_{gij}$ is the published correlation estimate for the $i^{th}$ trait in the $j^{th}$ article, $r^{*}_{gij}$ is the re-transformed correlation estimate for the $i^{th}$ trait in the $j^{th}$ article.

### Test of heterogeneity of parameter estimates

A meta-analysis done using a random effects model assumes some level of heterogeneity between the studies. A heterogeneity test is done to quantify the extent of between-study heterogeneity where the null hypothesis is that all the studies have only one true underlying parameter estimate and all the observed variance is because of the sampling error while the alternate hypothesis suggests that at least one study differs with respect to its parameter estimates. Higgins and Thompson's $I^2$ statistic (Higgins *et al.*, 2003) is used to obtain this variance.

$$I^2 = \left( \frac{(Q - df)}{Q} \right) \times 100 \tag{9}$$

where, Q is Cochran's Q statistic (Cochran, 1954) also known as the weighted sum of squares (WSS) which is calculated as Equation 10 and df are n-1 degrees of freedom with n number of articles.

$$Q = \sum_{j=1}^{j} \omega_j (\hat{\theta}_j - \hat{\theta})^2 \tag{10}$$

Q statistic follows a Chi-square distribution with degrees of freedom (j-1)and so takes only positive values. The degrees of freedom considered here give the value of Q which would be obtained if there was only sampling variance present. Thus, when the value of Q is higher than that then between study heterogeneity is present. When $I^2$ is >75% then there is substantial heterogeneity between the studies for a parameter estimate of a trait. The percentage of heterogeneity quantified by the $I^2$ can be categorized as low, moderate, and high if the values are 25%, 50%, and 75%, respectively (Higgins et al., 2003). Q depends on the number of articles and so $I^2$ is used which does not fluctuate with the number of articles but depends only on the precision of the estimate.

### Weighted Least Squares for the effect of factors affecting genetic parameters

Weighted least squares analysis is usually done to understand the effect of non-genetic factors on the genetic parameters for traits. Both fixed effects (Giannotti *et al.*, 2005; Akanno et al., 2013; Gathura et al., 2020; Medrado *et al.*, 2021a) and mixed-effects model (Vrindha *et al.*, 2022) have been used. For the fixed effects model the error term the random and also assumed to be independently and identically normally distributed (0, V), where V= $\sigma^2_e / w_n$ and $w_n$ is $1/ s^2_n$.

In the mixed-effects model the study effects are included as a random effect to account for all the factors affecting the trait and causing a between-study heterogeneity which could not be included in the meta-regression as this reduces the bias of estimates of other factors included in the model (St-Pierre, 2001). Meta-regression is different from a normal regression as weighted estimates for the traits are considered by giving appropriate weightage to the published estimates based on their standard errors. Thus, it takes into account the sampling error as well as the between study heterogeneity to get the values of the intercept and the regression coefficient such that they minimize the difference between the true estimates and predicted estimates.

**Example 13.1:** The mixed-effects model with factors as the fixed effects and between-study heterogeneity as the random effect could be represented as

$$P_{ijklmno} = B_i + M_j + D_k + A_l + L_m + \iota^2_n + e_{ijklmno}$$

where,

| | |
|---|---|
| $P_{ijklmn}$ | is the published genetic parameter estimate weighted by its standard error |
| $B_i$ | Breed of sheep categorized based on the utility (mutton, dual or wool) |
| $M_j$ | Model used for estimation of genetic parameter (animal or sire) |
| $D_k$ | Data origin (Farm or field) |
| $A_l$ | Age of data taken as a covariate (number of years prior to 2021 when the study was published) |
| $L_m$ | Latitude from the equator taken as a covariate |
| $\iota^2_n$ | Random between-study effect |
| $e_{ijklmn}$ | Random error assumed to be independently and normally distributed |

This analysis was also done using the 'meta' package in R software where the weights were assigned by inverse variance method. Meta-regression models help to understand how much heterogeneity is reduced by using this model in place of the initial random-effects model.

The amount of heterogeneity explained by the meta-regression model can be given by $R^2_*$ which can be calculated as described by Harrer *et al.*, 2019.

$$R^2_* = 1 - \frac{\hat{\tau}^2_{unexplained}}{\hat{\tau}^2_{total}} \qquad (11)$$

where, $R^2_*$ is the ratio of the unexplained between-study heterogeneity to the total heterogeneity.

**Table 13.2:** Pooled direct heritability ($h^2_a$) for growth traits obtained through a random effects model (Ambike et al., 2022)

| **Trait** | **N** | $h^2_a$ | **95% CI** | **RSE %** | **I² %** |
|---|---|---|---|---|---|
| W0 | 56 | 0.196 | 0.162-0.230 | 8.39 | 95.05 |
| W3 | 45 | 0.217 | 0.167-0.266 | 11.20 | 96.77 |
| W6 | 34 | 0.264 | 0.197-0.330 | 12.30 | 95.89 |
| W9 | 22 | 0.257 | 0.166-0.348 | 17.44 | 96.78 |
| W12 | 34 | 0.284 | 0.219-0.349 | 11.20 | 95.07 |
| W18 | 3 | 0.388 | 0.263-0.513 | 7.72 | 13.88 |
| ADG1 | 25 | 0.186 | 0.142-0.229 | 11.90 | 91.29 |
| ADG2 | 12 | 0.208 | 0.091-0.326 | 24.80 | 97.6 |
| KR1 | 16 | 0.121 | 0.059-0.184 | 24.11 | 94.68 |
| KR2 | 8 | 0.047 | 0.018-0.077 | 22.60 | 82.45 |

**Table 13.3:** Factors affecting heritability estimates of growth of sheep obtained through meta-regression in a mixed-effects model (Ambike *et al.*, 2022)

| **Trait** | **Model** | | **Origin of data** | | **Age of study** | **Latitude** | $R^2_*$ |
|---|---|---|---|---|---|---|---|
| **Heritability ($h^2_a$)** | **Animal** | **Sire** | **Farm** | **Field** | | | |
| W0 | 0 | 0.069 ± 0.089 | 0 | 0.090 ± 0.042 | -0.001 ± 0.002* | -0.005±0.002* | 21.51 |
| W3 | 0 | 0.167 ± 0.116 | 0 | 0.126 ± 0.062 | -0.003 ± 0.004* | -0.007±0.003** | 26.65 |
| W6 | 0 | 0.176 ± 0.163 | 0 | 0.053 ± 0.091 | -0.002 ± 0.005 | -0.008±0.004* | 7.31 |

Age of study and latitude was included as covariate, while Model and Origin of data where included as a fixed class.

## History of meta-analysis in animal breeding

- G.P. Davis (1993), Marshall (1994), Koots *et al.* (1994). Genetic parameters of beef cattle
- Fogarty (1995), Genetic parameters in sheep
- Lobo *et al.* (2000), Giannotti *et al.* (2005). Genetic parameters of beef and dairy cattle
- Safari *et al.* (2005), Genetic parameters in sheep
- Akanno *et al.* (2013), Genetic parameters in pigs
- Diaz *et al.* (2013), Feed intake traits in beef cattle

- Berry *et al.* (2014). Reproductive performance and genetic parameters in dairy and beef cattle
- Oliveira *et al.* (2017). Genetic parameters of Nellore breed
- Jembere *et al.* (2017). Genetic parameters of goats
- Gathura *et al.* (2020). Genetic parameters of beef cattle
- Medrado *et al.* (2021). Genetic parameters of buffaloes and sheep

## Advantages of meta-analysis

- Provides insights that individual studies may not be able to provide.
- Identifies between-study heterogeneity and moderators can be added which explain this variation.
- Deals with the large amount of information which is being generated.
- Know whether publication bias is present.
- Establishing relation between two parameters or summarizing a parameter estimate in a single group- Reliable estimate which can be generalized for the population.
- Meta-analysis is an efficient method of combining results from several studies
- Its properties can be particularly exploited for animal breeding where data is highly heterogeneous
- There has been a great increase in the number of meta-analyses published in the recent years but several avenues pertaining to animal breeding are still untouched and can be explored
- As multiple studies are combined together, the sample size increases and more powerful estimates can be obtained which can be used directly in the implementation phase of any breeding program.

## Forest Plot

The forest plot is a plot of effect sizes with confidence interval of all the studies included in the meta-regression. The vertical line indicates the pooled estimate of the genetic parameter with confidence interval.

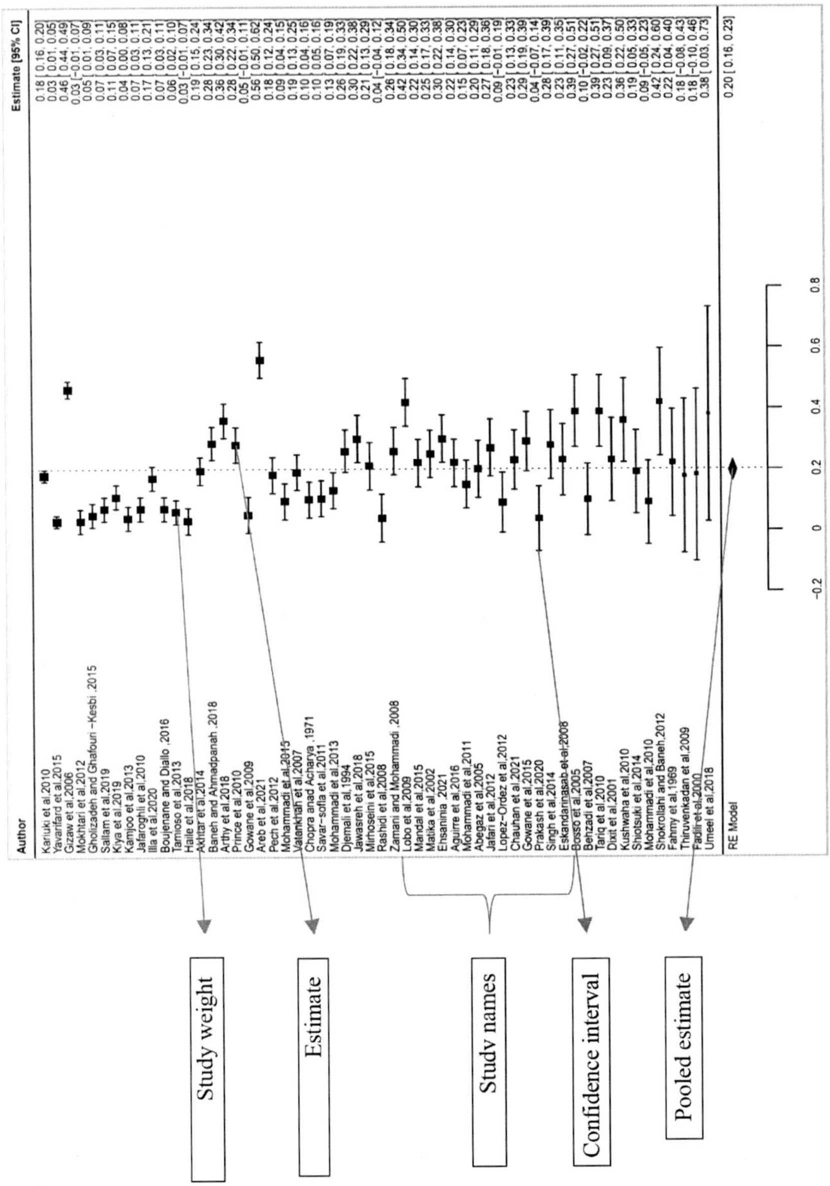


**Figure 13.1:** Forest plot

# 14

# Multivariate Analysis of Animal Breeding Data

This chapter describes various multivariate techniques which are useful in animal breeding. The genetic correlation with multiple response variables is already explained in the chapters on Correlation and Genetic Parameters. The other techniques including MANOVA, Principal Component Analysis, Factor Analysis, Cluster Analysis and Discriminant Analysis are explained.

Multivariate analysis is referred to a set of data with multiple response variables in general and such data is encountered often in animal breeding analysis. The simplest form of multivariate analysis is the genetic correlation where two or more traits are analysed together as response variables with factors affecting them on the right-hand side (RHS) and details of these are already explained in earlier chapters. Such multivariate data requires proper handling in order to obtain meaningful inferences and in this chapter are discussed some multivariate techniques like Multivariate Analysis of Variance, Principal Components Analysis, Factor Analysis, Cluster Analysis and Discriminant Analysis are explained. The codes used in commonly used software are also provided with examples. Rao (2007) has explained various multivariate techniques used in animal breeding.

## One - way MANOVA

One- way MANOVA is used when we have more number of response variables which are continuous and quantitative in nature and the source of variation (explanatory or cause variable) is discrete. Often more than two population means need to be compared. Random and independent samples, collected from each of g (say) populations, are arranged as

population 1: **x11, x12, x13, . . . , x1 n1**

population 2: **x21, x22, x23, . . . , x2 n2**

For g traits

population g: **xg1, xg2, xg3, . . . , xg ng**

Multivariate analysis of variance is used first to investigate whether the population mean vectors are the same and, if not, which mean components differ significantly.

For eg. we need to compare the vector of morphometric characters (Response variables) with source of variation as sex (male or female). The data could be represented as given in Figure 14.1.

| | BIRDNO | BODYWT | MF | BILLLENGTH | HEADWIDTH | NECKLENGTH | BODYLENGTH | SHANKLENGTH | WEBWIDTH | BREASTCIRCUM |
|---|---|---|---|---|---|---|---|---|---|---|
| 1 | 1.0000 | 1180.0000 | 2.0000 | 6.1000 | 2.2000 | 17.5000 | 22.2000 | 5.8000 | 6.3000 | 29.0000 |
| 2 | 2.0000 | 1530.0000 | 1.0000 | 7.1000 | 2.4000 | 18.8000 | 29.3000 | 5.5000 | 5.6000 | 30.3000 |
| 3 | 3.0000 | 1110.0000 | 2.0000 | 6.4000 | 2.0000 | 15.5000 | 26.5000 | 5.6000 | 5.5000 | 27.3000 |
| 4 | 4.0000 | 1377.0000 | 2.0000 | 6.2000 | 2.3000 | 17.7000 | 27.0000 | 5.5000 | 5.3000 | 28.7000 |
| 5 | 5.0000 | 1270.0000 | 2.0000 | 6.6000 | 2.3000 | 16.7000 | 26.4000 | 4.9000 | 5.5000 | 29.3000 |
| 6 | 6.0000 | 1530.0000 | 1.0000 | 6.6000 | 2.4000 | 17.5000 | 27.3000 | 5.4000 | 5.7000 | 30.8000 |
| 7 | 7.0000 | 1432.0000 | 1.0000 | 6.1000 | 1.9000 | 17.3000 | 28.6000 | 5.3000 | 5.9000 | 32.9000 |
| 8 | 8.0000 | 1447.0000 | 1.0000 | 6.6000 | 2.1000 | 19.1000 | 28.7000 | 5.0000 | 6.0000 | 30.1000 |
| 9 | 9.0000 | 1160.0000 | 2.0000 | 5.6000 | 1.9000 | 17.4000 | 23.4000 | 4.5000 | 6.1000 | 27.8000 |
| 10 | 10.0000 | 1472.0000 | 1.0000 | 6.1000 | 2.1000 | 17.8000 | 25.0000 | 5.9000 | 5.5000 | 30.3000 |
| 11 | 11.0000 | 1345.0000 | 2.0000 | 5.6000 | 2.3000 | 17.4000 | 26.3000 | 5.6000 | 4.7000 | 28.4000 |
| 12 | 12.0000 | 1325.0000 | 2.0000 | 6.6000 | 2.1000 | 16.4000 | 26.0000 | 5.1000 | 5.1000 | 30.9000 |
| 13 | 13.0000 | 1200.0000 | 2.0000 | 6.1000 | 1.9000 | 18.2000 | 26.4000 | 5.0000 | 5.8000 | 27.0000 |
| 14 | 14.0000 | 1452.0000 | 1.0000 | 6.6000 | 2.3000 | 17.5000 | 26.3000 | 5.1000 | 5.9000 | 30.6000 |
| 15 | 15.0000 | 1277.0000 | 2.0000 | 5.6000 | 1.9000 | 17.2000 | 24.1000 | 5.9000 | 5.6000 | 28.6000 |
| 16 | 16.0000 | 1150.0000 | 2.0000 | 6.2000 | 1.9000 | 17.6000 | 24.8000 | 5.3000 | 5.6000 | 30.8000 |
| 17 | 17.0000 | 1597.0000 | 1.0000 | 7.0000 | 2.3000 | 19.2000 | 30.2000 | 5.9000 | 5.9000 | 31.6000 |
| 18 | 18.0000 | 1203.0000 | 2.0000 | 6.2000 | 2.1000 | 15.6000 | 26.2000 | 5.1000 | 5.3000 | 29.9000 |
| 19 | 19.0000 | 1466.0000 | 1.0000 | 6.6000 | 2.4000 | 17.7000 | 26.9000 | 4.7000 | 4.9000 | 30.2000 |
| 20 | 20.0000 | 1135.0000 | 2.0000 | 5.9000 | 1.8000 | 15.4000 | 24.6000 | 4.7000 | 5.3000 | 28.1000 |

**Figure 14.1**

## Assumptions

- Independent discrete categorical variable with two or more groups
- Two or more dependent continuous quantitative variables
- Data are multivariate and normally distributed
- Independence of observations with
- Sample size (more cases in each group than the number of dependent variables)
- Equality of error variances

## Principal Components Analysis (PCA)

In animal breeding we often come across variables which are highly correlated and as such they are effectively "indicating the same". Analysing such data leads to confounding and errors in prediction PCA helps as a dimension reduction technique which minimises the large number of related variables to a few independent variables. To examine the relationships among a set of $p$ correlated variables, it may be useful to transform the original set of variables to a new set of uncorrelated variables called *principal components*. These new variables are linear combinations of original variables and are derived in decreasing order of importance.

Let x1, x2, x3, . . . , xp are variables under study, then first principal component may be defined as:

$$z1 = b11\ x1 + b12\ x2 + \ldots\ldots + b1p\ xp$$

subject to the condition that

$$b11^2 + b12^2 + \ldots\ldots + b1p^2 = 1$$

The second principal component is defined as

$$z2 = b21\ x1 + b22\ x2 + \ldots\ldots. + b2p\ xp$$

such that Var(z2) is as large as possible next to Var( z1 ) subject to the constraint that

$b21^2 + b22^2 + \ldots\ldots. + b2p^2 = 1$ and cov (z1, z2) = 0 and so on.

It is expected that the first few principal components account for most of the variability in the original data. If so, these few principal components can then replace the initial p variables in subsequent analysis, thus, reducing the effective dimensionality of the problem. An analysis of principal components often reveals relationships that were not previously suspected and thereby allows the interpretation that could not be found with the original variables. However, Principal Component usually serves as an intermediate step in much larger investigations by reducing the dimensionality of the problem and providing easier interpretation. It is a mathematical technique which does not require user to specify the statistical model or assumption about the distribution of original variates. It may also be mentioned that principal components are artificial variables and often it is not possible to assign physical meaning to them. Further, since Principal Component Analysis transforms the original set of variables to new set of uncorrelated variables, if the original variables are uncorrelated, then the principal component analysis will not give better results. Variables should probably be standardized if they are measured on scales with widely differing ranges or if measured units are not commensurate.

## Applications of Principal Components

- The most important use of principal component analysis is reduction of data. It provides the effective dimensionality of the data. If first few components account for most of the variation in the original data, then first few components' scores can be utilized in subsequent analysis in place of original variables.
- Plotting of data becomes difficult with more than three variables and principal component analysis enables us to plot the data in two dimensions.

Particularly detection of outliers or clustering of individuals will be easier through this technique and use of principal component analysis reveals grouping of variables which would not be found by other means.

- Reduction in dimensionality can also help in analysis where no. of variables is more than the number of observations, for example, in discriminant analysis and regression analysis. In such cases, principal component analysis is helpful by reducing the dimensionality of data and thus avoid the false positives and false discovery rate.
- Multiple regression can be dangerous if independent variables are highly correlated. Principal component analysis is the most practical technique to solve the problem through principal component regression.

## Factor Analysis

The essential purpose of factor analysis is to describe, if possible, the covariance relationships among many variables in terms of a few underlying, but unobservable, random quantities called *factors*. That is, all variables within a particular group are highly correlated among themselves but have relatively small correlations with variables in a different group. It is conceivable that each group of variables represents a single underlying construct, or factor, that is responsible for the observed correlations. As in PCA, if variables are uncorrelated, factor analysis will not be useful. Factor analysis is done in two parts, first solution is obtained by placing some restrictions and then the final solution is obtained by rotating this solution. There are two most popular methods available in the literature for parameter estimation, the principal component (and the related principal factor) method and the maximum likelihood method. The solution from either method can be rotated in order to simplify the interpretation of factors. It is always prudent to try more than one method of solution. If the factor model is appropriate for the problem at hand, the solutions should be consistent with one another.

If there are fewer than three sets of correlations above 3 in the correlation matrix, generally factor analysis is not recommended

The Bartlett Test of Sphericity compares the correlation matrix with an identity matrix and a small p-value is indicative for a higher correlation and thus factor analysis is recommended.

The Measure of Sampling Adequacy (MSA) does not produce a P value but a value over 0.8 and below 0.5 makes factor analysis undesirable.

Even though factor analysis is continued for larger correlations between variables, it is necessary to check for transformed variables or variables with very high correlation. This could be done by assessing the determinant of the correlation matrix, the value of which should be greater than 0.00001

**Cluster Analysis:** The main aim of cluster analysis is to allocate a set of individuals to a set of mutually exclusive, exhaustive, groups such that individuals within a group are similar to one another while individuals in different groups are dissimilar. The same analysis when it is done with a supervisory variable i.e. with existing data on the groups then is called the **Discriminant Analysis.**

Cluster analysis is non-parametric and distribution-free and is done based on similarity measures: It is necessary to measure "closeness" or "similarity" in order to produce a rather simple group structure from a complex data set. Important considerations include the nature of the variables as described in the earlier chapters (discrete, continuous, binary or scales normal, ordinal, interval, ratio). Measures of similarity are often called "similarity coefficients". Measures of *similarity* and *dissimilarity* are closely related in an inverse way. One of the measures of dissimilarity is the Euclidean distance.

The hierarchical structure is often represented by a two-dimensional diagram.

This diagram is called a tree diagram or dendrogram. A cluster tree may be defined as a nested sequence of partitions of the individuals in to 'g' groups, where 'g' varies from 1 to n, with a property that the partitions into 'g' and into (g+1) groups are such that (g-1) of the groups are identical while the remaining individuals from one group in the first case and two groups in the second case. Thus, a tree is a family of clusters for which any two clusters are either disjoint or one includes the other.

The different steps involved in the agglomerative hierarchical clustering for grouping N objects are;

1. Start with N clusters, each containing a single entity and an N x N symmetric matrix of distances (or similarities)
2. Search the distance matrix for the nearest (most similar) pair of clusters.

   Let the distance between "most similar" clusters **U** and **V** be dUV
3. Merge clusters U and V. Denote the newly formed cluster (UV). Update the entries in the distance matrix by
   i) deleting the rows and columns corresponding to clusters U and V
   ii) adding a row and column giving the distances between cluster (UV) and the remaining clusters
4. Repeat steps 2 and 3 a total of N-1 times. (All objects will be in a single cluster at termination of the algorithm.) Record the identity of the clusters

that are merged and the levels (distances or similarities) at which the mergers take place.

Many methods are available under agglomerative hierarchical clustering, viz. Single linkage (Nearest neighbor), Complete linkage (farthest neighbour), Average linkage (Average distances between the unit of one entity and the other unit of the second entity), centroid (Distance between means), Ward's distance (Error sum of squares). Different methods can give different results but use at least three methods and look for consensus clusters.

## Fisher's Discriminant Analysis

Discriminant analysis (DA) is a multivariate statistical technique used for classifying a set of observations into pre defined groups. It was developed by R.A. Fisher in 1936, and is similar to multiple linear regression except that it predicts an outcome that is discrete in nature (the groups). The dependent variable (Y) is **categorical**-dichotomous or multi-chotomous and the independent variables are metric, i.e., interval or ratio.

- ***Linear D A*** - when the criterion / dependent variable has two categories eg: chronic and acute mastitis
- ***Multiple D A*** - when three or more categories are involved eg: subacute, acute and chronic mastitis

## Properties and Assumptions for DA

- The sample size of the smallest group needs to exceed the number of predictor variables. As a "rule of thumb," the sample size should be at least 5-10 times the number of discriminant variables.
- Select discriminator variables (x1,x2) that are not highly intercorrelated If the correlation is greater than 0.3, indicate the violation of assumption.
- The number of variables should not exceed the number of groups
- Each predictor or discriminating variable should be normally distributed. This could be ascertained with histograms of frequency distributions.
- DA is very sensitive to the heterogeneity of variance-covariance matrices.
- The covariance or correlation between two groups should be similar to the corresponding covariance/ correlation in other groups and this could be ascertained using the Box's M statistics which tests the null hypothesis of equal population covariance matrices.
- The groups must be mutually exclusive, with every subject or case belonging to only one group.

- Each of the allocations for the dependent categories in the initial classification are correctly classified.
- Outliers should not be present in the data. DA is highly sensitive to the inclusion of outliers.

## Model for Discriminant Analysis

The **discriminant analysis model** involves linear combinations of the following form:

$D = b_1X_1 + b_2X_2 + b_3X_3 + \ldots + b_kX_k + c$

**Where**

**$D$ = discriminant score/ function (one less than the no of groups)**

**$b$ 's = discriminant coefficient or weight**

**$X$ 's = predictor or independent or discriminating variable**

**C = constant**

- Discriminant analysis – creates an equation that will minimize the possibility of misclassifying cases into their respective groups or categories. This maximizes the distance between the variance of the dependent variable.
- And minimize the variance of each group ie. as classified by the independent variable.

**Example**

Data file: Consider the morphometric data of a duck population (Figure 14.1)

## One – way MANOVA (Using SPSS)

Box's Test tests the null hypothesis that the observed covariance matrices of the dependent variables are equal across groups.

Box's Test of Equality of Covariance Matrices[a]

| | |
|---|---:|
| Box's M | 40.198 |
| F | 1.392 |
| df1 | 28 |
| df2 | 203298.605 |
| Sig. | .081 |

Levene's Test of Equality of Error Variances tests the null hypothesis that the error variance of the dependent variable is equal across groups

| | F | df1 | df2 | Sig. |
|---|---|---|---|---|
| BILLLENGTH | .335 | 1 | 248 | .563 |
| HEADWIDTH | .136 | 1 | 248 | .712 |
| NECKLENGTH | .012 | 1 | 248 | .911 |
| BODYLENGTH | .280 | 1 | 248 | .597 |
| SHANKLENGTH | .143 | 1 | 248 | .706 |
| WEBWIDTH | 6.050 | 1 | 248 | .015 |
| BREAST CIRCUMFERENCE | .017 | 1 | 248 | .896 |

- Since the significance value is less than 0.05, the assumption for this data set is fulfilled. That is the homogeneity of variance-covariance matrices is ascertained.

Multivariate Tests[a]

| Effect | | Value | F | Hypothesis df | Error df | Sig. | Partial Eta Squared |
|---|---|---|---|---|---|---|---|
| Intercept | Pillai's Trace | .999 | 31957.537[b] | 7.000 | 242.000 | .000 | .999 |
| | Wilks' Lambda | .001 | 31957.537[b] | 7.000 | 242.000 | .000 | .999 |
| | Hotelling's Trace | 924.392 | 31957.537[b] | 7.000 | 242.000 | .000 | .999 |
| | Roy's Largest Root | 924.392 | 31957.537[b] | 7.000 | 242.000 | .000 | .999 |
| MF | Pillai's Trace | .551 | 42.468[b] | 7.000 | 242.000 | .000 | .551 |
| | Wilks' Lambda | .449 | 42.468[b] | 7.000 | 242.000 | .000 | .551 |
| | Hotelling's Trace | 1.228 | 42.468[b] | 7.000 | 242.000 | .000 | .551 |
| | Roy's Largest Root | 1.228 | 42.468[b] | 7.000 | 242.000 | .000 | .551 |

a. Design: Intercept + MF

b. Exact statistic

The results of the analysis indicating Wilks Lambda and F value for the intercept and model indicate a significant difference between the sexes male and female.

### Factor Analysis Using SPSS (Correlation Matrix and Pca Extraction)

We shall consider the seven traits namely Bill length, Head width, neck length, body length, shank length, web width and breast circumference. The same data as shown in Fig 14.1.

Descriptive Statistics

| | Mean | Std. Deviation | Analysis N |
|---|---|---|---|
| BILLLENGTH | 6.078400 | .4075757 | 250 |
| HEADWIDTH | 2.123200 | .1616362 | 250 |
| NECKLENGTH | 18.032000 | 1.4838948 | 250 |
| BODYLENGTH | 24.854800 | 1.5512649 | 250 |
| SHANKLENGTH | 4.831200 | .4746448 | 250 |
| WEBWIDTH | 5.396000 | .4890611 | 250 |
| BREASTCIRCUM | 28.604800 | 1.4072307 | 250 |

Correlation Matrix

| | | Bill Length | Head Width | Neck Length | Body Length |
|---|---|---|---|---|---|
| Correlation | BILLLENGTH | 1.000 | .232 | .505 | .573 |
| | HEADWIDTH | .232 | 1.000 | .186 | .255 |
| | NECKLENGTH | .505 | .186 | 1.000 | .211 |
| | BODYLENGTH | .573 | .255 | .211 | 1.000 |
| | SHANKLENGTH | .297 | .140 | .091 | .379 |
| | WEBWIDTH | .396 | .096 | .172 | .449 |
| | BREASTCIRCUM | .548 | .266 | .334 | .510 |

Correlation Matrix

| | | SHANK LENGTH | WEB WIDTH | BREAST CIRCUM |
|---|---|---|---|---|
| Correlation | BILLLENGTH | .297 | .396 | .548 |
| | HEADWIDTH | .140 | .096 | .266 |
| | NECKLENGTH | .091 | .172 | .334 |
| | BODYLENGTH | .379 | .449 | .510 |
| | SHANKLENGTH | 1.000 | .448 | .259 |
| | WEBWIDTH | .448 | 1.000 | .343 |
| | BREASTCIRCUM | .259 | .343 | 1.000 |

- Several correlation values above 0.3 is indicative of an ideal data for dimension reduction

KMO and Bartlett's Test

| | | |
|---|---|---|
| Kaiser-Meyer-Olkin Measure of Sampling Adequacy. | | .788 |
| Bartlett's Test of Sphericity | Approx. Chi-Square | 447.818 |
| | df | 21 |
| | Sig. | .000 |

- KMO value is high, but significant rejection of Bartlett's test with low P-value indicates that we can proceed further

Communalities

| | Initial | Extraction |
|---|---|---|
| BILLLENGTH | 1.000 | .709 |
| HEADWIDTH | 1.000 | .292 |
| NECKLENGTH | 1.000 | .615 |
| BODYLENGTH | 1.000 | .628 |
| SHANKLENGTH | 1.000 | .644 |
| WEBWIDTH | 1.000 | .648 |
| BREASTCIRCUM | 1.000 | .581 |

Extraction Method: Principal Component Analysis.

- Higher values of communality indicate more contribution of the particular variable (similar to $R^2$)

Total Variance Explained by the components

| Component | Initial Eigenvalues | | | Extraction Sums of Squared Loadings | |
|---|---|---|---|---|---|
| | **Total** | **% of Variance** | **Cumulative %** | **Total** | **% of Variance** |
| 1 | 3.012 | 43.031 | 43.031 | 3.012 | 43.031 |
| 2 | 1.106 | 15.797 | 58.827 | 1.106 | 15.797 |
| 3 | .880 | 12.578 | 71.406 | | |
| 4 | .674 | 9.631 | 81.036 | | |
| 5 | .524 | 7.490 | 88.527 | | |
| 6 | .474 | 6.767 | 95.294 | | |
| 7 | .329 | 4.706 | 100.000 | | |

- There were two components extracted with eigen value above one. This is also evident from the screeplot and the total variance explained by these two components are 58.827 percent

Total Variance Explained

| Component | Extraction Sums of Squared Loadings | Rotation Sums of Squared Loadings | | |
|---|---|---|---|---|
| | **Cumulative %** | **Total** | **% of Variance** | **Cumulative %** |
| 1 | 43.031 | 2.060 | 29.433 | 29.433 |
| 2 | 58.827 | 2.058 | 29.394 | 58.827 |

Extraction Method: Principal Component Analysis.

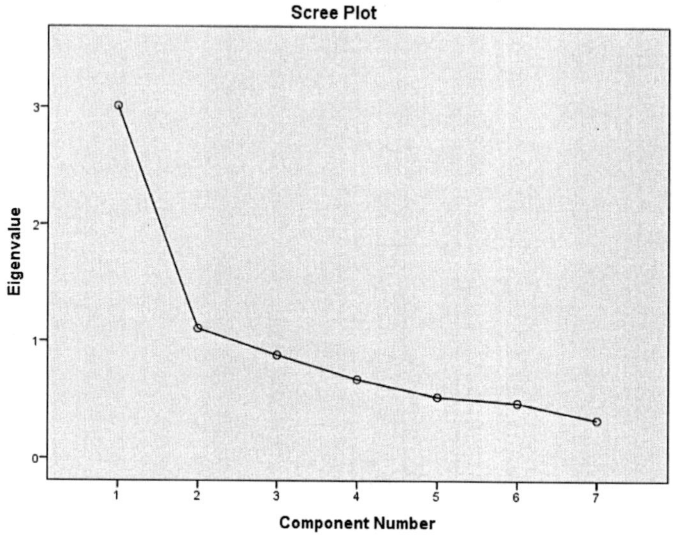


Component Matrix[a]

| | Component | |
|---|---|---|
| | 1 | 2 |
| BILLLENGTH | .816 | .210 |
| HEADWIDTH | .410 | .352 |
| NECKLENGTH | .529 | .579 |
| BODYLENGTH | .779 | -.145 |
| SHANKLENGTH | .561 | -.574 |
| WEBWIDTH | .651 | -.474 |
| BREASTCIRCUM | .744 | .163 |

Extraction Method: Principal Component Analysis.[a]

- The components matrix indicates the contribution of individual variables with the two components extracted. The component values change with better dimensions after rotation as given below

Rotated Component Matrix[a]

| | Component | |
|---|---|---|
| | 1 | 2 |
| BILLLENGTH | .725 | .428 |
| HEADWIDTH | .539 | .040 |
| NECKLENGTH | .783 | -.036 |
| BODYLENGTH | .449 | .653 |
| SHANKLENGTH | -.009 | .802 |

| | | |
|---|---|---|
| WEBWIDTH | .126 | .795 |
| BREASTCIRCUM | .642 | .410 |

Component Transformation Matrix

| Component | 1 | 2 |
|---|---|---|
| 1 | .708 | .707 |
| 2 | .707 | -.708 |

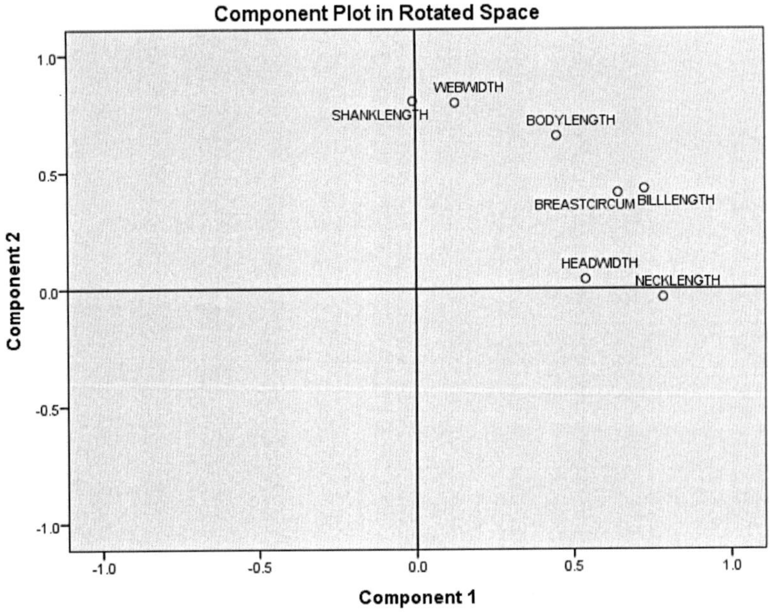


- The factor scores option saves the factor scores for the number of components extracted.

## Discriminant Analysis using SPSS

Example:

For the same data on the morphology of ducks (Figure 14.1) let us consider a discriminant analysis with sex as the dependent variable with two outcomes. The independent variables included were Bill length, Head width, neck length, body length, shank length, web width and breast circumference.

## Discriminant analysis tests the following hypotheses

H0: The group means for male and female groups are equal.

Against

H1: The group means for male and female groups are not equal

This group means is referred to as a ***centroid.***

Group Statistics for the two sexes

| MF | | Mean | Std. Deviation | Valid N (listwise) | |
|---|---|---|---|---|---|
| | | | | Un-weighted | Weighted |
| 1.0000 | BILLLENGTH | 6.315652 | .3414600 | 115 | 115.000 |
| | HEADWIDTH | 2.166957 | .1548750 | 115 | 115.000 |
| | NECKLENGTH | 19.125217 | 1.0947116 | 115 | 115.000 |
| | BODYLENGTH | 25.429565 | 1.5508330 | 115 | 115.000 |
| | SHANKLENGTH | 4.946957 | .4847357 | 115 | 115.000 |
| | WEBWIDTH | 5.576522 | .5073720 | 115 | 115.000 |
| | BREASTCIRCUM | 29.209565 | 1.2437898 | 115 | 115.000 |
| 2.000 | BILLLENGTH | 5.876296 | .3464548 | 135 | 135.000 |
| | HEADWIDTH | 2.085926 | .1584265 | 135 | 135.000 |
| | NECKLENGTH | 17.100741 | 1.0829407 | 135 | 135.000 |
| | BODYLENGTH | 24.365185 | 1.3785845 | 135 | 135.000 |
| | SHANKLENGTH | 4.732593 | .4443391 | 135 | 135.000 |
| | WEBWIDTH | 5.242222 | .4167154 | 135 | 135.000 |
| | BREASTCIRCUM | 28.089630 | 1.3350764 | 135 | 135.000 |

Tests of Equality of Group Means (F test for individual variables)

| | Wilks' Lambda | F | df1 | df2 | Sig. |
|---|---|---|---|---|---|
| BILLLENGTH | .710 | 101.201 | 1 | 248 | .000 |
| HEADWIDTH | .937 | 16.583 | 1 | 248 | .000 |
| NECKLENGTH | .536 | 214.865 | 1 | 248 | .000 |
| BODYLENGTH | .883 | 32.992 | 1 | 248 | .000 |
| SHANKLENGTH | .949 | 13.292 | 1 | 248 | .000 |
| WEBWIDTH | .883 | 32.711 | 1 | 248 | .000 |
| BREASTCIRCUM | .842 | 46.523 | 1 | 248 | .000 |

## Box's Test of Equality of Covariance Matrices

Test Results

| Box's M | | 40.198 |
|---|---|---|
| F | Approx. | 1.392 |
| | df1 | 28 |
| | df2 | 203298.605 |
| | Sig. | .081 |

- The Box's test tests the Null hypothesis: The covariance and variance matrix formed by the dependent variables should not differ between the groups.The test results should be non-signficant. We can continue with the discriminant function analysis as the hypothesis of equal variance-covariance matrix is accepted. If the group log determinants (also available in the results, not presented here) are similar, then a significant Box's M can also be ignored.

## Summary of Canonical Discriminant Functions

Eigenvalues

| Function | Eigenvalue | % of Variance | Cumulative % | Canonical Correlation |
|---|---|---|---|---|
| 1 | 1.228[a] | 100.0 | 100.0 | .742 |

a. First 1 canonical discriminant function was used in the analysis.

Wilks' Lambda

| Test of Function(s) | Wilks' Lambda | Chi-square | df | Sig. |
|---|---|---|---|---|
| 1 | .449 | 195.915 | 7 | .000 |

The discriminant function is tested using the Wilks' lambda and in this case is highly significant and thus the variables can discriminate between male and female.

- **Wilks' Lambda** indicates the significance of discriminant function. Sometimes also called the *U* statistic. Its value varies between 0 and 1. Large values of λ (near 1) indicate that group means do not seem to be different. Small values of λ (near 0) indicate that the group means seem to be different.
- It is used to measure how well each function separates cases into groups. It also indicates the significance of the discriminant function and **provides the proportion of total variability not explained.**

## Canonical Discriminant Function Coefficients

- The canonical correlation is the multiple correlation between the predictors and the discriminant function.
- For eg. 0.786 is the R square then 68.2 %.
- When it is large, we can say high correlation between the discriminant functions and the groups.
- The unstandardised canonical discriminant function given below in table is used to create the discriminant function equation.
- D = 0.654 X1 +.975 X2 +.....

| Unstandardised Canonical Discriminant Function Coefficients | Function |
|---|---|
| | 1 |
| BILLLENGTH | .654 |
| HEADWIDTH | .975 |
| NECKLENGTH | .744 |
| BODYLENGTH | .037 |
| SHANKLENGTH | .165 |
| WEBWIDTH | .573 |
| BREASTCIRCUM | .068 |
| (Constant) | -26.216 |

## Standardized Canonical Discriminant Function Coefficients

Discriminator variables on which more groups differ and on which the more groups differ receive the more weight, these weights are referred to as discriminate coefficient.

It determines the degree to which each discriminator variable is associated with differences among the group.

The sign indicates the direction of the relationship.

| Standardised Canonical Discriminant Function Coefficients | Function |
|---|---|
| | 1 |
| BILLLENGTH | .225 |
| HEADWIDTH | .153 |
| NECKLENGTH | .810 |
| BODYLENGTH | .054 |
| SHANKLENGTH | .076 |
| WEBWIDTH | .264 |
| BREASTCIRCUM | .088 |

## Structure Matrix

- Another way of indicating the relative importance of the predictors.
- Identify the largest loadings for each discriminant function.
- 0.30 is the cut off between important and less important variables.

| | Function |
|---|---|
| | 1 |
| NECKLENGTH | .840 |
| BILLLENGTH | .576 |
| BREASTCIRCUM | .391 |

| | |
|---|---|
| BODYLENGTH | .329 |
| WEBWIDTH | .328 |
| HEADWIDTH | .233 |
| SHANKLENGTH | .209 |

Functions at Group Centroids

| Group | Function |
|---|---|
| | 1 |
| 1.0000 | 1.196 |
| 2.0000 | -1.019 |

## Classification Statistics

Prior Probabilities for Groups

| **MF** | **Prior** | **Cases Used in Analysis** | |
|---|---|---|---|
| | | **Unweighted** | **Weighted** |
| 1.0000 | .500 | 115 | 115.000 |
| 2.0000 | .500 | 135 | 135.000 |
| Total | 1.000 | 250 | 250.000 |

**Classification Function Coefficients** (Fisher's linear discriminant functions)

| | MF | |
|---|---|---|
| | 1.0000 | 2.0000 |
| BILLLENGTH | 7.177 | 5.729 |
| HEADWIDTH | 58.315 | 56.155 |
| NECKLENGTH | 15.244 | 13.596 |
| BODYLENGTH | 3.861 | 3.779 |
| SHANKLENGTH | 8.648 | 8.283 |
| WEBWIDTH | 12.539 | 11.269 |
| BREASTCIRCUM | 10.553 | 10.403 |
| (Constant) | -491.889 | -433.627 |

The Classification function **Coefficients of Linear Discriminant Function** table interprets the Fisher's theory, and have following form

$$C_k = C_{k0} + C_{k1} X_1 + C_{k2} X_2 + ... + C_{km} X_m$$

where

$C_k$ is the classification score for group k

C's are the coefficients in table

For one observation, we can compute it's score for each group by the coefficients according to equation. The observation should be assigned the group with highest score. In addition, the coefficients are helpful in deciding which variable affects more in classification. Comparing the values between groups, the higher coefficient means the variable attributes more for that group.

Classification Results[a]

| | | MF | Predicted Group Membership | | Total |
|---|---|---|---|---|---|
| | | | 1.0000 | 2.0000 | |
| Original | Count | 1.0000 | 104 | 11 | 115 |
| | | 2.0000 | 19 | 116 | 135 |
| | % | 1.0000 | 90.4 | 9.6 | 100.0 |
| | | 2.0000 | 14.1 | 85.9 | 100.0 |

a. 88.0% of original grouped cases correctly classified.

- Thus based on the six variables the discriminant function helps in assigning the birds to different sexes, male or female.

# 15

# Software for Animal Breeding Data Analyses

The large volume, type and nature of animal breeding data and the complex nature of analytical requirement warrants additional tools for handling, storage, retrieval and solving complex equations. Accuracy, speed, computational requirement, applicability, etc., has resulted in the development of numerous software exclusive for animal breeding data analysis. The database management system is already explained in the chapter on 'Nature of animal breeding data and database management'. This chapter gives a note on the commonly used animal breeding software.

It is important to get acquainted with at least one database system for effective animal breeding analysis. Different software have been developed for unique objectives, including estimation of variance components, correction of fixed factors, formation of the numerator relationship matrix, pruning of pedigree, renumbering for uniform meaningful identification of animals, estimation of breeding value using BLUP and several other functions. Similarly, the method of estimation in different software or the algorithms used may vary and thus before using any software, it is important to understand the principles of animal breeding as most of the software will give a result irrespective of the type of inputs given. In order to ascertain that the software is being used for the right analysis, it is better to test it using a solved example from the textbook. For eg. the Nicholas (1982) BLUP example could be run using the WOMBAT BLUP option so as to know that we are using the software in the right manner. Therefore, users must look for features that would suit their individual circumstances before choosing software.

- Availability: Free availability of the software package. However, the paid ones have some advantages and could be made available through Institutional funds.
- Installation at the right machine and platform: Suitability of the environment where package work and availability. Working in UNIX is advantageous but many of us are more conversant with WINDOWS.
- Good user manual with theoretical inputs and step-wise guide to analyzing the data.
- Guidance or easy contact with developers or alternate sources for usage

and troubleshooting.

- Suitability of data including the nature of data and format of datafiles available.
- Database management system in use for storage and retrieval of data.
- Type of analyses to be carried out

## Animal Breeding Software

**Miztal (1994)** has reviewed various software used in Animal Breeding. **Harvey (1990)** has been one of the widely used software in animal breeding. There are 8 models and the analyses include fixed models, random models, mixed models, BLUP analysis and estimation of variance components by least squares, maximum likelihood and REML. The software requires a data and control file (the parameter file) with the necessary input commands and the output is obtained in the name as required by the user. Harvey, (1990), was a forerunner of all the present-day programs in animal breeding. However, being limited to the sire model and its inefficiency to support either the animal model or REML, is now outdated, but still in use at many places, where half-sib analysis is preferred. The degrees of freedom for the random effect, which is the main requirement for any breeder was too less to complete breeding analysis for large populations.

**WOMBAT and DFREML**: It is a free alternative to ASReml, written by Karen Meyer (2007). It can be downloaded via http://agbu.une.edu.au/~kmeyer/wombat.html. 32-bit and 64-bit Linux and windows executables are capable of analyzing complex models and large amounts of data. It is one of the most widely used animal breeding software for REML analysis of quantitative data. The software requires a data file, parameter file and pedigree file as input and several outputs in the form of pedigree information, variance components, fixed effects, numerator relationship matrix inverse and others are available. A manual covering all the basics as well as a number of more advanced options can be downloaded at http://agbu.une.edu.au/~kmeyer/download.php?file=WombatManual.pdf. Additional information related to running WOMBAT and REML estimation, in general, can also be found at the WOMBAT Wiki (http://agbu.une.edu.au/~kmeyer/dokuwiki/doku.php). Several models including the random regression models and qtl analysis are possible with this software. WOMBAT has replaced the earlier version of **DFREML** by Meyer (1988) which had different executables to run the univariate, multivariate and random regression models. This program was extensively used and became a gold standard in the 1990s till 2005. It used the likelihood ratio test to compare the significance of the variance components used in the model. It supported 10 models that also included complex random regression.

**MTDFREML**: Boldman *et al.* (1993) developed the Multiple Trait Derivative-Free Restricted Maximum Likelihood, denoted as MTDFREML, is a set of programs to estimate (co)variance components using animal models and derivative-free REML. It is a more general program and very easy to run, modify and interpret. These programs can be used for single trait, bivariate, and multiple trait animal models with repeated records including traits with sex limited expression. However, the program lacks some of the features like random regression.

**PEST and VCE:** (Prediction and Estimation) written by Groeneveld *et al.* (1994). Pest can give treatment of missing values and accommodate different incidence matrices for some or all traits, any number of fixed and random effects, any number of covariables, polynomials up to order 20, the inclusion of relationship among animals, treatment of inbreeding, genetic group models, heterogeneous variances, dumping of old solutions to be used for presetting the solutions vector for following runs as required in routine prediction of breeding values, Prediction error variances for BLUPs and standard errors of BLUEs. PEST accepts input data in a variety of formats, and is easier to use than other packages. VCE is a variance component program by Groeneveld that can be used standalone but works best with PEST for data preparation. VCE is modified and compiled for every model and data by a Unix script.

**MTGSAM**: For non-Guassian distributions, the Gibbs sampling Animal model is programmed by Van Tassell and Van Vleck (1995). Thet ability of this software is it can fit the priors to the probability to generate a posterior probability distribution function. Programs have been developed to implement the Gibbs sampling (GS) algorithm for Bayesian analysis of a broad range of animal models. The software can be downloaded at http://aipl.arsusda.gov/curtvt/mtgsam.html. The Threshold version of the MTGSAM program can be obtained at http://aipl.arsusda.gov/curtvt/thresh.html.

**ASREML:** ASReml is a very powerful statistical software developed by Arthur Gilmour in 1996 (Gilmour, 2006). It is specifically designed for fitting mixed models for large datasets, with unmatched model flexibility and high speed. ASReml's manual, provides details of usage in detail. This package is most suitable for the estimation of genetic parameters in animal breeding data for a wide variety of models. ASReml is a commercial product and it can be only used only on purchase (http://uncronopio.org/ASReml/ObtainingASReml). This software has the provision to run binary traits using appropriate link functions.

**DMU**: Developed by Jensen (1997) is also a Derivative free MUltivariate analysis algorithm based software. DMU includes a variance component program called DMUAI (based on ideas of R.) that uses Newton-Raphson maximization.

**MCMCglmm: It** is an R package for Bayesian mixed model analysis written by Jarrod Hadfield. It is free and distributed through CRAN (http://cran.r-project.org/). Information about the package, together with a user manual and vignettes are available at http://cran.r-project.org/web/packages/MCMCglmm/index.html. Users of both MCMCglmm and ASReml-R will require an up to date installation of the statistical package R (obtained http://cran.r-project.org/).

**BLUPF90 Family of Programs:** The BLUPF90 family of programs is a collection of free software in Fortran 90/95 developed by Ignacy Miztal

(http://nce.ads.uga.edu/wiki/doku.php?id=application_programs). The programs support mixed models with multiple-correlated effects, multiple animal models and dominance. The programs can do data and parameter file setting, estimate variances and calculate BLUP for very large data sets using REML and Bayesian Gibb's sampling. User manual can be downloaded (http://nce.ads.uga.edu/wiki/lib/exe/fetch.php?media=blupf90_all4.pdf). Masuda (2019) has explained the use of the BLUPF90 suite of programs through an Introductory manual.

**Pedigree Viewer:** A very user-friendly software developed by Brian and Sandy Kinghorn (2009) and several versions starting from 5.5 to 6.5f have evolved with new features coming in. The program displays the full pedigree on the screen. It can also be used to renumber the character fields in a pedigree file. The CSV file with new animal, sire and dam ids could be exported for use in further analysis. The software also has tools to estimate the inbreeding coefficient, coancestry and breeding value (BLUP). The 'matesel' option also helps in identifying the mate for breeding.

**ENDOG Ver. 3.0**: An useful program (Gutierrez and Goyache, 2005) to study the genetic variability in a population through pedigree analysis based on various parameters including (a) the individual inbreeding and average relatedness coefficients; (b) effective population size; (c) parameters characterizing the concentration of both gene and individuals origin such as the effective number of founders and ancestors, the effective number of founder herds; (d) F statistics and paired genetic distances for each subpopulation under study; (e) descriptors of the genetic importance of the herds in a population and (f) generation intervals. The program will help breeders and researchers to monitor the changes in genetic variability and population structure with limited costs of preparing datasets. The program, user's guide and example file can be downloaded free of charge from the World Wide Web at http://www.ucm.es/info/prodanim/Endog30.zip.

There are many software packages available for data analysis in animal breeding. The software explained above is only a list of commonly used ones and is not exhaustive. These have evolved as per the demand of the data structure, type of analysis, traits available, prior information availability, nature of the trait, statistical tools available, programming language evolution, computing facility and revolution in the IT industry. However, as far as the analysis of data for the purpose of obtaining genetic parameter estimates and breeding value of animals is concerned, all the packages are equivalent as far as output is concerned. The users may choose a suitable software package depending on their needs and switching of software may be done only for additional tools not available in the conversant package.

# Appendix

# Format for Registers to be Maintained in Different Livestock Species

## Cattle and Buffalo

**Daily Livestock Account Register (Separate Pages for Each Breed Every Month)**

Year :      Month :      Breed :

| Date | Opening Stock | | | | | | | | Total | Death | | | | Disposal / Transfers | | | | Sales | | | | Closing Balance | | | | Total | Re-mar-ks |
|---|---|---|---|---|---|---|---|---|---|---|---|---|---|---|---|---|---|---|---|---|---|---|---|---|---|---|---|
| | M | F | M | F | M | F | M | F | | M | F | M | F | M | F | M | F | M | F | M | F | M | F | M | F | | |
| | | | | | | | | | | | | | | | | | | | | | | | | | | | |
| | | | | | | | | | | | | | | | | | | | | | | | | | | | |

**Birth Register**

| S. No. | Breed | Tattoo No. | Sex | Colour | Date of Birth | Sire No. | Dam No. | Weight at Birth (kg) | Weaning Weight (Kg) | Remarks |
|---|---|---|---|---|---|---|---|---|---|---|
| | | | | | | | | | | |
| | | | | | | | | | | |

**Breeding Register**

| S. No. | Species / Breed | Tag No. | Date of Calv-ing | Date of A.I | | | Date of P.D | | State of Pregnancy | Expected date of calving | Date of Drying | Cal-ved on | Wei-ght of Calf | Sex of Calf | Remarks |
|---|---|---|---|---|---|---|---|---|---|---|---|---|---|---|---|
| | | | | 1st | 2nd | 3rd | 1st | 2nd | | | | | | | |
| | | | | | | | | | | | | | | | |
| | | | | | | | | | | | | | | | |

Treatment Register

| S. No. | Date | Breed & Species | Tag No. | History | Diagnosis | Treatment | Remarks |
|---|---|---|---|---|---|---|---|
| | | | | | | | |
| | | | | | | | |

Vaccination Register

| S. No. | Date | Name of Vaccination | Details of Vaccine | No. of animals vacci-nated | Route of Vaccine and Dose Rate | Next due date | Remarks |
|---|---|---|---|---|---|---|---|
| | | | | | | | |
| | | | | | | | |

| Deworming Register | | | | | | | | |
|---|---|---|---|---|---|---|---|---|
| S.No. | Date of Deworming | Name of the Medicine | Details of Medicine | No. of animals de-wormed | Route of Administration and Dose rate | Next due date | If any reaction | Remarks |
| | | | | | | | | |
| | | | | | | | | |

| Death and Disposal Register | | | | | | | | | | | | |
|---|---|---|---|---|---|---|---|---|---|---|---|---|
| Sl. No. | Animal Number | Breed | Date of Birth | Sex | Colour | Died / Sold | Cause of Death / Mode of Disposal | Date of Death / Sales | Book Value | P.M. Number | Body Weight (Kg) | Remarks |
| | | | | | | | | | | | | |
| | | | | | | | | | | | | |

| Milk Recording Register | | | | | | | | | | | | | | | | | | | | | | | | | | | | | | | | | | | | | | | | | | |
|---|---|---|---|---|---|---|---|---|---|---|---|---|---|---|---|---|---|---|---|---|---|---|---|---|---|---|---|---|---|---|---|---|---|---|---|---|---|---|---|---|---|---|
| S. No. | Cow No. | Date of Calving | Daily Milk Yield | | | | | | | | | | | | | | | | | | | | | | | | | | | | | | | | Total | | | | Progressive Total | | | Remarks |
| | | | | 1 | 2 | 3 | 4 | 5 | 6 | 7 | 8 | 9 | 10 | 11 | 12 | 13 | 14 | 15 | 16 | 17 | 18 | 19 | 20 | 21 | 22 | 23 | 24 | 25 | 26 | 27 | 28 | 29 | 30 | 31 | Days in Milk | Milk Yield (kg) | Daily average | Peak Yield | Days in milk | Milk Yield (Kg) | Peak Yield | |
| | | | M | | | | | | | | | | | | | | | | | | | | | | | | | | | | | | | | | | | | | | | |
| | | | E | | | | | | | | | | | | | | | | | | | | | | | | | | | | | | | | | | | | | | | |

**Weighment Register**

| S. No. | Animal Number | DOB | Birth Weight | Monthly Weight in (Kg) | | | | | | | | | | | | | | Remarks |
|---|---|---|---|---|---|---|---|---|---|---|---|---|---|---|---|---|---|---|
| | | | | 1st Month wt. | 2nd Month wt. | 3rd Month wt. | 4th Month wt. | 5th Month wt. | 6th Month wt. | 7th Month wt. | 8th Month wt. | 9th Month wt. | 10th Month wt. | 11th Month wt. | 12th Month wt. | 15th Month wt. | 18th Month wt. | |
| | | | | | | | | | | | | | | | | | | |
| | | | | | | | | | | | | | | | | | | |

# Cow Card

| Cattle / Buffalo Breed | |
|---|---|
| Number | |
| Name | |
| Herd Book No. | |
| Identification Mark | |
| Date of Birth | Place of Birth |
| Date of Purchase | Age |
| Purchased from | |
| Price | Age of Disposal |
| Disposal | |

| Incubated on | | | | | | | |
|---|---|---|---|---|---|---|---|
| Against | | | | | | | |
| At | | | | | | | |
| By | | | | | | | |

| Sire of Cow | Sire of Sire |
|---|---|
| Breed | Dam of Sire |
| Herd Book No. | |
| Sire Index | |
| Dam and Breed | Sire of Dam |
| Herd Book No. | Dam of Dam |

Dam of Cow

Dam of Cow – Lactation Details

| Order of Lactation | I | II | III | IV | V | VI |
|---|---|---|---|---|---|---|
| Milk Yield (Kg) | | | | | | |
| Days in Milk | | | | | | |
| Days Dry | | | | | | |
| 305 days yield (kg) | | | | | | |

**Veterinary History**

| Disease | Age | Period | | Treatment and Result |
|---|---|---|---|---|
| | | From | To | |
| | | | | |

| Calving | | Calf | | | Lactation record | | | | | | | Average Milk Yield per Day (kg) | | Peak Yield | | Half yearly weights and at each service | |
|---|---|---|---|---|---|---|---|---|---|---|---|---|---|---|---|---|---|
| Order | Date | Sex | Number | Disposal | Days in milk | Milk yield (kg) | Milk yield first 180 days (kg) | Milk yield first 305 days (kg) | Average fat % | Date of dry | Days Dry | Duration lactation | From calving to calving | Kilogram | Date | Date of weighing (kg) | Weight (kg) |
| | | | | | | | | | | | | | | | | | |
| | | | | | | | | | | | | | | | | | |
| | | | | | | | | | | | | | | | | | |
| | | | | | | | | | | | | | | | | | |
| | | | | | | | | | | | | | | | | | |
| | | | | | | | | | | | | | | | | | |
| | | | | | | | | | | | | | | | | | |
| | | | | | | | | | | | | | | | | | |
| | | | | | | | | | | | | | | | | | |
| | | | | | | | | | | | | | | | | | |
| | | | | | | | | | | | | | | | | | |
| | | | | | | | | | | | | | | | | | |
| | | | | | | | | | | | | | | | | | |
| | | | | | | | | | | | | | | | | | |
| | | | | | | | | | | | | | | | | | |
| | | | | | | | | | | | | | | | | | |
| | | | | | | | | | | | | | | | | | |
| | | | | | | | | | | | | | | | | | |
| | | | | | | | | | | | | | | | | | |
| | | | | | | | | | | | | | | | | | |
| | | | | | | | | | | | | | | | | | |

All the details regarding a breeding cow maintained in the farm can be recorded in the form of cow card

## Sheep and Goat

| Daily Stock Register | | | | | | | | | | | | | | | | | | | |
|---|---|---|---|---|---|---|---|---|---|---|---|---|---|---|---|---|---|---|---|
| Year : | | | | | | | | | | Month : | | | | | | | | | |
| Dates | Opening Stock | | | | | | Total | | Grand Total | Birth | | Breeding Sale | | | | Slaughter Sale | | | |
| | Adult | | Grower | | Suckling | | | | | | | Adult | | Grower | | Adult | | Grower | |
| | M | F | M | F | M | F | M | F | | M | F | M | F | M | F | M | F | M | F |
| | | | | | | | | | | | | | | | | | | | |

| Birth Register | | | | | | | | | | |
|---|---|---|---|---|---|---|---|---|---|---|
| S. No. | Breed | Tattoo No. | Sex | Colour | Date of Birth | Sire No. | Dam No. | Weight Birth (Kg) | Weaning Weight (Kg) | Remarks |
| | | | | | | | | | | |

| Young Stock Register | | | | | |
|---|---|---|---|---|---|
| Year : | | | | | |
| S. No. | Tag No. | Date of Birth | Sire No. | Dam No. | Remarks |
| | | | | | |

| Mating Register | | | | | | | | | | | | |
|---|---|---|---|---|---|---|---|---|---|---|---|---|
| S. No. | Animal Number | Date of Birth | Bred | Date of Matting | Ram / Buck Number | Date of Second matting (if applicable) | Ram / Buck Number | Date of lambing / kidding | Sex of the lamb / kid | Type of lambing / kidding | Tag number of the lamb / kid | Remarks |
| | | | | | | | | | | | | |

**Treatment Register**

| S.No. | Date | Breed & Species | Tag No. | History | Diagnosis | Treatment | Remarks |
|---|---|---|---|---|---|---|---|
| | | | | | | | |

**vaccination Register**

| S.No. | Date | Name of Vaccination | Details of Vaccine | No. of Animals Vaccinated | Route of Vaccine and Dose Rate | Next due date | Remarks |
|---|---|---|---|---|---|---|---|
| | | | | | | | |

**Deworming Register**

| S.No. | Date of Deworming | Name of the Medicine | Details of Medicine | No. of animals dewormed | Route of Administration and Dose rate | Next Due Date | If any reaction | Remarks |
|---|---|---|---|---|---|---|---|---|
| | | | | | | | | |

**Death and Disposal Register**

| S.No. | Animal Number | Breed | Date of Birth | Sex | Colour | Died / Sold | Cause of Death / Mode of Disposal | Date of Death | Date of Sales | Book Value | P.M. Number | Body Weight (Kg) | Remarks |
|---|---|---|---|---|---|---|---|---|---|---|---|---|---|
| | | | | | | | | | | | | | |

### Weighment Register

| S. No. | Animal Number | DOB | Birth Weight | 1st Month wt. | 2nd Month wt. | 3rd Month wt. | 4th Month wt. | 5th Month wt. | 6th Month wt. | 7th Month wt. | 8th Month wt. | 9th Month wt. | 10th Month wt. | 11th Month wt. | 12th Month wt. | 15th Month wt. | 18th Month wt. | Remarks |
|---|---|---|---|---|---|---|---|---|---|---|---|---|---|---|---|---|---|---|
| | | | | | | | | | | | | | | | | | | |

**Pig**

### Daily Stock Register (1st page)

| Year: | | | | | | | | | | | | | | | | Month: | | | |
|---|---|---|---|---|---|---|---|---|---|---|---|---|---|---|---|---|---|---|---|
| Date | Opening Stock | | | | | | Total | | Grand total | Birth | | Breeding sale | | | | Slaughter sale | | | |
| | Adult | | Grower | | Suckling | | | | | | | Adult | | Grower | | Adult | | Grower | |
| | M | F | M | F | M | F | M | F | | M | F | M | F | M | F | M | F | M | F |
| | | | | | | | | | | | | | | | | | | | |

### Daily Stock Register (2nd page)

| Year: | | | | | | | | | | | | Month: | | | | | | | | |
|---|---|---|---|---|---|---|---|---|---|---|---|---|---|---|---|---|---|---|---|---|
| Death | | | | | | Internal Transfer | | | | | | Closing Balance | | | | | | Total | | Grand total |
| Adult | | Grower | | Suckling | | Adult | | Grower | | Suckling | | Adult | | Grower | | Suckling | | | | |
| M | F | M | F | M | F | M | F | M | F | M | F | M | F | M | F | M | F | M | F | |
| | | | | | | | | | | | | | | | | | | | | |

### Birth Register

| S.No | Breed | Tattoo No | Sex | Colour | Date of birth | Sire No. | Dam No. | Weight birth (Kg) | Weaning Weight (Kg) | Remarks |
|---|---|---|---|---|---|---|---|---|---|---|
| | | | | | | | | | | |

| Adult Stock Register | | | | | |
|---|---|---|---|---|---|
| Year: | | | | | |
| S.No | Tag No. | Date of Birth | Sire No. | Dam No. | Remarks |
| | | | | | |

| Young Stock Register | | | | | |
|---|---|---|---|---|---|
| Year: | | | | | |
| S.No | Tag No. | Date of Birth | Sire No. | Dam No. | Remarks |
| | | | | | |

| Mating Register | | | | | | | | | | | |
|---|---|---|---|---|---|---|---|---|---|---|---|
| S. No | Animal Number | Date of birth | Breed | Date of mating | Boar Number | Date of second mating (if applicable) | Boar Number | Date of farrowing | Sex of the piglet | Litter Size | Remarks |
| | | | | | | | | | | | |

| Treatment Register | | | | | | | |
|---|---|---|---|---|---|---|---|
| S.No | Date | Breed & Species | Tag No | History | Diagnosis | Treatment | Remarks |
| | | | | | | | |

| Vaccination Register | | | | | | | |
|---|---|---|---|---|---|---|---|
| S.No | Date | Name of Vaccination | Details of vaccine | No of animal vaccinated | Route of Vaccine and Dose Rate | Next Due Date | Remarks |
| | | | | | | | |

| Deworming Register | | | | | | | | |
|---|---|---|---|---|---|---|---|---|
| S.No | Date of Deworming | Name of Medicine | Details of Medicine | No of animals dewormed | Route of Administration and dose rate | Next Due Date | If any reaction | Remarks |
| | | | | | | | | |

| Death And Disposal Register | | | | | | | | | | | | |
|---|---|---|---|---|---|---|---|---|---|---|---|---|
| S.No | Animal Number | Breed | Date of Birth | Sex | Colour | Died / Sold | Cause of death | Date of sale | Book value | P.M. Number | Body weight (kg) | Remarks |
| | | | | | | | | | | | | |

| Death And Disposal Register | | | | | | | | | | | | | | | | | | |
|---|---|---|---|---|---|---|---|---|---|---|---|---|---|---|---|---|---|---|
| S. No | Animal No | Date of Birth | Body weight | 1st month wt | 2nd month wt | 3rd month wt | 4th month wt | 5th month wt | 6th month wt | 7th month wt | 8th month wt | 9th month wt | 10th month wt | 11th month wt | 12th month wt | 15th month wt | 18th month wt | Remarks |
| | | | | | | | | | | | | | | | | | | |

**Rabbit**

| Breeding Register | | | | | | | | |
|---|---|---|---|---|---|---|---|---|
| Animal number | Date | | Number of kindlings completed | Date of last kindling | Buck assigned | Date of service | Date of kindling | Remarks |
| | Birth | First kindling | | | | | | |
| | | | | | | | | |

**Birth / Kindling Register**

| Animal number | Date | | Litter performance | | | | Number allotted to the young stock | |
|---|---|---|---|---|---|---|---|---|
| | Date of mating | Date of kindling | Litter size at | | Litter weight at | | | |
| | | | Birth | Weaning | Birth | Weaning | Male | Female |
| | | | | | | | | |

**Young Stock Register**

| S.No. | Tag. No. | D.O.B. | Birth weight | Litter weight | Litter size at birth | Sire No. | Dam No. | Litter weight at weaning | Weaning weight | Remarks |
|---|---|---|---|---|---|---|---|---|---|---|
| | | | | | | | | | | |

**Grower Stock Register**

| S. No | Tag. No. | D.O.B. | Sire No. | Dam No. | Birth weight | Weaning weight | Market weight | Adult weight | Remarks |
|---|---|---|---|---|---|---|---|---|---|
| | | | | | | | | | |

**Adult Stock Register**

| S. No. | Tattoo No. | D.O.B. | Birth weight | Sire No. | Dam. No. | Remarks |
|---|---|---|---|---|---|---|
| | | | | | | |

**Daily Stock Register**

| Date | Opening balance | | | | | Birth | Internal transfer | Disposal | Death | Closing balance | Remarks |
|---|---|---|---|---|---|---|---|---|---|---|---|
| | AM | AF | YM | YF | T | | | | | | |
| | | | | | | | | | | | |

**Feed Stock Register**

| Date | Opening balance | Receipts | Total | Issue | Closing balance | Remarks |
|---|---|---|---|---|---|---|
| | | | | | | |

**Feed Efficiency Register**

| Date | Feed amount<br>Opening balance | Feed purchased | Total | Feed issued | | | | | | Total feed issued | Closing balance |
|---|---|---|---|---|---|---|---|---|---|---|---|
| | | | | Total No. of Young | Total Feed | Total No. of Grower | Total Feed | Total No. of Adult | Total Feed | | |
| | | | | | | | | | | | |

**Health / Treatment Register**

| Date | Animal number | History | Observation | Treatment | Remarks |
|---|---|---|---|---|---|
| | | | | | |
| **Deworming** | | | | | |
| Date | Deworming drug used, Cost,D.O.M./D.O.E. | Type of animals, doses used | No. of animals | Reaction if any | Remarks |

**Growth / Weighment Register**

| Tag No. | Date of birth | Dam No. | Sire No. | Birth weight | Weaning weight | $3^{rd}$ month weight | $4^{th}$ month weight | $5^{th}$ month weight | $6^{th}$ month weight | Adult weight |
|---|---|---|---|---|---|---|---|---|---|---|
| | | | | | | | | | | |

**Mortality Register**

| S.No. | Date | Tag No. | Sex | D.O.B. | D.O.D. | Age | History | PM findings | Book value | Remarks |
|---|---|---|---|---|---|---|---|---|---|---|
| | | | | | | | | | | |

**Disposal Register**

| S.No | Date | Tag No. | Sex | D.O.B. | Date of disposal | Body weight | Amount realized | Receipt No. | Mode of sale Breeding/ Meat | To whom sold |
|---|---|---|---|---|---|---|---|---|---|---|
| | | | | | | | | | | |

**Doe Performance Register**

| Animal No. | | | Date of birth | | | | Sire | | | Dam | |
|---|---|---|---|---|---|---|---|---|---|---|---|
| Breed | | | | | | Date of purchase | | | | | |
| Reproductive performance | | | | | | | | | | | |
| Age at first mating | | | Weight at first mating | | | | Age at first lambing | | | | |
| Date of mating | Age at mating (days) | Sire number | weight at mating (Kg) | Date of kindling | Weight at kindling | Number of bunnies born | Bunny number | Sex | Birth weight (Kg) | Number of bunnies weaned | Remarks |
| | | | | | | | | | | | |

| Died/ sold | Date of death/ disposal | Total number of mating | Total number of bunnies born | Total number of bunnies weaned | weight of bunnies |
|---|---|---|---|---|---|
| | | | | | |
| Remarks | | | | | |

**Buck Performance Register**

| Animal number | | Date of birth | | Sire | | Dam | |
|---|---|---|---|---|---|---|---|
| Breed | | Date of purchase | | | | | |

**Reproductive performance**

| Age At First Mating | | Weight at First Mating | |
|---|---|---|---|

| Year | Month | Number of does mated | Number of does kindled | Number of bunnies born | | Conception rate (%) | Average birth weight of bunny | | Any abnormality | Remarks |
|---|---|---|---|---|---|---|---|---|---|---|
| | | | | Male | Female | | Male | Female | | |
| | | | | | | | | | | |

| Died/ sold | Date of death/ disposal | Total number of mating | Total number of bunnies born | Total number of abnormal bunnies | | Average birth weight of bunny (g) |
|---|---|---|---|---|---|---|
| | | | | | | |
| Remarks | | | | | | |

## Poultry

**Hatchability Register**

| S. No | Date of setting | Date of hatching | Fertility | | Early embryonic mortality | | Late embryonic mortality | | No. of Weak chicks | No. of Good chicks | Total No. chicks | Hatchability % | |
|---|---|---|---|---|---|---|---|---|---|---|---|---|---|
| | | | No. | % | No. | % | No. | % | | | | Total hatchability % | Fertile hatchability % |
| | | | | | | | | | | | | | |

**EGG Stock Register**

| Date | No. of eggs in the beginning (opening balance) | No. of eggs received | Total No. Eggs | No. of eggs Kept for incubation | No. of Table eggs | No. of unwanted eggs (small and large sized eggs) | No. of broken eggs | Total Disposal | Closing balance | Remarks |
|---|---|---|---|---|---|---|---|---|---|---|
| | | | | | | | | | | |

## II. Matrices in Animal Breeding

A matrix is an array of elements and is denoted by a single upper case letter eg., A. The number of rows and number of columns constitutes the order of a matrix. A matrix of order m x n means that there are m rows and n columns as:

$a_{11}$ $a_{12}$ $a_{12}$...................a1n

$a_{21}$ $a_{22}$ $a_{23}$...................a2n

$a_{m1}$ $a_{m2}$ $a_{m3}$.................$a_{mn}$

Where, $a_{11}$, $a_{12}$, etc. are called the elements of the matrix, $a_{12}$ means that the element lies in the 1st row and 2nd column, i.e., the first subscripts indicate the row number and second subscripts indicate column number of the element. The elements in the position where m=n form the diagonal elements. Matrices have been extensively used in animal breeding and it is important to understand the basics of matrix algebra so as to understand various aspects of animal breeding analysis.

- Row Vector or Row Matrix is a matrix with a single row
- Column Vector or Column Matrix is a matrix with a single column
- Square Matrix is a matrix with an equal number of rows and columns
- A rectangular matrix is a matrix with column numbers more than the row numbers
- A symmetrical Matrix is a matrix where the upper and lower triangular elements are mirror images with the diagonal as the plane. The element $a_{mn}$ will be equal to $a_{nm}$
- Null or Zero Matrix is a matrix with only zero as elements
- Unit or Identity Matrix is a matrix of '1' and '0', with '1' in the diagonal and zeroes in the off-diagonal positions.
- A diagonal Matrix is a matrix with non-zero diagonal elements and zeroes in the off-diagonal position.
- Scalar Matrix is a diagonal matrix with same diagonal elements.
- Upper Triangular Matrix are the elements above the diagonal.
- Lower Triangular Matrix are the elements below the diagonal.
- Determinant is a scalar quantity, which is used in obtaining the elements of the inverse matrix.
- Inverse of a matrix is a matrix, the product of which with the original matrix gives Identity matrix. If A is a matrix and $A^{-1}$ the inverse, then $A*A^{-1}$ gives Identity or Unit matrix. The inverse could be obtained using the 'minv' function in excel.

For eg.

| | | | | |
|---|---|---|---|---|
| | | 4 | 3 | 5 |
| A | = | 2 | 4 | 7 |
| | | 3 | 5 | 8 |

| | | | | |
|---|---|---|---|---|
| | | 0.428571429 | -0.14286 | -0.142857143 |
| $A^{-1}$ | = | -0.714285714 | -2.42857 | 2.571428571 |
| | | 0.285714286 | 1.571429 | -1.428571429 |

| | | | | |
|---|---|---|---|---|
| | | 1 | 0 | 0 |
| $A*A^{-1}$ | = | 0 | 1 | 0 |
| | | 0 | 0 | 1 |

- Singular Matrix is a matrix with no inverse and such a matrix has a zero determinant.
- Rank of a matrix is the largest order of a matrix for which a non-zero determinant is available.
- Trace of a square matrix is the sum of the diagonal elements.

## Matrix operations

**Addition** and **Subtraction** are done between the corresponding elements of two matrices and for which the order of the two matrices to be summed must be the same.

**Multiplication** in matrices requires an important condition that the number of columns of the first matrix is to be the same as the number of rows of the second matrix. The commutative rule of AB=BA does not hold well for matrix multiplication. The following is an example of matrix multiplication of $A_{2x3}$ and $B_{3x2}$ using 'mmult' function in excel.

| | | | | |
|---|---|---|---|---|
| A | = | 4 | 3 | 5 |
| | | 2 | 4 | 7 |
| | | | | |
| | | | | |
| | | | | |
| B | = | 3 | 4 | |
| | | 2 | 7 | |
| | | 6 | 3 | |
| | | | | |
| | | | | |
| A*B | = | 48 | 52 | |
| | | 56 | 57 | |

**Kronecker's product** is another form of multiplication in matrices where two matrices are transformed in to a large matrix through all possible products of the elements of A with B. It is useful in solving complex linear algebra.

## Application of Matrices in Animal Breeding

### Linear equations in matrices

Consider the simple linear equations for two variables x and y

$ax + by = 4$

$cx + dy = 7$

These two equations could be represented in matrix form as follows and using the multiplication rule will give the linear equations.

$$\begin{bmatrix} a & b \\ c & d \end{bmatrix} \begin{bmatrix} x \\ y \end{bmatrix} = \begin{bmatrix} 4 \\ 7 \end{bmatrix}$$

The left hand side (LHS) has two matrices, the first of which is the coefficient matrix or incidence matrix and the second matrix is the matrix of unknowns, while the third matrix right to the equation is the right hand side (RHS) or constants. The unknowns x and y can be found by multiplying the LHS and RHS with the inverse of the first coefficient matrix. This principle has been used extensively in obtaining solutions for large number of equations in animal breeding analysis.

**Incidence/Coefficient/Design matrices** are used to link the particular sources of fixed or random effects in linear models.

The **numerator relationship matrix (NRM)** has several applications including calculation of inbreeding coefficient (F) and obtaining the coefficient of relationship or coancestry between individuals in a population. More importantly, the inverse of this matrix is primary for the Best Linear Unbiased Prediction (BLUP) where Henderson could incorporate information from all the relatives in the population, proportionate to the degree of relationship in estimating the breeding value of an individual. He also devised ways to obtain the inverse NRM without forming the NRM as the dimensions of the NRM was very high and inversion using the conventional methods were not possible.

The **IBD or identity by descent matrices** are useful in estimation of genomic breeding value especially in genomic selection using SNP markers.

**Variance - covariance matrices** are the basis for multitrait analysis , especially in construction of selection index as solutions for the weighting factors (b) is obtained by solving the linear equation [P] [b]=[G][a], where P and G are the variance -(co)variance matrix for phenotypic and genotypic values respectively for the traits considered. [b] is the column vector of unknown weights to be determined and [a], the column vector for economic values of the traits considered.

**Eigen values** and Eigen vectors are important aspects of matrix algebra useful in animal breeding analysis. Eigen values of the covariance and correlation matrices are used in obtaining the principal components which is in turn used in dimension reduction techniques such as the factor analysis and principal component analysis.

The eigen functions obtained using the eigen values are eigen vectors of the random regression coefficients clarify the components and response in the particular longitudinal trait.

**Example script to obtain the eigen values and vectors of a matrix in R package**

```
> setwd("C:/Users/User/Desktop/eigen")
> x=read.table("eigen.txt", header=FALSE)
> x
      V1       V2      V3       V4
1  3.9171 -0.91280 -0.2724  1.08710
2 -0.9128  0.42040  0.1780 -0.20662
3 -0.2724  0.17800  0.2017 -0.03220
4  1.0871 -0.20662 -0.0322  0.31490
> newMat= as.matrix(x)
> newMat
         V1       V2      V3       V4
[1,]  3.9171 -0.91280 -0.2724  1.08710
[2,] -0.9128  0.42040  0.1780 -0.20662
[3,] -0.2724  0.17800  0.2017 -0.03220
[4,]  1.0871 -0.20662 -0.0322  0.31490
> newMat_eigen <- eigen(newMat)
> newMat_eigen
```

```
$values
[1] 4.4590911258 0.3157545827 0.0791718850 0.0000824065
$vectors
           [,1]       [,2]        [,3]       [,4]
[1,]  0.93628588 -0.1521839  0.10058969 -0.3001508
[2,] -0.22793469 -0.6974931  0.66599267 -0.1341752
[3,] -0.07138384 -0.6556858 -0.73890251 -0.1378534
[4,]  0.25752451 -0.2458040  0.01893574  0.9342928
```

# References


Akanno, E.C., Schenkel, F.S., Quinton, V.M., Friendship, R.M. and Robinson, J.A.B., 2013. Meta-analysis of genetic parameter estimates for reproduction, growth and carcass traits of pigs in the tropics. Livestock Science, 152 (2-3), 101-113.

Alderson G.L.H. 1992. A system to maximize the maintenance of genetic variability in small populations. In L. Alderson, and I. Bodo (eds.), Genetic Conservation of Domestic Livestock II, CABI, Wallingford, U.K. pp. 18-29.

Ali T E and Schaeffer L R. 1987. Accounting for covariances among test day milk yields in dairy cows. Canadian Journal of Animal Science 67, 637-644.

Ambike, 2022. "Random regressions in a Bayesian framework for modelling semen production and fertility traits in Holstein Friesian, Holstein Friesian-crossbreds and indigenous cattle". M.V.Sc., thesis submitted to the Tamil Nadu Veterinary and Animal Sciences University, Chennai

Ambike, V., Venkataramanan, R., Karthickeyan, S.M.K. and Tirumurugaan, K.G., 2022. Meta-analysis of performance and genetic parameter estimates for growth and body weight traits of sheep in the tropics. Small Ruminant Research, 206, p.106597.

Arango J A, Cundiff L V and Van Vleck L D. 2004. Covariance functions and random regression models for cow weight in beef cattle. Journal of Animal Science 82(1): 54-67.

Arthy V, Venkataramanan R, Sivaselvam S N, Sreekumar C and Balasubramanyam D. 2020. Suitability of random regression models for growth of Madras Red sheep under a field performance recording system. Small Ruminant Research 193: 106260.

Barkan, H. 2015. Statistics in clinical research: Important considerations. Ann. Card. Anaesth., 18(1): 74–82. doi: 10.4103/0971-9784.148325

Becker, W.A.1992. Manual of Quantitative Genetics (5th edn.). Washington State University. Washington.

Berry, D.P., Wall, E. and Pryce, J.E., 2014. Genetics and genomics of reproductive performance in dairy and beef cattle. animal, 8(s1): 105-121.

Blasco, A. 2001. The Bayesian controversy in animal breeding. J. Anim. Sci., 79, 2023–2046.

Boichard D., Maignel L., Verrier E.1997. The value of using probabilities of gene origin to measure genetic variability in a population. Genetics Selection Evolution 29: 5-23.

Borenstein, M., Hedges, L. V., Higgins, J. P., and Rothstein, H. R. (2011). Introduction to meta-analysis. John Wiley & Sons.

Brody S, Ragsdale A C and Turner C W. 1923. The rate of decline of milk secretion with the advance of the period of lactation. The Journal of General Physiology 5, 441-444.

Cochran, W.G., 1954. Some methods for strengthening the common $\chi$ 2 tests. Biometrics, 10(4): 417-451.

Cox, D.R., 1972. Regression models and life-tables. Journal of the Royal Statistical Society: Series B (Methodological), 34(2): 187-202.

Dag B, Keskin I and Mikailsoy F. 2005. Application of different models to the lactation curves of unimproved Awassi ewes in Turkey. South African Journal of Animal Science 35: 238-243.

Dave D B. 1971. First lactation curve of the Indian water buffalo. JNKVV Res J 5: 3

de Oliveira, H.R., Ventura, H.T., Costa, E.V., Pereira, M.A., Veroneze, R., de Souza Duarte, M. and e Silva, F.F., 2017. Meta-analysis of genetic-parameter estimates for reproduction, growth and carcass traits in Nellore cattle by using a random-effects model. Animal Production Science, 58(9), pp.1575-1583.

Diaz, I.D.P.S., Crews Jr, D.H. and Enns, R.M., 2014. Cluster and meta-analyses of genetic parameters for feed intake traits in growing beef cattle. Journal of Animal Breeding and Genetics, 131(3): 217-226.

Druet T, Jaffrézic F, Boichard D and Ducrocq V. 2003. Modeling lactation curves and estimation of genetic parameters for first lactation test-day records of French Holstein cows. Journal of Dairy Science 86(7): 2480-2490.

Dunner S., Checa M.L., Gutiérrez J.P., Martín J.P., Canón J. 1998. Genetic analysis and management in small populations: the Asturcon pony as an example. Genetics Selection Evolution 30: 397-405.

Eisenhart, C.1947. The assumptions underlying the analysis of variance. Biometrics 3: 1-21.

Falconer, D.S. and Mackay, T.F.C. 1996. Introduction to Quantitative Genetics, Longman, Harlow.

Fischer T M and Van der Werf J H J. 2002, August. Effect of data structure on the estimation of genetic parameters using random regression. In Proc. 7th World Cong. Genet. Appl. Livest. Prod., Montpellier, France: 19-23.

Fisher, R. A. (1918). The correlation between relatives on the supposition of Mendelian inheritance. Proc. R. Soc. Edin. 52: 399

Fisher, R. A. 1921. On the mathematical foundations of theoretical statistics. Phil. Trans. R. Soc. Lond., 222, 309–368.

Fisher, R.A. 1925. Statistical Methods for Research Workers (1st Edn). Oliver and Boyd, London.

Fogarty, N.M., 1995. Genetic parameters for live weight, fat and muscle measurements, wool production and reproduction in sheep: a review. Anim. Breed. Abstr., 63, 101-143.

Foulley JL and Robert-Granié C (2002). Heteroskedastic random coefficient models. Proceedings of the 7th World Congress on Genetics Applied to Livestock Production, Montpellier, France.

Garrick, D.J. 2010. An animal breeding approach to the estimation of genetic and environmental trendsfrom field populations. J. Anim. Sci., 88, E3-E10.

Gathura, D.M., Muasya, T.K. and Kahi, A.K., 2020. Meta-analysis of genetic parameters for traits of economic importance for beef cattle in the tropics. Livestock Science, 242, p.104306.

Giannotti, J.D.G., Packer, I.U., Mercadante, M.E.Z., 2005. Meta-analysis for heritability of estimates growth traits in beef cattle. Rev. Bras. Zootec. 34, 1173–1180.

Gianola, D. and Fernando, R. L. 1986. Bayesian Methods in Animal Breeding Theory. J. Anim. Sci., 63:217-244.

Gianola, D., 2000. Statistics in animal breeding. Journal of the American Statistical Association, 95(449), pp.296-299.

Gilmour, A.R., Cullis, B.R., Harding, S.A. and Thompson, R., 2006. ASReml Update: what's new in Release 2.00. VSN International Ltd, Hemel Hempstead, UK.

Glass, G.V., 1976. Primary, secondary, and meta-analysis of research. Educational researcher, 5(10), pp.3-8.

Grossman, M., A. L. Kuck and H.W. Norton.(1986). Lactation Curves of Purebred and Crossbred Dairy Cattle. Journal of Dairy Science, 69: 195-203.

Guo, Z. and H.H. Swalve (1995). Comparison of different lactation curve sub-models in test day models. Proc. Interbull Mtg. Vienna Austria Interbull Bull.No.16.

Gutierrez, J.P. and Goyache, F. 2005. A note on ENDOG: A computer program for analyzing pedigree information. Journal of Animal Breeding and Genetics 122, 172–176.

Gutiérrez, J.P., Altarriba, J., Díaz, C., Quintanilla, R., Cañón, J. and Piedrafita, J., 2003. Pedigree analysis of eight Spanish beef cattle breeds. Genetics Selection Evolution, 35(1), pp.43-63.

Gutierrez, J.P., Cervantes, I. and Goyache, F. 2009. Improving the estimation of realized effective population sizes in farm animals. Journal of Animal Breeding and Genetics 126, 327–332.

Harrer, M., Cuijpers, P., Furukawa, T.A. and Ebert, D.D., 2021. Doing meta-analysis with R: A hands-on guide. CRC press.

Hartley, H.O. and Rao, J.N.K. 1967. Maximum likelihood estimation for the mixed analysis of variance model, Biometrika, 54, 93-108.

Harvey, W.R. 1960. Mixed Model Least-squares and Maximum Likelihood Computer Programme. Ohio State University, Columbus.

Hedges, L.V. and Vevea, J.L., 1998. Fixed-and random-effects models in meta-analysis. Psychological methods, 3(4), p.486.

Henderson, C. R. 1950. Estimation of genetic parameters. Ann.Math. Stat., 21,309.

Henderson, C. R. 1973. Sire evaluation and genetic trends," Proceedings of the Animal Breeding and Genetics Symposium in Honour of Dr Jay L. Lush, 10-41, Champaign: American Society of Animal Science and the American Dairy Science Association.

Henderson, C. R. 1975. Best Linear Unbiased Estimation and Prediction under a selection model. Biometrics, 31, 423-449.

Henderson, C. R.; Kempthorne, 0., Searle, S. R., Von krosigk,C. N. 1959. Estimation of environmental and genetic trends from records subject to culling. Biometrics, 15, 192-218.

Henderson, C. R.1953. Estimation of Variance and Covariance Components. Biometrics, 9, 226-252.

Henderson, C. R.1976. A simple method for computing the inverse of a numerator relationship matrix used in prediction of breeding values, Biometrics, 32, 69-83.

Henderson, C.R. 1984. Applications of Linear Models in Animal Breeding. University of Guelph, Guelph, Ontario.

Higgins, J.P., Thompson, S.G., Deeks, J.J. and Altman, D.G., 2003. Measuring inconsistency in meta-analyses. Bmj, 327(7414), pp.557-560.

Hill W G. 1998. Inferences from evolutionary biology to livestock breeding. In: Proc. Sixth World Congr. Genet. Appl. Livest. Prod. 23, Armidale, Australia: 32–39.

Hoeschele I (1988) Genetic evaluation with data presenting evidence of mixed major gene and polygenic inheritance. Theoretical and Applied Genetics 76, 81–92.

IntHout, J., Ioannidis, J.P. and Borm, G.F., 2014. The Hartung-Knapp-Sidik-Jonkman method for random effects meta-analysis is straightforward and considerably outperforms the standard DerSimonian-Laird method. BMC medical research methodology, 14(1), pp.1-12.

Iwaisaki H, Tsuruta S, Misztal I and Bertrand J K. 2005. Genetic parameters estimated with multitrait and linear spline-random regression models using Gelbvieh early growth data. Journal of animal science 83(4): 757-763.

James J.W.1972. Computation of genetic contributions from pedigrees. Theory and Applied Genetics 42: 272-273.

Jamrozik, J., and L. R. Schaeffer. 1997. Estimates of genetic parameters for a test day model with random regressions for yield traits of first lactation Holsteins. J. Dairy Sci. https://doi.org/10.3168/ jds.S0022-0302(97)75996-4.

Jembere, T., Dessie, T., Rischkowsky, B., Kebede, K., Okeyo, A.M. and Haile, A., 2017. Meta-analysis of average estimates of genetic parameters for growth, reproduction and milk production traits in goats. Small Ruminant Research, 153, pp.71-80.

Kesbi F G, Eskandarinasab M and Shahir M H. 2008. Estimation of direct and maternal effects on body weight in Mehraban sheep using random regression models. Archives Animal Breeding 51(3): 235-246.

Kirkpatrick M and Heckman N. 1989. A quantitative genetic model for growth, shape, reaction norms, and other infinite-dimensional characters. Journal of Mathematical Biology 27: 429–450

Knapp, G. and Hartung, J., 2003. Improved tests for a random effects meta-regression with a single covariate. Statistics in medicine, 22(17): 2693-2710.

Koots KR, Gibson JP, Smith C, Wilton JW (1994a) Analyses of published genetic parameter estimates for beef production traits. 1. Heritability. Animal Breeding Abstracts 62, 309–338.

Koots KR, Gibson JP, Wilton JW (1994b) Analyses of published genetic parameter estimates for beef production traits. 2. Phenotypic and genetic correlations. Animal Breeding Abstracts 62, 825–853.

Kruuk, L.E.B, 2004. Estimating genetic parameters in natural populations using the animal model. Phil. Trans. R. Soc. Lond. B., 359, 873-890.

Lacy R.C.1989. Analysis of founder representation in pedigrees: founder equivalents and founder genome equivalents, Zoo Biology 8: 111-123.

Leon-Velarde, C.U., I. McMillan, R.D. Gentry and J.W. Wilton (1995). Models for estimating typical lactation curves in dairy cattle. Journal of Animal Breeding and Genetics, 112(5-6): 333-340.

Lobo, R.N.B., Madalena, F.E. and Vieira, A.R., 2000, June. Average estimates of genetic parameters for beef and dairy cattle in tropical regions. In Animal breeding abstracts (Vol. 68, No. 6, pp. 433-462).Giannotti, J.D.G., Packer, I.U., Mercadante, M.E.Z., 2005. Meta-analysis for heritability of estimates growth traits in beef cattle. Rev. Bras. Zootec. 34, 1173–1180.

Luo, Z., 1992. Computing inbreeding coefficients in large populations. Genetics Selection Evolution, 24(4), pp.305-313.

Macciotta, N.P.P., D. Vicario and A. Cappio-Borlino (2005). Detection of different shapes of lactation curve for milk yield in dairy cattle by empirical mathematical models. Journal of Dairy Science, 88: 1178–1191

Mahala S, Saini S, Kumar A, Sharma R C and Gowane G R. 2020. Genotype× environment interaction affects sire ranking for live weights in Avikalin sheep. Small Ruminant Research 186: 106092.

Maignel L., Boichard, D. and Verrier, E. 1996. Genetic variability of French dairy breeds estimated from pedigree information. Interbull Bulletin 14, 49-54.

Malhotra P K, Singh R P and Singh R N. 1980. Estimating lactation curve in Karan-Swiss cattle [dairy cattle, India]. Indian Journal of Animal Sciences 50, 799--804.

Marshall DM (1994) Breed differences and genetic parameters for body composition traits in beef cattle. Journal of Animal Science 72, 2745–2755.

Masuda Y. 2018. Introduction to BLUPF90 suite programs. University of Georgia. http://nce.ads.uga.edu/wiki/doku.php?id=documentation

Medrado, B.D., Pedrosa, V.B. and Pinto, L.F.B., 2021a. Meta-analysis of genetic parameters for economic traits in sheep. Livestock Science, 247, p.104477.

Medrado, B.D., Pedrosa, V.B. and Pinto, L.F.B., 2021b. Meta-analysis of genetic parameters for economic traits in buffaloes. Livestock Science, 251, p.104614.

Menezes G R O, Torres R A, Torres Jr, R A, Silva L O C, Gondo A, Euclydes R F. 2013. Estimation of genetic parameters for growth traits in Tabapua cattle using a multi-trait model. Braz. J. Anim. Sci. 42: 570–574

Meyer K. 2004. Scope for a random regression model in genetic evaluation of beef cattle for growth. Livestock Production Science 86(1-3): 69-83.

Meyer K. 2005. Random regression analyses using B-splines to model growth of Australian Angus cattle. Genetics Selection Evolution, 37(6): 1-28.

Meyer K. 2007. WOMBAT- A tool for mixed model analyses in quantitative genetics by restricted maximum likelihood (REML). Journal of Zhejiang University Science B 8(11): 815-821.

Meyer, K. 1989. Restricted maximum likelihood to estimate variance components for animal models with several random effects using a derivative-free algorithm. Genet. Sel. Evol., 21, 317-340.

Meyer, K. and Thompson, R.1984. Bias in variance and covariance component estimators due to selection on a correlated trait. Tierz. Zuchtungs biol. 101, 33-50.

Meyer, K., 1992. Variance components due to direct and maternal effects for growth traits of Australian beef cattle. Livestock Production Science, 31(3-4), pp.179-204.

Misztal I, S Tsuruta D A L Lourenco, Y Masuda, I Aguilar, A Legarra, Z Vitezica. 2018. Manual for BLUPF90 family programs. University of Georgia. http://nce.ads.uga.edu/wiki/doku.php?id=documentation Montpellier, France. 28: 21–22

Misztal I, Strabel T, Jamrozik J, Mäntysaari E A and Meuwissen T H E. 2000. Strategies for estimating the parameters needed for different test-day models. Journal of Dairy Science 83(5): 1125-1134.

Misztal, I., 1994, August. Software packages in animal breeding. In 5th World Congress: Genetics Applied to Livestock Production, Guelph, Canada.

Moher, D., Shamseer, L., Clarke, M., Ghersi, D., Liberati, A., Petticrew, M., Shekelle, P. and Stewart, L.A., 2015. Preferred reporting items for systematic review and meta-analysis protocols (PRISMA-P) 2015 statement. Systematic reviews, 4(1): 1-9.

Mota R R, Marques L F A, Lopes P S, Silva L P, Araujo Neto F R, Resende M D V, Torres R A. 2013. Genetic evaluation using multi-trait and random regression models in Simmental beef cattle. Genetics and Molecular Research 12: 2465–2480.

Mrode, R.A., 2014. Linear models for the prediction of animal breeding values. Cabi.

Mrode, R. A. (1996). Linear Models for the Prediction of Animal Breeding Values. CAB international, UK.

Nelder J A. 1966. Inverse polynomials, a useful group of multi-factor response functions. Biometrics 22, 128-141.

Nemutandani K, Snyman G, Olivier W and Visser C. 2018. Estimation of variance components and heritabilities for body weight from birth to six years of age in Merino sheep using random regression models. In Proceedings of the World Congress on Genetics Applied to Livestock Production (Vol. 11).

Nicholas, F. W. (1982). Veterinary Genetics. Clarendon Press, Oxford.

Nobre P R C, Lopes P S, Torres R A, Silva L O C, Regazzi A J, Torres Júnior R A A and Misztal I. 2003. Analyses of growth curves of Nellore cattle by Bayesian method via Gibbs sampling. Arquivo Brasileiro de Medicina Veterinária e Zootecnia 55: 480-490.

Nobre P R C, Misztal I, Tsuruta S, Bertrand J K, Silva L O C and Lopes P S. 2003a. Analyses of growth curves of Nellore cattle by multiple-trait and random regression models. Journal of animal science 81(4): 918-926.

Patterson, H. D. & Thompson, R. 1971 Recovery of interblock information when block sizes are unequal. Biometrika, 58: 545–554.

Prakash, V., Gupta, A.K., Singh, M., Ambhore, G.S., Singh, A. and Gandhi, R.S., 2017. Random regression test-day milk yield models as a suitable alternative to the traditional 305-day lactation model for genetic evaluation of Sahiwal cattle. Indian J Anim Sci, 87(3), pp.340-344.

Rao, A.R. (2007). Multivariate analysis of animal breeding data. Compendium of National Training Programme on Genetic Analysis of Animal Breeding Data Using Advanced Software Packages. NDRI, Karnal.

Rieman, B.E. and Allendorf, F.W., 2001. Effective population size and genetic conservation criteria for bull trout. North American Journal of Fisheries Management, 21(4), pp.756-764.

Safari, E., Fogarty N.M.and Gilmour A.R. 2005. A review of genetic parameter estimates for wool, growth, meat and reproduction traits in sheep. Livest. Prod. Sci., 92, 271–289.

Scalez D C B, Fragomeni B D O, Santos D C C D, Passafaro T L, Alencar M M D and Toral F L B. 2018. Random regression models with B-splines to estimate genetic parameters for body weight of young bulls in performance tests. Revista Brasileira de Zootecnia 47(0)

Schaeffer, L. R., and J. C. Dekkers. 1994. Random regressions in animal models for test-day production in dairy cattle. Pages 443–446 in Proc. 5th World Congr. Genet. Appl. Livest. Prod., Guelph, ON, Canada. University of Guelph, Guelph, ON, Canada.

Schwarzer, G. and Schwarzer, M.G., 2012. Package 'meta'. The R foundation for statistical computing, 9.

Searle, S.R. 1989. Variance components - some history and a summary account of estimation methods. J. Anim. Breed. Genet., 106, 1-29.

Shaw, R.G. 1987: Maximum-likelihood approaches applied to quantitative genetics of natural populations. Evolution 41, 812-826.

Sikka L C. 1950. A study of lactation as affected by heredity and environment. Journal of Dairy Research 17, 231--252.

Silva F G, Torres R A, Brito L F, Euclydes R F, Melo A L P, Souza N O, Ribeiro Jr J I and Rodrigues M T. 2013. Random regression models using Legendre orthogonal polynomials to evaluate the milk production of Alpine goats. Genetics and Molecular Research 12(4): 6502-6511.

Sorensen, D. and Kennedy, B.W. 1984. Estimation of genetic variances from unselected and selected populations. J. Anim. Sci., 59, 1213-1223.

St-Pierre, N.R., 2001. Invited review: Integrating quantitative findings from multiple studies using mixed model methodology. Journal of dairy science, 84(4), pp.741-755.

Strucken E M, Laurenson Y C and Brockmann G A. 2015. Go with the flow—biology and genetics of the lactation cycle. Frontiers in genetics 6:118.

Sutton, A.J., Abrams, K.R., Jones, D.R., Jones, D.R., Sheldon, T.A. and Song, F., 2000. Methods for meta-analysis in medical research (Vol. 348). Chichester: Wiley.

Thompson, R. 1973. The estimation of variance and covariance components with an application when records are subject to culling. Biometrics 29: 527-550.

Turner, H.N. and Young, S.S.Y. 1969. Quantitative Genetics in Sheep Breeding. MacMillan Co., Melbourne, Australia. pp: 1-132.

van der Werf, J.H.J. and de Boer, I.J.M. 1990. Estimation of additive genetic variance when base populations are selected. J. Anim. Sci. 68,3124.

Van der Werf, J.H.J., 2001. Random regression in animal breeding. Course Notes. Jaboticabal, SP Brazil (http://www-personal.une.edu.au/~jvanderw/CFcoursenotes.pdf) dowloaded on 25/06/2014

Venkataramanan R. 2016. Random regressions to model growth in Nilagiri sheep of South India. Small Ruminant Research 144: 242-247.

Viechtbauer, W. and Viechtbauer, M.W., 2015. Package 'metafor'. The Comprehensive R Archive Network. Package 'metafor'. http://cran.r-project.org/web/packages/metafor/metafor.pdf

Wang, Z. and Goonewardene, L. A. 2004. The use of mixed models in the analysis of animal experiments with repeated measures data. Can. J. Anim. Sci., 84, 1–11.

Wilmink J B M. 1987. Adjustment of test-day milk, fat and protein yield for age, season and stage of lactation. Livestock Production Science 16, 335--348.

Wood P D P. 1967. Algebraic model of the lactation curve in cattle. Nature 216, 164--165.

Wright, S. 1931. Evolution in Mendelian populations. Genetics 16, 97–159.

Wright, S., 1921. Systems of mating. II. The effects of inbreeding on the genetic composition of a population. Genetics, 6(2), p.124.

Yadav M P, Katpatal B G and Kaushik S N. 1977. Components of inverse polynomial function of lactation curve, and factors affecting them in Hariana and its Friesian crosses. Indian Journal of Animal Sciences 47, 777-

Zamani P, Moradi M R, Alipour D and Ghafouri-Kesbi F. 2016. Combination of B-Spline and Legendre functions in random regression models to fit growth curve of Moghani sheep. Small Ruminant Research 145: 115-122.

Zarkovich, S., 1979. Stability of variance patterns. Jomal da Sociedade Indiana de Estatísticas Agrícolas, 31: 23-48.